What others are saying:

Because of the times we're living in, never has it been more important to have men and women exercising the prophetic gifts to help the people of God navigate their lives both personally and corporately. Connie Hunter-Urban is one such person who has submitted herself to the Holy Spirit's work through her. In both writing and speaking, Connie's insight into the prophetic shines through. She has the ability to look into the Spirit realm and then communicate the truths she finds there into the physical realm. Throughout the country, lives have been changed, confidence has been instilled, and understanding has been gained by individuals and the body of Christ as a whole who have benefitted from Connie's ministry. As a frontrunner of those boldly exploring the supernatural, Connie is training a new generation of believers to venture confidently into the prophetic.

—Lynda Hunter-Bjorklund
Christian Author

Connie has spoken and ministered at our church a couple times. Her ministry is refreshing and enlightening. She operates fluently in words of knowledge, which have been confirmed. Her prophetic ministry brings revelation of Jesus, which is truly the spirit of prophesy. When she came to our church, I so enjoyed her ministry that I bought a case of her book, *God's Plan for Our Success, Nehemiah's Way*, so all our women could have one. I have full confidence in her relationship with Jesus and her ministry. She bears awesome fruit.

—Pastor Larry Townsend
Bethel Acres Assembly
Tecumseh, Oklahoma

THE
ELIJAH
ANOINTING

Connie Hunter-Urban

THE ELIJAH ANOINTING

EMPOWERING THE PROPHETIC GIFT

TATE PUBLISHING
AND ENTERPRISES, LLC

Published by Tate Publishing & Enterprises, LLC
127 E. Trade Center Terrace | Mustang, Oklahoma 73064 USA
1.888.361.9473 | www.tatepublishing.com

Tate Publishing is committed to excellence in the publishing industry. The company reflects the philosophy established by the founders, based on Psalm 68:11,
"The Lord gave the word and great was the company of those who published it."

Book design copyright © 2014 by Tate Publishing, LLC. All rights reserved.
Cover design by Allen Jomoc
Interior design by Honeylette Pino

Published in the United States of America

ISBN: 978-1-63306-588-8
1. Religion / Biblical Studies / Prophets
2. Religion / Christianity / Holy Spirit
14.10.07

ACKNOWLEDGMENTS

I'd like to thank the following:

- My Father for His Spirit's leading.
- My husband, Wade, for his support in all God's directives and his proofreading help. He's truly my helper as much as I am his.
- My daughters, Jennifer and Jillian, for their continual loving support of where God has sent me during their lives and their allowing me to share so many of their stories which reflect God's messages to me.
- My stepdaughter, Lissa; her husband, Mike; and our grandsons, Isaac and Ian—for their spiritual support and affirmation as I began my journey as a Christian author.
- My brothers Phillip and Jason and my sisters, Lynda, Becky, Liz, Anita, and especially Suzy, who have always been there and provided me with much love and life lessons.
- My close friends, who always support me with prayers, encouragement, and help: Margie, Curtis, Bonnie, Jo, Kristi, Nancy, Connie, Sharon, and Kara Lynne.
- My pastors, Richie and Stacey Ware, whose sermons and worship have given many nuggets to fill my pages.

- Our Times of Refreshing and *Restoration Ministries Streaming* family who cover me with love, support, and prayers.
- My late parents, Ernest and Audrey Sampson-Hunter, who started me on my own prophetic journey by their love for Holy Spirit and His gifts. I miss you both!
- My mother-in-law, Joan, and late father-in-law, Gordon Urban, who loved me like a daughter the minute I came into their farmhouse.

CONTENTS

FOREWORD

Gifted teachers have a way of making their subject both interesting and enriching. The love that Connie Hunter-Urban has for the Word of God is easily recognizable in her book, *God's Plan for Our Success, Nehemiah's Way*. I have an appreciation for any book that you can read and immediately apply it to your life situation. In the New Testament, there are two Greek words used for knowing. Paul used these two words repeatedly in the Corinthian letters. One is to see and to have a mental concept of what is in the line of sight. The second word means to be intimate with or to have a relationship with. It would be hard to write a book like this if you only had a mental concept of the gates of the ancient city.

Connie proves in her first book that she has more than just a video image in her mind of what she has written. You can only know these things by obeying and experiencing in matters of a heart for God. This new book, *The Elijah Anointing*, promises that same balance. Those who operate in the prophetic can learn much about their gifts through Elijah's life that Connie has interpreted here. I highly recommend this reading.

—Cleddie Keith
Pastor of Heritage Fellowship,
Serving the Greater Cincinnati Tri-State

INTRODUCTION

Interstate 75 stretched on, dark, desolate, and long that night. The prophetic class I'd taught in Dayton, Ohio, had lasted longer than I'd anticipated after putting the prophetic into practice and ministering in the gifts of Holy Spirit with words of knowledge and healing. I'd be getting into Lexington well after midnight and needed to be up early the next morning to set up a book table at a conference. I was tired but exhilarated about the good time we'd had teaching about and ministering in Holy Spirit's power. South of Cincinnati, the Lord first tugged on my awareness. It had been nearly a year since God had told me to write a book about Elijah. Between my husband, Wade's, and my ministry travel, our finishing a co-authored book, and my preparing for God-prompted sermons, I'd sandwiched in the Elijah research. I planned to teach it first at a home Bible study; then, like my other books, I'd write it. Six months later, I had finished most of those notes when God whispered to me, "I said to write a book." I had done things my way when I assumed I'd teach it first, so Wade and I shifted our plans. He would teach a different study, and I started slowly putting my notes into paragraph form. Very slowly. A couple months after His first reminder, Holy Spirit again whispered in my ear: "Put the book on the front burner." I heard Him loud and clear. With all my commitments, and most of them for ministry, I needed to prioritize.

A few months later, driving to Lexington that night, I'd just finished my fourth draft. In Dayton, I'd been with Christians who cared so much about the prophetic that they'd formed a church group devoted to that purpose. Whenever believers love and learn about their gifts and seek ministry opportunities, Holy Spirit responds. Their dedication to the prophetic started the wheels in my mind turning as God nudged my heart. They loved everything concerning Holy Spirit as I love everything about Holy Spirit because He's my essence too. I wear many hats: a teacher, a mother, a wife, a sister, a preacher, a friend, a writer. But most of these are what I do. I was created to *be* a prophet: "Before [I was] born,…[I was] ordained [as] a prophet to the nations" (Jer. 1:5). It's in my DNA. The prophetic is not what I do but who I am.

ELIJAH

So, why Elijah? He is an enigma referred to in Scripture as Eliah, Elijah, and Elias; and though genealogies include those names, most scholars agree those men are not Elijah the prophet. He appears to have no lineage, like Melchizedek, a king and priest with whom Abraham took communion and to whom he paid tithes (see Gen. 14:18-20). He wasn't a supernatural being, yet he had extreme supernatural abilities through Holy Spirit. So why would God tell a prophet like me to study the common prophet Elijah when the Bible devotes much more Word to others? That night as I drove down the interstate, I heard God tell me why He wanted me to write this book. Elijah's life is a clear parallel to all our prophetic journeys. His odyssey can help us understand how the prophetic operated in him and us too. He prophesied mostly during Ahab's reign (874-853 BC). During that time, many prophets existed through schools of the prophets, but because Ahab promoted Baal instead of God, unlike many Old Testament prophets, neither Elijah nor the others were acknowledged as official prophets. Like Elijah, though we're shunned and denigrated because we don't speak in the name of tolerance or political correctness, we should all still resound God's words, not what's pleasing to man.

But, why Elijah, why now? He's a man we can learn from whether we operate in the prophetic or not. The prophetic must be practical, and Elijah not only spoke words of events to come, but he also brought signs and wonders to earth by his great faith walk. He touched others' lives by bringing God's miracles into being. Elijah dealt with people in a "now" way, not with end-time or messianic prophecies, which had little meaning for their lives right then. He didn't fit into other prophets' molds, and he didn't foretell Jesus's coming, but his life reflected what Jesus would preach one thousand years later. Elijah cared for people just like Jesus cared for people. His purpose, making lives better while bringing correction which would lead to repentance, should define what's happening today in twenty-first-century America, but sadly it doesn't. The nation and even much of the church have forgotten that it's about people, not the other way around.

His ministry is every man's and woman's. His shortcomings mirror ours. His events are real-life stories. His life, like ours, experienced one crisis after another; yet those crises gave him opportunities to shine in his gifts. He wasn't popular or in vogue and rather strange-looking for the times. He wasn't politically correct and had a long-running relationship with leadership who persecuted him, yet he also had regular experiences and relationships with regular people. He challenged the prevailing religious ideology. Elijah promoted godliness, revealed judgment, and brought repentance. He dealt with economic hardship during drought and famine, and yet he thrived. He had a time of great testing and failed. Sound familiar? This describes many with prophetic gifts today, including me.

Yet, the most important principle we can take from Elijah is how he made it work. Despite shortcomings or emotional lows, he knew that by tapping into God's secrets, he could do all things. He understood a faith walk and how to put it into practice because he placed no limitations on what God could do. He knew how to bring God's fire or how to operate in wonders like being translated. After Peter had noticed the dried fig tree, Jesus said, "Whoever says to this mountain, 'Be removed and be cast into the sea,' and does not doubt in his heart, but believes that those things he says will be done, he will have whatever he says" (see Mark 11:23). Jesus's lesson about His times' powerless and dead religion was the same message for Elijah's time and for today too. Religion has opted for a type of godliness without power (see 2 Tim. 3:5) because Holy Spirit is no longer a reality for much of the Christian world. Cursing nonproductive things like fig trees and speaking life through faith can accomplish much. Elijah did just that.

THE PROPHETS

Many operate in the prophetic, but a prophet's hat isn't one size fits all. In the Old Testament, a prophet was *nabi*, "one who proclaims or tells a message—a spokesman, herald, announcer."[1] This word has over three hundred references and usually means "Yahweh's commissioned spokesmen."[2] Many in the Old Testament are described as prophets—Jeremiah, Micah, Daniel, even David and Abraham. These spokesmen include women too. The feminine form, *nebiyah*, refers to prophetesses such as Noadiah (see Neh. 6:14), Deborah (see Judg. 4-5), and Isaiah's wife (see Isa. 8:3). What a power couple they were! The New Testament word for prophet is *prophetes*, "primarily a forth-teller, one who speaks forth a divine message—foretelling future events."[3] These biblical prophets received revelation from God to relay on earth.

New Testament prophecy isn't as clearly defined as Old Testament because different levels operate. Today, people have prophetic callings in three ways: a divine calling for the office of the prophet, a motivational gift of the prophet, and a gift of Holy Spirit. Only those prophets who operate in the office of the prophet deserve the title of "prophet." As Jesus ascended, He gave the five-fold ministry—apostles, prophets, evangelists, pastors, and teachers (see Eph. 4:11). This prophet's ministry gift is a role often misunderstood. Many who actually operate in this office shy away from that designation because others claim that title who haven't actually been called to the office of prophet but operate on a lower prophetic level. This misunderstanding has given this ministry a dubious name when actually Jesus Himself acknowledged and operated in it. One who functions in this prophetic calling must be mature for this huge responsibility: to speak God's words from his/her mouth (see Matt. 4:4). So, this prophet's words are God's words which He communicates to men.

God has told Wade that our ministry is to equip equippers. Like Elijah, this type of prophet functions as a teacher, bringing individuals along in the prophetic and instructing others how to use prophetic gifts. These prophets can be blessing or building. Blessing prophets give words of encouragement and direction, while building prophets bring along protégés, teach how to hear from God for themselves, and provide a platform for others to become equipped for Holy Spirit's ministry through their lives. This prophet's words are weighty. He can bring correction and direction, and often his word ushers in a new move of God. God reveres this prophet and honors his/her words. As Elijah proclaimed, God doesn't reopen the heavens until the prophet speaks it (see 1 Kings 17:1). What a powerful calling this is!

Another level of prophetic gift is the motivational gift of the Father. This gift includes prophecy, ministry (serving), teaching, exhorting, giving, leading, and showing mercy (see Rom. 12:6-8). Prophecy is first on this list, showing God's view of its importance. These gifts reflect a person's character and define him/her. You probably know someone whom one of these describes. Take, for example, a teacher. One with a teaching motivation finds any opportunity to teach—with grandkids, at the laundromat, in the grocery aisle. Prophetic motivation is the same. Those possessing that motivation hold an innate ability to know God's heart and speak what their heart is fixed on too. They're always tuned in to Holy Spirit, hearing God's voice and describing what's on His heart. This is body ministry where each plays a crucial role toward making the body operate properly by cooperating one with another. These gifts minister to others and demonstrate that no one thinks higher of himself than another (see Rom. 12:3-4).

The last level of prophecy is the Gift of Holy Spirit (see 1 Cor. 13:2-3), part of a Holy Spirit walk and thus available to all Spirit-filled believers. This gift of prophecy involves speaking "exhortation, edification, and comfort" (see 1 Cor. 14:3). When operating in prophecy as a gift of Holy Spirit, believers hear prophetic words but don't function in the office of prophet. Many are labeled as prophetic because they operate in spiritual gifts: words of wisdom, words of knowledge, discerning of spirits, prophecy, tongues, interpretation of tongues, faith, gifts of healings, and working of miracles (see 1 Cor. 12:8-10). Paul said believers should desire to operate in all the gifts of the Spirit but especially prophecy (see 1 Cor. 14:1, 5). Moses too, wanted all to be prophets as God filled them with Holy Spirit (see Num. 11:29). He labeled dreamers and visionaries as prophets (see Num. 12:6), and those gifts are so common even children operate in them. Since anyone can serve in this level of prophecy, these gifts aren't as profound as the office of prophet, who speaks what's crucial into existence. Because the immature can operate in the Holy Spirit prophetic, no one should be led by another's single prophetic word and should always receive confirmation. People often learn about this gift by practice; and they make errors as they learn, like we all did.

THE PROPHETIC

Knowing these three types of prophetic gifts is important in order to keep perspective since all believers have access to one or more of these levels of prophecy. Though some may be operating at a higher, more authoritative level, the word "prophetic" has become generally synonymous with a Spirit-filled walk and operating in the gifts. Other gifts, like words of knowledge, become prophecy when one speaks them or acts on them. Dreamers and visionaries are called prophets because they receive a prophetic revelation from God then speak it forth by Holy Spirit's power. Those catalysts of revelation and speaking gifts move into power gifts.

Actions authored by Holy Spirit, often called prophetic actions, are what He tells us to do to bring His results. Just as Jesus ministered in the spirit of prophecy (see Rev. 19:10), so we too are called to speak what we hear Holy Spirit saying and to act out what we see Him doing. Prophetic actions begin with hearing from God, then obeying to initiate the miraculous. When we obey, we create prophecy and power. Prophetic actions, common in Scripture, bring supernatural results: Moses held his rod over the Red Sea (see Exod. 14:21), and Jesus put mud on the blind man's eyes (see John 9:6). Elijah's ministry also used prophetic actions: he built an altar for fire to fall, bowed on the ground to bring rain, stretched his body across a dead boy to bring a resurrection, and hit the Jordan with his mantle. In our ministry, God often speaks for someone to do a prophetic action, and wondrous occurrences happen as a result.

THE ANOINTING

To understand your prophetic walk, you should recognize how the anointing fits. I like Kenneth Copeland's definition of the anointing: "'God on flesh doing those things that flesh cannot do.' It is God doing those things only He can do, and doing them through a flesh-and-blood, earthly vessel."[4] The anointing is a "treasure in earthen vessels, that the excellence of the power may be of God and not of us" (2 Cor. 4:7). That's a beautiful picture of how wonders are accomplished as that anointing engulfs us—His power as a treasure inside this earth body. Isaiah prophesied:

The Spirit of the Lord God is upon Me, Because the Lord has anointed Me To preach good tidings to the poor; He has sent Me to heal the brokenhearted, To proclaim liberty to the captives, And the opening of the prison to those who are bound.

Isa. 61:1

Jesus quoted Isaiah as He declared Himself, His anointing, and His mission (see Luke 4:18).

The Old Testament word for "anointed" is *mashach*, "to rub with oil, i.e. to anoint; by impl. to consecrate."[5] The New Testament word for anointing is *chrio*, meaning basically the same thing but adding that the consecration is "to an office or relig. service."[6] This word is derived from *chraomai* which adds clarity about our prophetic anointing: "to furnish what is needed; to employ or (by extens.) to act toward one in a given manner:— entreat, use."[7] These definitions together show the anointing has been spiritually rubbed upon us to furnish what's needed, when it's needed for service to God. That's why you'll hear an anointed speaker, worshipper, or service today, then the same speaker, singer, or scriptures don't impact you tomorrow because it's not "employed" by Holy Spirit to bring results by "acting toward one in a given manner," for a given purpose. The anointing is Holy Spirit's impartation, enabling through words and actions to bring powerful, necessary results as He deems. That anointing also teaches us how to move in our Holy Spirit gifts (see 1 John 2:27).

Many believe the origin of anointing came from shepherds. David compares God's provision and protection to a shepherd's role when he says "You anoint my head with oil" (Psalm 23:5). This familiar scripture means much more in the context of Holy Spirit's anointing. In ancient times, sheep were prey to parasites which crawled onto their heads and eventually into their ears, causing death. Shepherds carried oil to pour on sheep's heads because the oil's texture made parasites unable to climb up their heads, thus saving the sheep's lives. This practice evolved into the symbolism of anointing with oil for preservation, healing, empowerment, protection, and blessings.[8] Doesn't that thrill you? The anointing covers us and keeps things which could kill us from getting into our heads. Satan wants to permeate our thinking, but the anointing keeps us safe for God's communication and purposes.

Biblical uses of anointing were for priests (see Lev. 4:3), prophets (see 1 Kings 19:16), the tabernacle (see Exod. 40:9), and sacred vessels (see Exod. 30:16). Later, anointing kings became common practice. Like a king was anointed to fill a role, the anointing seals us prophets for His purpose too. Doesn't that speak volumes to us kings and priests? Samuel anointed two kings, Saul and David (see 1 Sam 10:1, 16:13), and Holy Spirit rushed upon David during this ceremony. This demonstrates a principle of the anointing. When one is chosen and anointed, he becomes empowered. In other words, when he's anointed, he becomes anointed. Eventually, this anointing practice became associated with Holy Spirit's anointing.

THE INGREDIENTS

That anointing oil had specific ingredients: myrrh, cinnamon, sweet cane, cassia, and olive oil (see Exod. 30:23-24), all representing our anointing. Myrrh was fragrant but bitter and utilized as a medicine, perfume, cosmetic, or pain suppressant (see Mark 1:23). It was costly and often used in burial preparation for bodies of people of means.[9] Cinnamon was an expensive, imported spice used for cooking and perfume.[10] Sweet cane or calamus, used for sacrifice (see Jer. 6:20), was precious because it came from far away India and was used in trading.[11] Cassia too was another exotic spice from far away and used for trading. It was for cooking or as a perfume, incense, medicine, and aphrodisiac.[12] The final ingredient and greatest quantity in the mixture was olive oil, itself connected with anointing. The olive tree, symbolizing peace, prosperity, and God's blessing, is valuable in the Holy Land, and much work and time go into its maturing. The fruit was a staple for cooking, ointments, and remedies for whatever ailed them. Harvesting the olive comes by shaking or striking the branches. Olives are associated with Jesus because Gethsemane means "olive press" and Jesus ascended from the Mt. of Olives.[13]

All these ingredients represent aspects of our own anointing and, like our anointing, are precious and sought after because others see its value. Experiencing the anointing comes with seeking and being willing to pay the required cost. As God uses it to bless others, it blesses us too beyond what's imaginable, and creates sufficiency to heal our pain. It speaks of intimacy with our beloved Father (see Prov. 7:17), for anointing comes from spending time with Him. Just as myrrh anoints for burial, the anointing is a type of dying to self as we present ourselves for God to use for His, not our purposes. It brings death to the carnal as it takes us into new dimensions of Holy Spirit. This anointing isn't of the flesh but of the Spirit, so it can't be imitated. The oil wasn't to be counterfeited but was to be used exclusively for holy purposes (see Exod. 30:32). Time is required before an olive tree can produce just like we mature over time. Our anointing comes through trials' bitterness to create growth then more anointing in us as we commune with the Father, like Jesus did in that Garden and the fragrance of His suffering reached Heaven. It comes with a shaking as Holy Spirit gets our attention and moves in and through us to release His empowerment.

The anointing breaks Satan's yoke (see Isa. 10:27) and brings power to preach, heal, deliver, comfort, and free others (see Luke 4:18). We "can do all things through Christ which strengtheneth [us]" (Phil. 4:13, KJV). That word for "Christ" is *Christos,* or "anointed."[14] I like the King James version of this scripture because its use of "which" instead of "who" implies the anointing strengthens us as overcomers in *all* situations. This can be restated as "I can do all things through The Anointed One's anointing because the anointing operating on and through me has boundless possibilities." So, we're anointed to accomplish God's purpose in each prophetic role we fill. As we speak His words, Holy Spirit has rubbed His anointing onto us, enabling us to fulfill His assignment for us. After Elijah's ascension, sons of the prophets said, "The spirit of Elijah is upon Elisha" (2 Kings 2:15). I believe these men were referring to the anointing they frequently saw and felt on Elijah and Elisha, just like others see and feel His anointing operating in us.

THE BOOK

So, the anointing is important in our lives, just like in Elijah's. Both before and during the book's writing, God not only brought out scriptural nuggets about Elijah, but He also pressed me to finish quickly multiple times. Once as I was praying, He showed me the word, "hie." Uncertain of its meaning or if it was truly a word, I looked it up. It meant "hurry." In other words, put this on the front burner. Again. I believe this study was a priority because understanding Elijah's ministry and anointing can clarify much in our own prophetic excursion as end-time revival comes. Being aware of how our anointing and gifts work is crucial as we enter this wondrous phase of human history.

When the Lord first told me to study Elijah, my husband suggested I write about both him and Elisha. However, though that made sense, I knew God had spoken Elijah's name alone. As I went through chapters about him, gleaning information, I understood why. Those scriptures, even word choice and phrase usage, had so much wealth, that limiting his story to one book was difficult. I've been greatly blessed by the assignment about this amazing man. As I drove down the interstate that dark night months ago, I knew the anointing for this book was for now so those feeling disenfranchised or at loose ends could find direction through seeing their own ministries mirrored in Elijah's. May God speak to you as you read these words, just like He enriched my life during this study. May you see yourself, your anointing, and your own prophetic destiny, no matter where you are on your prophetic journey.

WHO IS HOLY SPIRIT?

My parents accepted Jesus because of a miraculous healing in our family. From the start they became tongue-talking, Spirit-filled believers who thought this realm of using the gifts was normal. By the time I arrived, they were ensconced in that life and expected that of their kids too. Dad and Mom drove their family down the road on His revelation. Which church should we go to tonight? Where should summer vacation be? Whether through dreams, Scripture, or unctions, we recognized when Dad chewed on his eyeglasses' earpiece or Mom pursed her lips, scrunched her eyebrows, and looked off into space, that they were hearing God and would act on that. I've been operating in Holy Spirit nearly my entire life, yet I constantly find ways He shows Himself new and fresh.

Who is Holy Spirit? That question is as big as the universe, and people have come to understand just a bit of the wonder of this Person of the Godhead. Many dedicate their lives to pneumatology, study of Holy Spirit, yet I've heard comments that the more they learn, the more they discover they don't know. Amen! How do you explain anything unseen—wind, gravity, love? We recognize signs—leaves tossing gently, a book falling to the floor, a hand inside her love's hand as they stroll down the street. But those signs don't explain each complicated concept. Nor do signs of Holy Spirit working—speaking in tongues or discerning spirits—tell Who He is. He's God in His power and might. People look for revelation in many ways from tarot cards, to fortune cookies, to petals on a daisy, yet they overlook the true Tool Who can direct their lives. Jesus came for salvation and to usher in Holy Spirit to dwell in us. Elijah's life shares exciting principles about that Holy Spirit walk.

NEW TESTAMENT ROLE

Holy Spirit is a mystery and misunderstood by much of America's church and secular world. However, He permeates the Bible. Though Jesus operated through Holy Spirit during His time on earth, His return to the Father preceded Holy Spirit's coming in His fullness to dwell in believers. Except for a few who were filled with Holy Spirit earlier, that infilling happened on the Day of Pentecost to those in the Upper Room when tongues fell (see Acts 2:4). That manifestation still demonstrates our infilling with Holy Spirit. With that Upper Room event, Holy Spirit's gifts were given for living as overcomers. Those gifts represent His ability and are divided into three categories (see 1 Cor. 12:8-10):

- Revelation-words of knowledge, words of wisdom, discerning of spirits
- Speaking-tongues, interpretation of tongues, prophecy
- Power-faith, gifts of healings, working of miracles

Grouping them is misleading though, since they're interdependent with one another. We often speak a prophecy because of a word of wisdom. A word of knowledge may result in healings and miracles. The gifts work in tandem.

The New Testament also reveals Holy Spirit by His fruit, His character (see Gal. 5:22-23):

- Love
- Joy
- Peace

- Long suffering
- Kindness
- Goodness
- Faithfulness
- Gentleness
- Self control

The gifts of Holy Spirit verify and validate the love nature of God's character. How can we possibly wrap our minds around His ability and His character's awesome, unlimited nature?

Many believe Holy Spirit's work ended after the death of early apostles. On the contrary, much of Paul's writing deals with how He works now, and other scriptures confirm His purpose. Jesus spoke of and demonstrated Holy Spirit often in the Gospels, and His life showed Holy Spirit's pervasiveness. He was conceived by Holy Spirit (see Matt 1:18), and John the Baptist proclaimed that Jesus would baptize in Holy Ghost and fire (see Matt. 3:11). Holy Spirit sent Jesus for His wilderness testing (see Mark 1:12), and Matthew quotes from Isaiah that God will put His Spirit upon His Son to declare justice to Gentiles (see Matt. 12:18, Isa. 42:1-4). Jesus rejoiced in Holy Spirit (see Luke 10:21), and the Spirit led Him to Galilee to begin His ministry (see Luke 4:14). He told disciples to cast out demons by Holy Spirit (see Matt. 12:28) and to baptize in the name of Father, Son, and Holy Spirit (see Matt. 28:19).

Jesus prophesied that Holy Spirit's power would come on the disciples (see Luke 24:49). He said that what's born of flesh is flesh, but of the Spirit is spirit (see John 3:6) and that we must worship God in spirit and truth (see John 4:24). He said that Holy Spirit will convince the world of sin, righteousness, and judgment; guide us into truth; and glorify Jesus (see John 16:8-14). He left so the Helper could come (see John 14:16) and breathed on disciples to receive Holy Spirit (see John 20:22). His words and experiences aren't the only New Testament Holy Spirit references though. An angel told Mary, Holy Spirit would come upon her (see Luke 1:35). Elizabeth and John were filled with Holy Spirit while he was in her womb and leaped upon hearing Mary's voice (see Luke 1:15, 41). His dad, Zacharias, became filled with Holy Spirit when his tongue was loosed after John's birth (see Luke 1:67). Holy Spirit came upon Simeon and revealed he wouldn't die until he saw Christ. He saw that prophecy fulfilled when Holy Spirit led him to the temple the day Jesus's parents brought Him (see Luke 2:25-27). The Upper Room wasn't Holy Spirit's only appearance. He didn't show up suddenly when Jesus went back to Heaven but saturates the New Testament. He's always been there.

OLD TESTAMENT ROLE

Yes, Holy Spirit fills many New Testament pages, but references to Holy Spirit permeate the Old Testament too. The book of Ezekiel is so laden with Holy Spirit allusions, it has been called "'The Acts of the Holy Spirit' in the Old Testament."[1] The Spirit of the Lord translated Ezekiel multiple times (see Ezek. 3:12, 14; 11:1); and the Spirit of the Lord fell on him for a prophetic word (see Ezek. 11:5). To receive his dry bones revelation, the Hand of the Lord came on Ezekiel and brought him out in the Spirit of the Lord into the valley of bones (see Ezek. 37:1).

David embodies a Spirit-filled believer, with relationship and intimacy with the Father. While Samuel anointed David as king, "the Spirit of the Lord came upon David from that day forward" (1 Sam. 16:13). Think of that. Years before the Upper Room, David was Spirit-filled, probably speaking in tongues as he cared for his sheep, annihilated lions, and walked boldly before giants and demon-possessed kings. Jesus said, "David himself said by the Holy Spirit" (Mark 12:36) that God would make our enemies our footstools. From our Lord's very words, Holy Spirit was alive and active before Jesus came, died, arose, and ascended to make way for all to receive Holy Spirit. The Spirit gave David plans for building God's temple (see 1 Chron. 28:12) and enabled him to do extraordinary feats because of Holy Spirit's ability. What a great example of Holy Spirit's ministry and purpose.

Holy Spirit played a role from the first, as part of creation, for before God spoke light into existence, "the Spirit of God was hovering over the face of the waters" (Gen. 1:2). Imagine what this scripture is saying. Creation was accomplished because Holy Spirit was lingering there. When we want to activate the creative process to birth answers, we must be moved on by Holy Spirit. So, miracles, healings, deliverances, divine revelation, and even ideas, start with God's Spirit. Through Holy Spirit, we conceive those—ministries, healings, destinies—then birth them.

Samson was another man who operated in Holy Spirit. After his birth, the Spirit of the Lord moved on Samson (see Judg. 13:25) and helped him tear apart a lion (see Judg. 14:6), kill thirty men at Ashkelon (see Judg. 14:19), then escape from the Philistines by breaking his bonds (see Judg. 15:14). Isaiah too had Holy Spirit's abilities as he declared the "Lord God and His Spirit had sent" him (Isa. 48:16) and the "Spirit of Lord God [was] upon" him (Isa. 61:1). He prophesied that the Spirit of the Lord as well as the Spirit of wisdom, understanding, counsel, might, knowledge, and the fear of the Lord would rest on Jesus (see Isa. 11:2). He said God had put His Spirit upon Him (see Isa. 42:1) and declared God's Spirit would be poured on Jacob's descendants (see Isa. 44:3). Other Old Testament prophets like Daniel and Jonah declared Holy Spirit wasn't just a name in the Godhead but also mightily at work.

Besides these references, Holy Spirit is specifically mentioned often. He's called the Spirit of God (see Gen 41:38, 1 Sam. 11:6) and the Spirit of the Lord (see Judg. 3:10). He's referred to as My Spirit (see Hag. 2:5, Zech. 4:6) as in Joel 2:28-29, also quoted in Acts 2:17 when God said He "will pour out My Spirit on all flesh; [and]...pour out My Spirit in these last days." He's designated as Your Spirit (see Psalm 51:12) and His Spirit (see Psalm 106:33). Holy Spirit is the Hand of the Lord (or God) (see 2 Kings 3:15, Neh. 2:18) and the glory of the Lord (see 2 Chron. 5:14). Most fruit of the Spirit listed in Gal. 5:22-23 are also mentioned in Exod. 34:6-7. These unveiled Old Testament references to Holy Spirit show clearly He wasn't a new concept but has always been because He's God's Spirit. He's referenced both overtly and covertly in Elijah's life too.

ELIJAH

Each Holy Spirit reference in the Old and New Testaments is worthy of a chapter or book itself, but Holy Spirit led me to write this book to show how Elijah demonstrates His Person. Though he prophesied around 870 to 850 BC,[2] his experiences instruct those operating in Holy Spirit's gifts in the twenty-first century. Unconcealed Holy Spirit references exist in Elijah's ministry—the Spirit of the Lord carried Elijah to different locations (see 1 Kings 18:12). After his ascension, sons of the prophets wanted to find Elijah in case the Spirit of Lord had deposited him elsewhere (see 2 Kings 2:16). The word of Lord came to Elijah (see 1 Kings 17:2, 5, 8, 16), the fire of the Lord consumed the sacrifice on Mount Carmel (see 1 Kings 18:38), and the hand of Lord came upon Elijah as he outraced Ahab back to Jezreel (see 1 Kings 18:46). Other more subtle references acknowledged Holy Spirit. Elisha asked that a double portion of Elijah's spirit come on him (see 2 Kings 2:9), and students recognized that Elijah's spirit enabled Elisha to roll back Jordan's waters (see 2 Kings 2:15). Holy Spirit's operation through Elijah is the same ability indwelling in us, causing miraculous demonstrations through us too.

SYMBOLS FOR HOLY SPIRIT

As you can see from New and Old Testament references, Scripture refers directly to Holy Spirit often. However, other references are veiled. As you know, Jesus spoke in parables because God loves symbols. When asked why He taught in parables, Jesus said, "it has been given to [us] to know mysteries of the kingdom of heaven, but to [the world] it has not been given (Matt. 13:11). God shares His wisdom with His kids but puts it into parable form so we have access the unbeliever doesn't. He also wants us to seek it as if it were valuable: a treasure in a field or a beautiful pearl (see Matt. 13:44-45). Everything God has is a prize to be sought after. Holy Spirit's symbols show a wealth of His Person and meaning about His character. Though many symbols exist, Elijah's ministry demonstrates several:

FIRE AND LIGHT

Fire often represents Holy Spirit's passion, strength, force, illumination, and heat. His fire literally comes into believers' assemblies today. I've heard about it falling as worshippers lifted their voices and fire became so visible outside the building that someone called the fire department. One night in our service, those on the room's south side grew exceptionally hot. No one said anything until we later saw pictures. Several showed a progression in the back window of a face with fire emerging from His mouth. Holy Spirit's fire often comes as heat in hands. Frequently, when I lay hands upon someone for healing, he/she will feel heat, often so hot the person has trouble holding my hands.

One morning, I'd been ministering at the end of service. Church was over when Steve, who played on the worship team, walked to where I'd been praying. He stood for a moment while I finished talking with someone, then asked another prayer partner and me to pray for his shoulder he'd injured in sports when he was younger. Now, when he drummed on Sunday mornings, his shoulder hurt until Wednesday. Before we prayed, I knew he came in a way that was a prescription for healing—in faith; in humility; in desperation, pressing in though he had to wait; and in holiness, asking to be made whole so he could play better for God. I placed my hands on his shoulder, and he felt intense heat emanating from them. Lying against his shoulder, my hand issued forth heat which burned out pain and restored injured tissue. Before he left church, he had to sit down because the heat permeated his body; and his shoulder felt different immediately. He e-mailed me a couple days later and said he couldn't remember how wonderful being pain-free was because he'd hurt for thirty-four years.

Fire references are often signs of Holy Spirit. Moses encountered the burning bush on Mt. Sinai (see Exod. 3:2). He saw another aspect of Holy Spirit's fire, direction, as a pillar of fire led them in the wilderness by night (see Exod. 13:21). In the Upper Room, Holy Spirit came to apostles as tongues of fire and sat on each of them (see Acts 2:3). John proclaimed Jesus would baptize with Holy Ghost and fire (see Matt. 3:11). Elijah operated with Holy Spirit's fire on three different occasions. When he challenged Baal's prophets, the fire he called down from heaven on the sacrifice consumed everything (see 1 Kings 18:38). He also called it down twice to burn up Ahaziah's men. On the mountain of God, he expected the Lord to speak through fire. As he ascended, not tasting death, a chariot of fire drawn by horses of fire took Elijah away. Another example related to Elijah was when a fire symbol, light, came at the Transfiguration. Jesus's face shone as the sun and His clothes became as white as a light as Holy Spirit enveloped him in glory (see Matt. 17:2). Each example shows Holy Spirit's representation through fire, powerful and consummate.

WATER

Water, which flows, cleanses, and brings life, is another common Holy Spirit symbol. Like water, Holy Spirit is essential for believers. I can't imagine a day without His direction. Isaiah says, God "will pour water on him who is thirsty, And floods on dry ground; and...[His] Spirit on your descendants" (Isa. 44:3). Paul says by one Spirit, we're baptized into one body, drink into one Spirit (see 1 Cor. 12:13), and are washed in the water of the Word (see Eph. 5:26). Water which flowed from the rock Moses struck represented Holy Spirit coming forth for new life (see Exod. 17:6). Old Testament references to water are usually *mayim*, used 570 times in the Old Testament with many meanings including life, favor, sustenance, refreshing, cleansing, and fertility,[3] all Holy Spirit descriptions.

Just as rain rejuvenates from dryness and barrenness to bring crops, plenty, and restoration (see Joel 2:23-29), Holy Spirit sends rain to barren lives' fields through revelation, speaking, and power gifts (see Acts 2:17). A river symbolizes Holy Spirit, John's rivers of living water (see John 7:37-39). The dove of Holy Spirit descended upon Jesus during His baptism in the Jordan (see Matt. 3:16). Moses looked over the Jordan River to see the Promised Land (see Deut. 34:4), and Elijah had a Jordan experience. Before he ascended, he traveled to several places; one was to the Jordan to cross over with Elisha. The Jordan for Elijah, Elisha, Moses, and Jesus, was entrance into the Promised Land. Our Promised Land is life in Holy Spirit.

Elijah's *mayim* filled his ministry. He proclaimed drought. Then he hid in the Brook Cherith, his sanctuary and sustenance, as he ate food from ravens and drank water from the brook. When he ran from Jezebel, an angel fed him cake and water. The Widow of Zarephath also gave him a cake and water. His Baal showdown used water, and he took Baal's prophets to be killed in the Brook Kishon. When he called an end to the drought, rain fell from a cloud which rose from the sea. Then, he beat Ahab's chariot back to Jezreel in a storm. Each water reference in Elijah's life describes Holy Spirit: He's a necessity upon earth, is sustenance and sanctuary, and supernaturally provides. Holy Spirit precedes and causes the miraculous. He covers our sacrifice and washes away what's not of Him. He comes gently as the sea's waves or violently as a storm, but through Him, God brings salvation and an end to spiritual drought. Elijah's ministry was immersed in Holy Spirit.

WIND

Another symbol representing Holy Spirit is wind. *Pneuma*,[4] from the New Testament, and *ruach*,[5] from the Old Testament, are translated as "spirit" (see Acts 2:4; Mal. 2:15), "wind" (see John 3:8; 1 Kings 18:45), or "breath" (see Acts 17:25 [derivative of *pneuma*]; Psalm 18:15). Both are closely associated with Holy Spirit. On the Day of Pentecost, a rushing, mighty wind (derivative of *pneuma*) permeated the house and people were filled with Holy Spirit (see Acts 2:2). John makes the connection between wind and Holy Spirit when He says "wind [pneuma] blows...and you hear the sound...but cannot tell where it comes from and where it goes. So is everyone who is born of the Spirit" (John 3:8). We don't know His origin, but we feel Him and see His results. *Ruach* of life, or breath of life, is generally used as Holy Spirit (see Gen. 6:17).[6] In Elijah's ministry, *ruach* was both a great wind as the storm raged and ended the drought, and as his depression came, it tore mountains and broke rocks into pieces. Also, a whirlwind accompanied his chariot ascension.

OIL AND WINE

Oil and wine represent a believer's joy, power, calling, and anointing. Ministers use oil to pray for the sick (see James 5:14) because it symbolizes Holy Spirit's healing anointing, but Holy Spirit often deposits His own oil and miraculous power into people's hands. As mentioned in my "Introduction," much Scripture indicates oil as an anointing agent, or calling. Moses mentioned that anointing oil (see Exod. 30:31). Jesus quoted Isaiah 61:1 when He said the Spirit of Lord anointed Him to preach (see Luke 4:18). The consummate example of oil representing anointing was at Bethany when Mary anointed Jesus's feet with expensive spikenard, costly oil used only for special times, and wiped them with her hair (see John 12:3). How that should speak to us. Like individual ingredients listed in the "Introduction," Holy Spirit's oil is precious. Each time we operate in His anointing is an extraordinary occasion.

Jesus refers to putting new wine into old bottles as an analogy to putting Holy Spirit into established religion (see Luke 5:37). He alludes to Holy Spirit during the Passover feast when He says He "will no longer drink of the fruit of the vine until that day when [He drinks] it new in the kingdom of God" (Mark 14:25). Jesus's first miracle in Cana involved wine (see John 2:1-11), and His last words to disciples were for them to stay in Jerusalem until they were "endued with power from on high" (Luke 24:49), a reference to Holy Spirit. What an amazing revelation that the first, last, and everything in between in Jesus's ministry revealed Holy Spirit. Oil and wine are also apparent in Elijah's ministry. He's fed by the widow of Zarephath, who made bread from flour and oil. He performed the miracle of her oil being replenished, like Holy Spirit's unending anointing is available to us too. The implication of wine comes in Naboth's story since his vineyard would produce it. Naboth symbolizes those whom the enemy wants to destroy to keep them from coming into a Holy Spirit walk.

Cloud and Hand

A cloud, representing life-giving water and glory, is another Holy Spirit symbol. God was present in a cloud travelling before the Children in the Wilderness in the daytime (see Exod. 13:21-22). God's glory cloud often shows up now too, like when a cloud descended as God's presence, the Ark, was brought into Solomon's temple (see 1 Kings 8:10). Priests couldn't keep ministering because of a glory cloud (see 2 Chron. 5:14), and a cloud filled the Temple's inner court (see Ezek. 10:3-4). Moses stayed on the mountain with the Lord for forty days as God's glory appeared as a cloud (see Exod. 24:18). He also spoke to Moses from a cloud on Mount Sinai (see Exod. 19:9) and in a cloud covering the mountain with lightning and a trumpet sound (see Exod.

19:16). The cloud accompanying the Children in the Wilderness parallels Holy Spirit's presence in our own wilderness journey.

One name for Holy Spirit is Hand of the Lord. A hand represents power, and Spirit-filled believers understand how powerfully Holy Spirit uses hands as we "lay hands on the sick, and they…recover" (Mark 16:18). Jesus laid hands on the sick and healed them (see Mark 6:5). Apostles also used this Holy Spirit tool to do signs and wonders (see Acts 5:12), impart Holy Spirit into people's lives (see Acts 8:17; 19:6), and give a calling to those being sent forth (see Acts 13:3). Hands are for helping, and Holy Spirit is our ultimate Helper (see John 14:16). Elijah's ministry used both clouds and hands. His servant saw a cloud which looked like a hand. God talked through a cloud that overshadowed Jesus, Elijah, Moses, and the disciples at the Transfiguration. Elijah asked for bread from the widow's hand because Holy Spirit gives provision as we sow with our own hand. Elisha is described later as the one who washed Elijah's hands (see 2 Kings 3:11). What symbolism that speaks of. During ministry, my hands are often points of contact as I infuse power into another person. As Elisha washed Elijah's hands, that anointing power was transferred with each contact.

CLOTHING

Holy Spirit is also represented through clothing, demonstrating calling and authority. Joseph's phases toward his destiny are reflected through clothes he wore—pampered son, betrayed brother, forgotten prisoner, elevated Egyptian leader. I love the detail when he finally fulfilled his calling, he changed in just one day from prison garbs to those in which he met Pharaoh (see Gen. 41:14). Although we may occupy a lower station during our journey toward our destiny, God's calling remains sure. We will be promoted and our clothes (anointing) will show that. Elijah was also recognized by his clothes when he sent the message to Ahaziah, and so are we all recognized by our callings. He wore a leather belt, or girdle, to keep his robe from tripping him as he traveled. He girded his loins as he beat Ahab's chariot. He also had a mantle of anointing and authority, Holy Spirit's power to step boldly into ministry. During the Transfiguration ceremony with Elijah and Moses, Jesus's clothes were white as light (see Matt. 17:2). Whether clothing represents covering, empowerment, calling, authority, or God's glory, Holy Spirit envelops us in every case.

NUMBERS

Several numbers represent Holy Spirit in Scripture, but some reflected in Elijah's ministry are fifty, forty, twelve, seven, and three. Fifty can mean Holy Spirit's anointing and organization. Obadiah saved one hundred prophets during the drought, fifty in two caves. His hiding them fifty at a time demonstrates God's organization because He does nothing haphazardly nor chaotically. Nor does Holy Spirit or Jesus, Who organized five thousand hungry men plus women and children into groups of fifty before distributing loaves and fishes (see Mark 6:40). Our ministry or operating in our gifts isn't haphazard either. King Ahaziah sent fifty men plus one captain several times to kill Elijah. Holy Spirit's power and anointing spared the prophetic. Forty is also a prophetic number, meaning probation or testing. Before his ministry began, Moses worked forty years in the desert for his father-in-law (see Acts 7:30); he was on the mountain receiving the tablet forty days and nights (see Exod. 34:28); and Israel was tested in the wilderness for forty years. Jesus fasted forty days and nights before He began His ministry (see Matt. 4:2). Elijah journeyed forty days to Horeb on the sustenance of angels' food where he too received revelation after testing.

Twelve usually means divine governmental perfection and order, like twelve tribes and apostles, but it can also mean abundance. Elijah's ministry speaks of the prophetic and Holy Spirit's abundance. He built the Mt. Carmel altar for sacrifice with twelve stones, representing the tribes of Israel. He poured twelve barrels of water on the sacrifice, just as Holy Spirit saturates our sacrifices too. When Elijah went to Shaphath to give Elisha his calling, Elisha was plowing with twelve yoke of oxen, an abundance for a farmer. After Jesus fed the five thousand, twelve baskets were left (see Mark 8:19); and after feeding the four thousand, seven baskets remained (see Mark 8:19-20).

Therefore, Holy Spirit abundance is also demonstrated through the number seven. Seven, when used about Holy Spirit, means completeness, perfection, and fullness. Holy Spirit is complete— He was, is, and will be. Completeness is integral in Holy Spirit: creation took seven days, Elisha lay across the child seven times and brought him back to life, and the child sneezed seven times (see 2 Kings 4:35). Joshua had victory as seven priests blew seven trumpets, and they marched seven times on the seventh day (see Josh. 6:20). Elijah sent his servant back seven times looking for rain. What Holy Spirit starts, He completes.

Three also means completeness, plus resurrection, fullness, witness of God, and divine perfection. Jonah stayed in the fish's belly and Jesus lay in the tomb three days before each was resurrected and stepped into God's fullness. Holy Spirit is part of the perfect Trinity. For Elijah, three men participated in the Transfiguration (which occurred before the resurrection), and three were watching (witnesses). Ahaziah sent men to kill Elijah three times before the angel approved his coming down to speak judgment to Ahaziah. Elijah had water poured on the sacrifice three times. He stretched his body three times over the Widow of Zarephath's dead son before the resurrection was complete.

Three is also significant in his ministry in conjunction with one-half. This number recurs biblically and represents a season of testing and fulfillment of God's words. Jesus had a three-and-a-half-year ministry. Daniel describes a three-and-a-half-year tribulation (see Dan. 9:24-27), and the beast which would reign for "time and times and half a time" (see Dan. 7:25, 12:7; Rev.12:14). The Bible also refers to three and one-half years as forty-two months (see Rev. 11:2, 13:5) and one thousand two hundred and sixty (or ninety) days (see Dan. 12:11-12; Rev. 11:3, 12:6). Revelation references include 11:2 (witnesses prophesy), 11:11 (witnesses resurrected), 12:6 (woman fled in the wilderness), 12:14 (woman nourished in the wilderness), and 13:5 (power given to beast). For Elijah, in Revelation 11:3, the witnesses [Elijah and Moses] will walk around Jerusalem for three-and-a-half years. Elijah's drought lasted three-and-a-half years. With so much allusion to prophetic events, this number represents a season of testing then Holy Spirit's words being fulfilled.

CONCLUSION

Holy Spirit isn't a vague "thing" which showed up for a limited time and never before or after. He's a Person of the Godhead Who's been around since the beginning of time, and now He lives within us and operates through His Gifts. He gives direction, for "the Spirit also helps in our weaknesses. For we do not know what we should pray for as we ought, but the Spirit Himself makes intercession for us with groanings which cannot be uttered" (Rom. 8:26). Whether He's giving prayer language or direction for which road to turn on, He's all about helping His children.

Elijah's life is synonymous with the prophetic and a testimony of Holy Spirit. We hear nothing about him until he showed up doing miraculous feats and already understanding the gifts. Whether Elijah entered the prophetic as a student at a school of the prophets; as a protégé for another prophet; or just as an operator in Holy Spirit, the consummate Teacher (see John 14:26), he used his Holy Spirit gifts amazingly. He intimately understood Holy Spirit's ways of operating through a man as he heard from God and stepped out to speak with authority. His pronouncements impacted natural events on earth, and he had such intimacy with God he didn't taste death. We can learn from Elijah.

ELIJAH AND THE DROUGHT

1 King 17:1-7

Prophetic Principles:
Declaring God's Word, Coming into Our Calling,
Learning Obedience, Understanding Provision,
Growing, God Raising a Mighty Prophet to
Counter Mighty Evil, God's Unfolding Plan

Holy Spirit's Role:
Spirit of Judgment (Isa. 4:4);
Holy Spirit As Prophet (2 Pet. 1:21)

My first day back from summer vacation each year as an Indiana high school teacher included a motivational speaker, introduction of new staff and faculty, and a short speech by the school board president. That year, the president was a believer who had the audacity to say a prayer for a good school year. Afterwards, I heard negative comments, even from believers, concerning separation of church and state and how inappropriate his prayer was. Are you kidding? Our school needed help—low test scores, high dropout rates, classroom discipline issues, teen pregnancies, absentee parents. Many students had such enormous problems that expecting them to sit and pay attention was impossible. And praying wasn't appropriate? Sometimes my heart grows weary of what's done in the name of political correctness and tolerance of all groups, except Christians. News stories proclaim Christian persecution, from personal assaults to lawsuits removing any vestige of God from public sites. That day, I shared the old adage with my colleagues: "If not now, when? If not us, who?"

Today's Christians must take a stand for righteousness. That often puts us in the minority and the butt of jokes from liberal politicians and celebrities. Elijah must have felt that isolation too as he became God's lone voice to speak His judgment. When we take a prophetic stand, much of the world and even the church joins against us. Then God allows a drought to come so change happens. Dry times are often created by disobedience and its consequences—refusing to move to the next assignment when God says go, marrying outside His will, choosing a career not in His plan. Israel's drought fell because of their choices too. Everything that brought on and perpetuated the drought could be summarized in one word—Baal. Israel's king and queen worshiped him and made others turn aside from God. He wanted His people back, and He chose Elijah as His representative for that job.

ELIJAH

The drought came through the words of a man who's referred to only as "Elijah the Tishbite, of the inhabitants of Gilead" (1 Kings 17:1). "Tishbite" means "that makes captive,"[1] and Elijah became a force which took captive the things of Satan. This identification probably means he lived in Tishbe, a town east of the Jordan in the region of Gilead, meaning "the heap or mass of testimony."[2] Tishbite also means "recourse."[3] Recourse, "access or resort to a person or thing for help or protection,"[4] is what Elijah did through Holy Spirit. He tapped into the Helper's resources like no one else in the Bible except Jesus. This Holy Spirit man was a testimony, and "Holy Spirit also testifies to us" (Heb. 10:15,

NIV). We're called as watchers on the wall, prophets seeing what's coming. Elijah was a watcher to speak God's words to man.

He was an "inhabitant" of Gilead. "Inhabitant" is *towshab*, "a dweller; espec. (as distinguished from a native citizen and a temporary inmate or mere lodger) resident alien:—foreigner— sojourner, stranger."[5] Wow! Like Elijah, Christians just don't fit in. We're aliens passing through. The writer of Hebrews said fathers of faith "all died in faith, not having received the promises, but having seen them afar off were assured of them, embraced them and confessed that they were strangers and pilgrims on the earth" (Heb. 11:13). They were sojourners like Elijah; and like them, we're strangers and pilgrims en route to a better place. We can't get too comfortable in our temporary assignments. When God called Abram from his cushy life in Ur to dwell the rest of his days as a nomad in tents, he knew he was a sojourner (see Gen. 12). This world isn't home, and its temporary comforts mean little unless they're part of the eternal.

Elijah came to Ahab proclaiming Israel's punishment for following Baal's prophets: "'there shall not be dew nor rain these years, except at my word'" (1 Kings 17:1). Dew is *tal*, meaning "to cover."[6] In 1 Kings 17:1 and 18:1, "rain" is *matar*, meaning "rain (upon)."[7] The other rain in Elijah's story is what God sent at the drought's end, not *matar* but *geshem*, "to shower violently"[8] (see 1 Kings 17:7, 14; 18:41, 44, 45). When you lose sight of the Lord and chase after other gods, you step outside the realm of God's everyday coverings and showers of blessings. When you turn around, get rid of your idols, and make Him Lord again, He'll cause unimaginable abundance to rain in your life.

Elijah's authoritative proclamation and its coming to pass make him seem already experienced in the prophetic, with an understanding of how God's Spirit operated to bring divine occurrences. Interestingly, he wasn't called a prophet until after the drought. That word wasn't used for Samuel either, until he'd learned obedience to speak hard words to Eli. After he gave those words, God elevated him so all of Israel recognized him as a prophet (see 1 Sam. 3:20). God gives assignments, and some are not-so-pleasant, so we can come into our destiny. Samuel and Elijah faithfully spoke despite potential consequences, and then God advanced them to the office for which He'd destined them. This message should speak to us ordinary people whom God chooses. Whether or not we have a title, God brings us into our calling if we obey. Elijah isn't recorded as calling himself a prophet. Yet around three thousand years later, we still know what he was. Samuel was just a child and Elijah was just a man, but these prophets' callings were powerful. Oh, what can just a man or woman do when partnered with Holy Spirit?

AHAB AND ELIJAH

Ahab became king of Israel after his evil father, Omri, died (see 1 Kings 16:28). Ahab was more evil and angered God worse than any king before him had done (see 1 Kings 16:33). His wife, Jezebel, was a heathen worshipper and wicked woman; and like many who consort with evil, he followed her lead. God has a reason for telling us not to mix with the ungodly. He understands human nature better than we do. He said not to intermarry because we're often drawn toward their pagan lifestyles and eventually serve their gods. Whether worshipping Baal or skipping church to go boating, we change, and usually not for the better. Ahab worshipped Jezebel's gods, built a temple, made a wooden image, and set up an altar for Baal in Samaria (see 1 Kings 16:32-33).

Yet, God answers pervasive wickedness with a remarkable man or woman—Noah, Gideon, Deborah, Samson—to counter atrocious evil. Now the terrible Jezebel and Ahab were addressed by one of God's generals—Elijah. With such insidious ungodliness, no wonder God chose Samaria, where Ahab and Jezebel lived, for this amazing man of God to present himself to the king to proclaim no rain or dew in Israel (see 1 Kings 17:1). God often sends us right into the lions' lair to show His might.

The nation would experience drought and famine because God was responding to the sin and famine of souls during Ahab's reign. As Elijah showed up to proclaim God's judgment in Chapter 17, thus, the journey of these men began.

THE PROPHET

Elijah arrived on the scene and brought the message to a backslidden Israel that Jehovah was still God regardless of so many following the politically correct path delineated by the king and queen. Sounds like our nation during these latter days. We Elijahs need to be the voice to identify sin and step out in faith despite what's popular. In this first encounter, as Elijah spoke to Ahab and authoritatively proclaimed drought, he swore by the Lord: "As the Lord God of Israel lives, before whom I stand" (1 Kings 17:1).

"Lord" means Jehovah, "(the) self-Existent or Eternal."[9] His authority was God's, Elohiym's, "the supreme God";[10] so he wasn't afraid of Ahab's ability to kill him. We're emissaries of Jehovah Elohiym, Who is Supreme, and always was and will be. Elijah answered to Him, not Ahab. This event gives a principle for our own Holy Spirit giftings: speaking and obeying is crucial because we stand before God, rather than men. Elijah approached his enemy Ahab, risking all, to declare God's word because he understood that along with his ability to receive revelation came responsibility to share that word (see Jer. 23:28). Our obedience is an act of faith which starts us toward our destiny.

THE WORD

God's word is important to Him, whether His *logos* or *rhema* through His prophets' mouths. His word is birthed by Holy Spirit (see 2 Pet. 1:21). We're in partnership with Holy Spirit. Therefore, God "does nothing, unless He reveals His secret to His servants the prophets…The Lord God has spoken! Who can but prophesy?" (Amos 3:7-8). Before God allows events to occur, He tells His prophets. He cherishes them enough to tell them His secrets. All His prophets. We're not the only ones who hear from God, nor was Elijah. He revealed His plans to many, including Abraham when He sent two heavenly messengers to warn him of Sodom's destruction because He didn't want to keep those plans from him (see Gen. 18:17). As intimacy and relationship with God grow, so does His sharing. He informed Elijah, Abraham, and many other prophets of His plans, even occurrences hundreds of years later. Today, God's still revealing His intentions through Holy Spirit because even now He doesn't want to hide what He's doing from us.

Like God commissioned Ezekiel, "Son of man, eat what you find; eat this scroll, and go, speak to the house of Israel" (Ezek. 3:1), we eat His words and they become part of our being. Our job is to share that, and Amos said we can do nothing else. Jeremiah also understood how God's word is innate as he chewed the words which brought joy and rejoicing of heart (see Jer. 15:16). He used a great analogy to describe Amos's and Ezekiel's comments about how that word becomes the prophet's obsession: "His word was in my heart like a burning fire Shut up in my bones; I was weary of holding it back, and I could not" (Jer. 20:9). Can you relate to times when God gives a word you need to deliver or you feel you'll burst?

Jesus was God's Word Who became flesh (see John 1:14) as He walked among those in need. Now, as we go about the Father's business, we're that word that's made of flesh and dwelling among people to meet needs and speak God's word through Holy Spirit. Elijah proclaimed drought because he was a prophet, God's word in the flesh, and a prophet's being has God's word "shut up in [his] bones." It's our essence. Fire shut up in the bones has an interesting meaning. Bones are not only our skeletal support system. The center of large bones contains marrow with stem cells which produce blood cells and fat, bone, and cartilage. Blood vessels and capillaries, plus production of cells make marrow crucial to blood like no other body part. God's word is our core, living in our marrow. We must speak that living word.

Elijah later said he had done these things at God's word (see 1 Kings 18:36). He understood Holy Spirit is a creative force, preparing the way for God's Word (see Gen. 1:1-3). Therefore, as Elijah spoke the Spirit's word forth, it became an unstoppable force to bring forth God's will. He created Elijah's words, essential to bringing an entire nation to repentance. God then honored Elijah's prayers and proclamations and brought the three-and-a-half-year drought. Drought brings famine and generates the need for food, and this nation had been starving in both body and soul. The state of Israel at this time reminds me of Eli the priest who was so spiritually out of tune, that the "word of the Lord was rare in those days" (1 Sam. 3:1). He didn't have the ark (God's presence) in Jerusalem and interpreted Hannah's sincere prayer as drunkenness. Leaders, especially prophets, stay attuned to God by dwelling in His presence. There, they hear God's words from His mouth and can bring God's word, His light, back to the land.

God's word comes for mighty phenomena like beginning and ending a drought, but it also comes to direct us, as when He told Elijah to get away from Ahab and then to leave Cherith (see 1 Kings 17:2, 8). Usually, a prophet experiences occasional revelations which affect nations. But God usually reveals direction about ours, our family's, and others' lives because we all matter to Him. The key is to obey and to act on that word from the Lord whether the message is personal or universal. God and the prophet are in partnership, so Elijah spoke as God's mouthpiece to bring atmospheric changes "according to the word of the Lord which he spoke by Elijah" (1 Kings 17:16). God's words, Elijah's mouth. In God's eyes, His words are weighty whether He speaks audibly or through His prophets. I love when the Gospels discuss prophecies about Messiah and say God worked out details to validate the prophets' words (see Matt. 1:22). Through prophets' mouths, His commands go forth through His swift word (see Psalm 147:15). What an awesome prophetic responsibility.

LIVING WATER

Interestingly, the word "drought" isn't used in this chapter, but "famine" is mentioned in the next chapter. Lack of water doesn't seem to be the main issue. When Cherith dried up, God led Elijah to other waters. The widow had water to give him but only a little oil and flour because of famine. Elijah poured plenty of water on his sacrifice. Angels fed Elijah with cakes and water. When he went to confront Ahab to declare the drought's end, Ahab and Obadiah were looking in "springs of waters and to all the brooks; [to]…find grass to keep the horses and mules alive" (1 Kings 18:5). Those brooks and springs are plural and referred to as "all," indicating more than one. The problem they're addressing isn't water supply, but rather insufficient grass from lack of rain.

This Middle Eastern area has ample water sources which could have been utilized. At Jerusalem, the Spring of Gihon gushed several times a year and provided seemingly endless fresh water. The Jezreel Valley has fertile farmland and many natural springs.[11] This region also has limestone layers, which allow underground springs' development.[12] In the Old Testament, groundwater from springs and brooks is called *chay mayim*, "living water."[13] The New Testament word is *dwzao hudor*.[14] Both refer to abundant, natural sources of water—fountains, springs, and wells. With effort, even if brooks dried up during drought, people could dig and find sources of living water to irrigate crops.

John quoted Jesus that, "'He Who believes in [Jesus], as the Scripture has said, out of his heart will flow rivers of living water.' But this He spoke concerning the Spirit" (John 7:38-39). John clearly defined "living water"—Holy Spirit. Jeremiah said people had forsaken living waters and built cisterns rather than using what God gave naturally (see Jer. 2:13). That speaks of today's body of Christ who opt to drink from manmade systems of religion they've grown comfortable with instead of abundant Living Water of Holy Spirit. As a result, drought and famine have come to the body of Christ. Living water was available in Elijah's day and to us today in ample supply through God's Spirit.

Isaiah spoke of Holy Spirit Whom God would use to "pour water on him who is thirsty, And floods on the dry ground...and pour [His] Spirit on your descendants, And [His] blessing on your offspring" (Isa. 44:3). Through His Spirit, we have plenty to drink; but if we want vegetation to grow, we'll have to dig to find that water. Because rain or dew weren't falling, crops, grass, livestock and people could starve. Today, famine is not only of teaching *logos* but also ignoring Holy Spirit's living *rhema.* Without *rhema*, we spiritually dry up and die. Even our Promised Land will become parched without an influx of Holy Spirit, which makes us never thirst again. We must allow Holy Spirit to quench the thirst with His living water.

CHERITH

As soon as Elijah spoke the Lord's judgment, he received direction from God. That should be a lesson to us. Often, we want God to move us into our destiny when we haven't obeyed him about doing something at a previous assignment. No matter where God sent Elijah, obedience was imperative, and he was saved by following God's directive. God gave Elijah clear instructions: He was to leave Samaria, go east, "and hide by the Brook Cherith" (1 Kings 17:3). I like His using the word *"hide."* There's a time to stand and a time to hide. That word is *cathar,* "to hide (by covering)."[15] The land wasn't covered by dew or rain, but God's obedient ones were covered and provided for in their hiding places during the drought. When we obey Him and walk in our calling, He'll be our covering, and the wicked one can't touch us (see 1 John 5:18). **He's gotcha covered!**

Elijah retreated to Cherith (see 1 Kings 17:5). For the person seeking to do God's will and his footsteps be ordered of God, location is crucial. My sister, Lynda, for example, knew God wanted her to step into ministry but didn't know when, where, or what. As she gave those decisions to Him, she obeyed Him, step-by-step, as she took care of her children and worked in her local church. Within a short time, He'd led her from Cincinnati to Colorado where she located a job with a Christian organization which led to her destiny in Him. God's not just interested in what we do for our ministries but also in everything related to our lives (see 2 Pet. 1:3). God cared that my sister discovered a good location to bring up her young family and where she could grow into the mature Christian she is today.

God told Elijah where to go and what to do when he arrived. When we're obedient in small assignments, He elevates us to greater ones and leaves nothing to chance. But this story shows another aspect of God taking us into our destinies. He doesn't usually give more of the picture than we need to know. Why? I'd probably mess it up by moving too quickly or trying to make it happen my way when God's way is oh, so much better. Abraham and Sarah did it their way and got an Ishmael instead of Isaac. God told Elijah about His Cherith provision but didn't tell him he'd be there just a while before he'd go elsewhere. God works in seasons. Here in the Midwest, each season is varied and beautiful. Spring brings hope after long winter days with ice, sleet, and lots of snow. But spring couldn't come if summer and autumn hadn't preceded winter, for if old leaves don't fall, new ones can't come. When God unfolds our life's picture in His time, His way, know that He'll take care of His prophets during their Cherith season, and then in whichever season comes next.

In his Cherith season, God spared Elijah's life and did a work in him too. Cherith means "cutting; piercing; slaying."[16] He was already hearing from God, but that doesn't mean issues that could impact his ministry weren't still there and needed cut away. That's a lifelong process, even for mature prophets. A refining occurred in him, a cutting, just as circumcision cuts away flesh. God often uses our droughts to cut away what needs to be eliminated. One day, a childhood friend showed up at our house and told me his life hadn't gone well: he'd made poor choices which lost him his job, wife, and home. Now, he was living in his truck. My first reaction was to pity him and to offer him a bed in our house. However, I felt a check in my spirit. As I listened to his story, Holy Spirit impressed me that He could teach my friend more by sleeping in the back of a truck than he could learn by sleeping on a feather mattress. David said, "Before I was afflicted I went astray, but now I keep Your word" (Psalm 119:67). Even Jesus learned obedience through His suffering (see Heb. 5:8). Our furnace of affliction, our own drought season, burns away issues that could keep us from entering our destiny while God cuts out what's not of Him.

The concept of our Christian progression is shown throughout Scripture—Ezekiel's River, Nehemiah's Gates, Moses's Tabernacle. Our journey's purpose is to arrive at our destiny, but a crucial component is in the expedition itself. What will each experience, each season, build in us? Patience? Faith? Love? Trust in Him? Confidence in our gifts? God takes us through each event to remove flaws from us or put things into us. Here, God cut away Elijah's dependence on himself while creating covenant with the Father. No matter how far along Elijah was in his role as prophet, he was still a work in progress because even as a refined prophet, he operated in the flesh. God cuts and purges until we're ready to do things His way and accomplishes a mighty work in us during our solitary Cherith seasons. Like Elijah, we may already be operating in our prophetic gifts, but those solitary seasons refine our gifts and character while building relationship and trust. During hardship, we often see only drought or famine but forget those are allowed by God to bring change. During his drought time, Elijah would become adept at making prophetic pronouncements, performing miracles, mastering translations, and having a resurrection. Quite a résumé, and we don't know what else God did in and through him that's unrecorded. What is God cutting out of or putting into your life during your Cherith season, as He brings forth His purpose?

THE RAVENS

As Elijah hid at the brook, God proved His covenant to provide for His servants. See, God will "supply all your need according to His riches in glory by Christ Jesus" (Phil. 4:19). God's supply is beyond ample because He's really rich—He owns even the beasts in the forest and cattle on the hillsides (see Psalm 50:10). He provides commensurately with what He has, and that's everything. In His abundance, He didn't forget a weird prophet in a drought. Water flowed into the brook. Then, he was fed a two-course meal of bread and meat twice a day by ravens. Doesn't that thrill you that although the world was experiencing drought and famine, God provided Elijah with abundant sustenance? We too can be fed bread and meat (word) while we drink water (Holy Spirit) as long as we stay where God tells us. Provision may be brought by an unlikely source—a sour neighbor, our toddler, an unexpected letter. No matter whom or what God chooses, He'll sustain us during growing and hiding times. He supplies our needs but also "provides food for the raven, When its young ones cry to God, And wander about for lack of food" (Job 38:41). His creations are all important to Him, so He provided for those ravens; then they in turn could provide for the prophet.

I chuckle when I think of Elijah's sustenance. I understand how ravens could potentially find meat, but the bread makes me wonder. Where were they getting it twice a day? Since during the drought Jezebel supported 850 pagan prophets of Baal and Asherah (see 1 Kings 18:19), my guess is that those prophets ate lots of bread. I can imagine cooks fretting because every time they took bread from the oven to cool, those darn ravens stole some. Brook Cherith was about twenty-five miles from the Jezreel palace. A raven can travel from twenty-two to twenty-eight miles per hour,[17] so they could easily have made that twice-a-day trip to redistribute the kings' wealth for God's prophet's benefit. Isaiah says, "Therefore your gates...shall not be shut day or night, That men [or ravens] may bring to you the wealth of the Gentiles, And their kings in procession" (Isa. 60:11). Isn't that like God to take from Gentiles to give to His own, even when that Gentile is Jezebel? She had devoted herself to his destruction but was instead probably feeding him her bread for his survival! God certainly has a sense of humor!

Throughout Elijah's story, he was miraculously fed three times—by ravens, angels, and a widow. A raven seems to be an unusual choice since God could have sent angels but chose instead a common, unclean creature (see Lev. 11:15), treated as sinister in literature. However, God knew what He was doing. Because much of its existence revolves around finding food, the raven was a perfect choice. David described it when he said that God "gives to the beast its food, And to the young ravens that cry" (Psalm 147:9). Common in Israel, they're intelligent, vocal, and voracious hunters; will eat nearly anything; and fly in constant search for food.[18] Ravens hide food for later and steal from other animals to survive. When they find a kill, they call others to share, even if one they call is a prophet by a brook.[19] Because of their scavenger nature, Noah sent one from the ark probably to find if waters had receded (see Gen. 8:7) or if dead bodies were above water level. That's also possibly why God selected them when He commanded them to feed Elijah at Cherith (see 1 Kings 17:4). It's their nature.

I guess while Father, Son, and Holy Ghost were creating, They said, "There'll be a prophet in a few thousand years who'll need miraculously fed. Let's make a bird with a scavenger character." This wasn't the only time God used His animals' proclivities to help His people. As Lazarus the beggar lay on the street, a dog licked his sores (see Luke 16:21). Though I've always read that detail as a contrast with the rich man's wealth, it could also show God's provision. Within a dog's saliva is a natural healing substance.[20] The dogs' licking probably relieved Lazarus's pain. Ravens and dogs, though not God's best, became His perfect choice to accomplish His purpose. Now, whom does that sound like? God doesn't pick those the world would choose but finds His perfect choice for the job He needs done. God will save us, but it may come through lowly things—a talking donkey, dirty river, nasty dog, or bread-seeking ravens. Whatever He chooses though, when God sends you to do His work, He'll provide.

HIS PROVISION

I love how God made promises to Elijah and how He's faithful to His word. He promised provision and made good through ravens. He promised drought and then rain and did just what He said. He stands by His word, so when you need something, you should find promises in the Word and stand on them. For example, if you, like Elijah, have an enemy with life and death power over you, you can rest because "'No weapon formed against you shall prosper, And every tongue which rises against you in judgment You shall condemn. This is the heritage of the servants of the Lord" (Isa. 54:17). You don't need to fret about your enemy's weapons because God takes care of you. He promised, and, after all, it's the "heritage of the servants of the Lord." When you're in His service, you can expect He'll care for you.

My family discovered that firsthand. My parents lived by faith, including not going to doctors. Therefore, when I entered kindergarten, I'd never been to a doctor until I was sent for a smallpox shot. It didn't take. The school sent me again with the same results. After that, no one considered it again for my thirteen years of public education. However, before starting college, Miami University said I needed another shot. Again, nothing happened.

When I told Mom the doctor said I had a natural immunity, she pursed her lips like I'd seen her do often. "Huh. I thought you had smallpox," she said simply.

She told me that when I was a baby, she and Dad had done missionary work in Mexico. Though borders were closed because of smallpox, somehow my parents had unlimited access to do what God had instructed them. They worked there then traveled back home to Ohio, excited about what God had done during those visits. Then, I became sick. A library book told Mom I had symptoms and was within the incubation time to have contracted the disease. At first, she was taken aback by that word—smallpox. Certain words shake our faith walk; but as we gain relationship with God, we learn to step beyond fear. My mom's woman-of-faith character kicked in because she'd fallen in love with a Savior Who took care of His children. Who kept His word when He gave a heritage to His kids. Who sent you into assignments with His provision. Who let you be taken care of, even by dirty birds. Who didn't endanger your children. She cried to God, and He answered with a healing and a natural immunity.

More than anything, I know God's hand protects and saves us (see Psalm 138:7) as we follow His directives in His appointed place, time, way, and purpose. He can send us anywhere to accomplish that purpose. But if we stay in His will, we don't have to worry about ours or our family's safety, although our enemies send predators to every known land to find us as Ahab did during the drought. God saves His way and often by using what the world considers foolish (see 1 Cor. 1:27)—things like ravens, smallpox viruses, or people like you and me who don't qualify to work for Him by man's standards. Yet, He orchestrates every detail.

CONCLUSION

One spring, God spoke to us to leave the church Wade and I attended and go to the South to seek His will. We told our pastor, and in June, we left. We held meetings in several states and were gone for nearly a month before we rolled back into Connersville, not knowing details but certain God would guide us in the next step of our journey. We'd been home a few days when He told us to remodel our kitchen. Its outdated, hodgepodge cabinets, cracked plaster, and burnt floor from one of Jennifer's cooking experiments had long since gone beyond character. It badly needed intense sprucing up, so Wade and our neighbor began a building project. During that time, we visited different churches to find a new one in which to put down roots. At one of them, the pastor preached about Nehemiah's walls. At home, as I looked up his references, the Lord led me to do a study on the Gates in those walls being rebuilt. I was thrilled as that study unfolded into a picture of how those Gates correlate to places we grow in our walk toward our godly destiny. In a few weeks, I was approached to start a Bible study. By September, I not only had one ready to teach in our home, but we had a new kitchen to fellowship in afterwards. Had we not gone where God led us, we may have missed the blessing that ended in my book, *God's Plan for Our Success, Nehemiah's Way*, published through Destiny Image. That Bible study changed Wade, others, and me, and it started with simple obedience to step where He told us.

Have you ever been in a dry time? No matter how much you sped ahead, you ended up spinning your wheels? If you were going by God's chart in the closet, it would be a long time between growth spurts. You might wonder if you'd become stunted, or if you'd reached the maximum potential you'd ever achieve. Then, one day, you step to those marks on the wall. You hadn't noticed even slight gains, but suddenly you'd grown tremendously. Drought's fallowness did something and brought indiscernible change along the way. Like in Elijah's life, drought will come, but oh the wonders God accomplishes in those dry times.

Elijah and the Widow of Zarephath

1 Kings 17:8-24

Prophetic Principles:
Bringing Provision, Being Refined, Receiving a
Prophet's Reward, Sowing and Reaping, Following God's
Direction, Understanding Deeper Signs and Wonders

Holy Spirit's Roles:
Revealer (1 Cor. 2:12-16);
Creator of Signs and Wonders (Rom. 15:19)

I don't like change. I've lived in the same house for twenty plus years, and I worked on the same job for thirty plus. I don't like to rearrange my furniture or keep up with fashions. When I change, I feel like I'm at the mercy of the ocean's wave. For a moment, it sweeps me off my feet, and I find no terra firma on which to stand. Although I know that wave will set me down in a few seconds and eventually deposit me on the beach, panic still grips me momentarily from lack of solidity. But this trait isn't God's way. When one season's wave moves, He wants us to follow. Often His will is apparent because He tells us through a dream, scripture, or confirming word. Maybe, though, circumstances say the time to move has arrived. Maybe our Cherith stops flowing.

THE NEW ASSIGNMENT

The Brook Cherith dried up after six months. Doesn't that sound like how it goes? You're praising God for marvelous raven provision, and then it's gone. Maybe someone who sows into your ministry stops sending a monthly check. Maybe the job you're counting on downsizes and you're left with nothing. Moses learned the principle of faith and divine supply (see Exod. 16-17). They needed food, so God sent manna and quail. Their needed water came from a rock. God doesn't have a single source of supply, but we do. Him! He knows how to provide as we leave our comfort zone and go to our next assignment. God sent Elijah to Zarephath to the house of a heathen widow God raised up "to provide for [him]" (1 Kings 17:9). God can save us during our own times of drought and famine through many resources—an ungodly landlord, an unexpected financial windfall, a chance encounter at the grocery, a raven, or even a destitute widow. He doesn't send His prophets on a journey to let them be casualties but prepares ways of escape before they ever need it.

Wade and I had worked in many ministry capacities—pastors, teachers, evangelists, writers—yet we relied on the provision my paycheck brought in each month. That's why when God spoke that it was time for me to retire and be full-time in the ministry, I hesitated. How could we go from my contributing over half of our income to a monthly retirement check that was a fraction of what I earned. Though logic said I needed to stay, God confirmed that it was time to go; we acted in faith and I turned in my retirement letter. Despite that step, though, I was filled with insecurities. What else could I do after thirty-three years of teaching? How could we afford not only our home expenses but also the extra required for ministry travel? How would we find open doors for ministry opportunities? Before the end of that first summer, God had begun to implement His plan as He led me into my Gates research, teaching, and writing. Since then, He has opened doors for us to share His message, given timely *rhema* for sermons, and provided income time and again through unexpected sources. Though my retirement check is much smaller now, God knows the perfect way to supplement. By obeying when He said to leave Cherith and go to Zarephath, He has catapulted both Wade and me into ministry we never dreamt of.

Ministry seasons change as we obey—obedience led Wade and me into a new facet of ministry. God didn't send Elijah to Cherith until he stepped out in faith and made the proclamation to Ahab, but He didn't send him to Zarephath until the Cherith season was finished. When the time to leave arrived, God spoke to Elijah to "Arise, go to Zarephath...and dwell there" (1 Kings 17:9). This order has awesome principles. Elijah reacted to God's command like we should. When God told Elijah to "arise," "he arose and went to Zarephath" (1 Kings 17:10). Obedience is the only accurate response when God gives directives. Abraham answered likewise when God told him to sacrifice the son he'd awaited twenty-five years, born to parents well past child-bearing years. When God spoke, he didn't bemoan his loss but got up early the next morning and saddled his donkey to get on his way (see Gen. 22:3). Some want God's blessings but forget their response should be unquestioning, immediate obedience.

The second aspect of that quote is that God told Elijah to *dwell* in Zarephath. He was described as an *inhabitant*, a sojourner, in Gilead. This word *dwell*, though, is stronger—*yashab*, "to dwell, to remain; caus. to settle, to marry—abide."[1] When Elijah arrived on God's business, Zarephath was his true dwelling. He staked a claim to live there. We prophets are sojourners and don't fit in with the rest of the world, but we're at home when we're about the Father's business. Years ago, Wade and I realized we were sojourners in this life. We had jobs to do, children to rear, chores to accomplish, but our hearts were wherever He led us. Our *yashab* isn't about geographical location but rather pursuing His will. We stay when He says and go when He says. His assignments take us on varied roads, but the destination where we settle is where we can put down roots and grow in Him. It's our *yashab*.

During the bulk of drought time, God provided for Elijah through a desperate widow. But he wasn't the only one about whom God cared. The whole land had gone through months of famine, so the widow's need was dire too. A Christian's job is to care for "orphans and widows" (James 1:27). Therefore, though her responsibility was to give to Elijah, his job was to provide for her too. Our words should be coupled with actions as we speak and actually give blessings to the needy (see James 2:15-16). However, sometimes we have no finances, clothes, or food to offer. Then we can give prayers and power through our gifts. Tangible earthly goods are one thing, but spiritual wealth produces unending supply. Peter said, "Silver and gold I do not have, but what I do have I give you" (Acts 3:6). Elijah's provision wasn't from earthly goods because he had none. His came from the Father. Releasing the eternal allows Christians to eat fish and learn to catch them too. Elijah's spiritual silver and gold gave miraculous provision of Holy Spirit. He had eaten bread in his Cherith season so now he had that to share in Zarephath. We prophets also have great spiritual wealth we can share with others.

When we're led by the Spirit, often God will allow one area of our lives and ministry to dry up so another can come forth. He's the ultimate Multitasker, Who orchestrates blessing and direction for us, but not exclusively. He speaks into billions of His children's lives. Our own trip from Cherith to Zarephath, deeper into the desert of despair, could be God's way of making divine, life-changing intersections for us as well as others. He's often sent Wade and me many miles to minister to a small congregation, but that group included an individual desperately needing something in his own drought. We become Elijahs speaking life into dead or nearly dead situations.

ZAREPHATH

When we become comfortable in our Cheriths, we often neglect the bigger picture. Disciples suffered such intense persecution in Jerusalem, they fled to other locations. During their desperate time of drought, they prospered. Everywhere they went, they performed the Great Commission and used their Holy Spirit gifts to promote His kingdom. As a result, Christianity spread much more extensively than if they'd stayed comfortably established in Jerusalem. Often we get content in our Cherith seasons and see it as a finish line rather than a stepping stone to God's greater destiny. Some even start Cherith churches and can't move on when the Holy Spirit cloud relocates. The Children in the Wilderness had many encampments, but those weren't their destiny. We need to proceed when God leads us. He can move us easily or through difficult circumstances if we don't obey. Wade and I have discovered that going when He says to go is a whole lot easier than having Him create circumstances which force obedience!

Elijah's Zarephath was a small village in the region of Sidon, Jezebel's home. Again, God's sense of humor tells the evil one "in your face!" Remember when He sent David for sanctuary in Goliath's hometown (see 1 Sam. 21:10-15)? Don't be surprised if God's assignment takes you even closer to those who have persecuted you; Elijah was literally in the enemy's territory. The danger dynamic wasn't Elijah's only issue, though. In Zarephath, he was at the home of a destitute woman and her son. Sometimes God provides through someone as bad off or worse than we are. If Elijah considered this assignment with carnal eyes, he may have become discouraged. Instead, he trusted God's bigger plan, just as he'd relied on Him in his Cherith months.

A city on a hill shines brightest in the dark.

61

The Hebrew word "widow" is *almanah*, "a desolate place:—desolate house,"[2] which perfectly describes this woman and her son's existence. We in the prophetic are often sent to hard cases, not to those who'll financially support us or who have their lives together. When God puts us into ministry, we may anticipate mega churches, worldwide television exposure, and name recognition; then God leads us to a "desolate place." We go where He says no matter where that journey takes us. God responds to desperate situations—for Hannah (see 1 Sam. 1:10), for David's Adullam group (see 1 Sam. 22:1), for the woman who approached Jesus for her demon-possessed daughter (see Matt. 15:22). He hears desperation and brings deliverance as desolate people in desolate places call on Him, then listen to and obey the prophet's words.

Zarephath means "refinement...purge away, try."[3] Imagine that! The widow and her son were tried by this season of drought and needed refinement. They had barely survived during those first six months while Elijah had thrived physically and spiritually. He might have even been a little chunky after all the carbs in that bread! However, he was right in the middle of the drought at Zarephath because he too needed refinement. Trials produce that. We don't know what God was doing in him. Maybe an attitude of gratitude. Maybe total trust on God. Maybe, since Zarephath also means "ambush of the mouth,"[4] He was refining Elijah's words. We operators in the gifts must learn the "mouth lesson—" watching that our words reflect faith and not fear, not letting conversations become idle words or gossip, or not repeating what should be confidential. Prophets must be aware that "Death and life are in the power of the tongue" (Prov. 18:21). Our mouths can speak God's words and produce blessings or can ambush His purpose. Jesus said it's not what we take in but rather what comes from our mouths that defiles us (see Matt. 15:11). God wants to use our mouths to speak life, so the lesson of the mouth is crucial. Could your own Zarephath season be refining that in you?

CHOSEN

That widow was desperate yet chosen. Jesus says,

> Many widows were in Israel in the days of Elijah, when the heaven was shut up three years and six months, and there was a great famine throughout all the land; but to none of them was Elijah sent except to Zarephath, in the region of Sidon, to a woman who was a widow.

> Luke 4:25-26

After this, Jesus added the same thing about Elisha and Naaman's healing from leprosy (see Luke 4:27). Plenty in Israel were experiencing drought and leprosy, but these prophets were sent to heathens so God could show Himself mighty. They were chosen. He chooses whomever He decides upon, and we don't always understand why. Both Christians and unbelievers may think He's forgotten their seemingly meaningless existence, but He's allowed suffering for a reason.

And we were chosen too, not because we're exceptional Christians, educated or trained at the seminary. Sometimes, unremarkable people, places, and events create extraordinary results. This widow didn't have a significant biblical role. As a matter of fact, neither she nor her son is mentioned by name though they became closely acquainted with Elijah in the ensuing three years. By the world's standards, they were unimportant, but not to God. She intimately knew a great man of God and was mentioned by Jesus. That's important! Her actions rather than her lineage show how to receive blessings.

When Elijah arrived in Zarephath after his one-hundred-mile journey, she was "gathering sticks" (1 Kings 17:10). Gathering (symbolizes human effort) sticks (symbolize man) represents her attempt to meet their needs to the best of her knowledge. That word "gather" is *qashash*, "to become sapless through drought."[5] She gathered what had no sap. Doesn't that sound like what people collect and think it will save them? We try to bring life back into situations by gathering dead, sapless items to bring results—relationships, money, beauty, sticks. When nothing else can change your situation, God has restoration. He wanted the widow to learn that her knowledge and effort weren't sufficient because He's the Provider, not her. Unlike Elijah, she lived by human devices during her drought experience; but after Holy Spirit showed up, He took over. When all our own ideas fail, God has a plan.

ELIJAH'S REQUESTS

Elijah approached her with two difficult requests—a little water in a cup and bread from her hand. Neither dew nor water had fallen for six months, and she'd depleted her food supply to just enough for her and her son's last meal before they died. Now this prophet asked her to give away what would keep them alive for another few days! This request to a woman who was getting sticks to fix a meal to eat and die seems unfeeling but instead was powerful. Doing actions the same way produces the same results. When we allow others to stay in their current patterns without giving liberating truth, we promote death instead of life. At Samaria, Jesus asked another woman without a husband for a drink of water. When He said she'd never thirst again (see John 4:14), He spoke of Holy Spirit, Who takes us through droughts and gives permanent provision. Elijah's request for a little water (see 1 Kings 17:10) was that Holy Spirit connection which would serve during and beyond current circumstances.

Jesus said that even more than our bodies need food, our spirits need to hear the word from God (see Matt. 4:4). His use of "word" is *rhema*, that spoken word to bring life into now situations. Elijah's words became the widow's *rhema* for what God would do if she obeyed. Then his statement, "Do not fear" (1 Kings 17:13), sealed that deal. When God speaks, we obey because we revere God more than fearful outcomes. Like Egyptian midwives feared God's wrath if they killed His babies more than Pharaoh's retribution,[6] the widow revered God's word. He responds to faith, not fear of how we can survive when logic says the *rhema* doesn't make sense. Faith and action bring His words to pass. Those with Holy Spirit assignments are charged with caring for others, yet ours isn't the only responsibility necessary to initiate God's will. Others must both hear and do God's word (see James 1:22). Though this "word" is speaking of *logos*, those who've had a *rhema* spoken to them also know they must either receive or reject that word. If we obey God's *logos* and *rhema* despite circumstances which say obeying will negatively impact us and our families, He'll be faithful. God must be first (see Matt. 6:33), but often putting Him in that place comes at a cost.

THE COST

King David had disobeyed God and numbered Israel to know its strength. This is like the widow relying on her own ability by gathering sticks to get through the drought. She and David learned their strength wasn't in numbers, wood, or cakes, but in God. When David repented, God forgave but sent a plague which killed seventy thousand (see 2 Sam. 24:15). To atone, David planned to build a tabernacle to the Lord. He went to purchase the threshing floor from Araunah the Jebusite, but Araunah offered to give it to him instead. David refused because he couldn't build a temple, "nor will I offer burnt offerings to the Lord my God with that which costs me nothing" (2 Sam. 24:24). How can we think our effort pleases God if it "costs [us] nothing"? Our worship comes with a price—our tithes, time, some friends, moving away from family, our last meal for us and our son. Araunah's land was associated with sacrifice. There, on Mt. Moriah, Abraham brought his beloved Isaac to sacrifice (see Gen. 22:1-14). There, Solomon built his temple (see 1 Chron. 22:11-20). There, also was Mt. Calvary, according to certain scholars. What a sacrifice God made there! The Christian journey is based on sacrifice. When we sacrifice to God, we can be sure He will give much more than we relinquish.

Prophets sacrifice for their calling because they usually aren't wealthy or popular, but obeying the prophet cost that widow too. It could have cost hers and her son's lives if the prophet's words hadn't come to pass. When she gave up what would feed them, she was probably criticized. Maybe others condemned her because they were jealous that she had ample food while the rest experienced famine. They probably found fault with her for allowing a man to live in her home. Since Zarephath wasn't part of Israel, they most likely told her that Elijah's God wasn't their God and alienated her for that too. They may have scolded her for harboring the region's Number One Enemy. We must weigh the cost, whether life and death or our friends' opinions, before we begin our journey. Jesus said, "which of you, intending to build a tower, does not sit down first and count the cost, whether he has enough to finish it" (Luke 14:28). When we begin our Elijah or even our widow's journey, we should always start with the intention of finishing.

THE SEED

God sometimes asks for something easy but often something difficult. The widow obeyed immediately when Elijah asked for water, but when he requested bread, she said she had too little for them, let alone the prophet. However, though she at first protested, she believed his word when Elijah promised provision and did what he asked (see 1 Kings 17:15). Can you imagine what raced through hers and her son's thoughts as they watched Elijah—hungry himself from his journey—eat that meal? Their own growling stomachs probably made them wonder why she'd acquiesced instead of eating what could have prolonged their lives if only for a short time. Sometimes extreme acts of faith are followed by questioning. When we can't measure immediate results, knowing something must change because nothing has worked so far, gives us a faith boost. That's how God often teaches the difference between faith and fear, obedience and rebellion— trusting Him rather than ourselves.

Like Elijah required her to "bring [him] a morsel of bread in [her] hand" (1 Kings 17:11), God requires a seed from our own hand too. Her seed came in the form of a cake she had to sow into the prophet for provision to come back to her and her son. We Hoosiers understand seed since our Indiana countryside is rich in farmland. As you travel by the fields, you see what seed that farmer has sown. If he planted corn, soybeans won't grow. If he sowed wheat, that comes forth. With no seed, nothing grows. We can sow that seed to get more or eat the seed and have nothing to plant and ultimately harvest. Sometimes, circumstances make us see with our emotions instead of our Spirit man, so we need a prophet to identify our seed. God needed to help Moses recognize his when he looked for how to get through to Pharaoh. God said, "What is that in your hand?" (Exod. 4:2). Moses had his old rod, useful for flocks, but hadn't recognized its power. God will identify our own seed that's in our hand.

Just as Elijah told the widow to bring bread with her own hand, if we want to get unending supply, we must sow with our own hand. What's in your hand? Money, talents, bread? We activate miracles by sowing those then awaiting God's results. What we sow from our hand determines what we reap. Friendship, we reap friendship. Finances, we reap finances. Love, we reap love. That widow needed food and had to sow food, a hard request for a starving woman. Elijah gave directions for how to bring the widow's miracle into being: she was to make the cake and bring it to Elijah (see 1 Kings 17:13). She had to put legs to her faith and obey for the prophecy to come to pass. We each can receive our promise, but before it will come to fruition, we must act—come forward in response, walk around the city's walls, bake a cake and take it to the prophet.

Like Elijah had a little oil and meal with which to bring the miraculous, a little can create great things. Your seed is sufficient for God to take over, but often He asks us to give Him all. Elijah said if she'd first make him a cake, her seed, "the bin of flour shall not be used up, nor shall the jar of oil run dry until the day the Lord sends rain on the earth" (1 Kings 17:14). By human logic, especially to us moms, giving everything is foolish and against our nature, yet God's wisdom far exceeds ours. Because of logic, many don't act in faith by planting their fields. During the wilderness journey, when the children first saw manna, they said, "What is it?" (Exod. 16:15). Sometimes we need to stop questioning God's provision and just take it. When we let logic rule, we miss many blessings. Though the widow balked at first, God doesn't look at where we start, but rather where we finish. Her sacrifice made God's mighty blessings possible. His principle of sowing and reaping saved her and her son more than once during Elijah's years in Zarephath.

When the widow sowed her seed rather than devouring it, she and her son didn't have long to see harvest. Both hers and Elijah's obedience brought great results. She, Elijah, and her household "ate for many days" (1 Kings 17:15). That's a great harvest when she'd expected just one more meal from her supply. Though she'd been ready for death after six months of drought, she had plenty for the next three years. The food didn't last the rest of her life—just until God sent rain. Provision was limited for the Children in the Wilderness too. God miraculously provided for them during their wilderness experience with wondrous manna. When they crossed over the Jordan though, the manna stopped (see Josh. 5:12). Wilderness living was sustenance, just daily provision. Living in the Promised Land activated seedtime and harvest. Once there, they needed to sow other ways because God gave them ability in the Promised Land. You can have abundance, depending upon what you sow. Now instead of just enough, in Christ, you can store up and have harvest for others too. During your Zarephaths, your oil won't be used up or run dry. Then, you step into a new season.

A friend of mine maintains a wilderness mentality that all she can reap has to fall upon her like manna. She doesn't tithe because she can't afford to, yet she wants God to bless her financially. She wants a job but doesn't fill out applications. She wants a ministry but doesn't cherish her talents or pursue openings which would allow her success. Once, she asked me to pray for her to lose weight. When I told her she could walk each morning and those pounds would come off, she looked at me like she'd never heard of exercise. Of course, God can make each of those occur, but He didn't intend for anything to remain stationery and dormant— not bodies, not water, not spiritual lives, not Children in the Wilderness, not widows. His will is for us not to stagnate and be satisfied with sustenance but to step into the Promised Land of Holy Spirit where there's more than imaginable. He'll open the heavens and bless the work of our hands (see Deut. 28:12). We'll sow our seed then believe He'll bless what we plant to produce harvest. Do you still have a wilderness mentality of sustenance when you could step into Holy Spirit's bounty?

OUR WORDS

Elijah came to Zarephath bringing life, but after a while, the widow's son grew sick and died (see 1 Kings 17:17). That sounds like a typical trick of Satan who responds to our blessing with a catastrophe. Her reaction mirrored many when everything falls apart. She blamed the prophet: "What have I to do with you, O man of God? Have you come to me to bring my sin to remembrance, and to kill my son?" (1 Kings 17:18). Her accusation said Elijah's being there had brought God's attention to her sins, so her son's death was her punishment. Don't you hear this during adversities when some blame God for whatever happens? When trials come, we can surely believe God didn't spare our child or ministry or marriage only to let it die a short time later. In reality,

God *had* singled her out when He chose her to survive that famine with plenty, not for her to lose her child. He watches out for His chosen ones. Remember, Zarephath was the "ambush of the mouth" to change Elijah's words, but her words also needed changed. When she first met Elijah, she said she was making bread so she and her son "may eat it, and die" (1 Kings 17:12). My husband often says we prophecy our own pathways by our words. Job acknowledged that he had feared those things which ultimately happened to him (see Job 3:25). Sometimes our fear or faith words are that seed we sow. Isaiah says a word which goes forth "shall not return...void" (Isa. 55:11), so the promised harvest will come, whether good or bad. When we sow words into situations, they accomplish their purpose.

The widow sowed her words of death. Fear-laden statements spoken into the atmosphere created reality for her when her son died. If you want to change your circumstances, change your words. Now, as she approached Elijah, she desperately needed God's touch. Amazingly, even in her accusation of Elijah, she had called him a "man of God" (1 Kings 17:18). She wasn't a Jew, but a Phoenician who didn't believe in God, His supremacy, and certainly not His prophet.[7] She'd come to recognize Elijah's God during their years together. Yet, she still had misgivings. It would take a resurrection to bring her total belief in God to fruition.

THE RESURRECTION

Like at other times, Elijah didn't shy away from knowing he served the God of the impossible. He took her son from the widow's arms, carried him to a familiar place (his own room), and laid him on the bed. How can we operate in miraculous signs and wonders when the place of the miraculous is foreign to us? How can we expect to receive great answers if we aren't dwelling where miracles and intimacy with Holy Spirit are common? As he began to pray, Elijah reminded God that his assignment was to care for the widow and cried out, "O Lord, my God" (1 Kings

17:20). Jehovah *Elohiym*. For something as significant as bringing life back, we call on the mighty, Supreme God Who can do anything. Elijah then let power go from him into that dead boy as he stretched three times over the son's body. God rose to Elijah's expectation level as he prayed, "'Let this child's soul come back to him.' Then the Lord heard the voice of Elijah; and the soul of the child came back to him, and he revived" (1 Kings 17:21-22). When our voices call to God, He hears and answers! Jehovah *Elohiym* is awaiting our call. Like Elijah stretched across the dead to renew life, we prophets must stretch ourselves across the need, beyond our comfort zones (see Isa. 54:2) if we want to see miracles like drought, supernatural provision, and resurrections. That stretching is sometimes painful when we go into uncharted waters, but if God is Master of our vessel and our lives' waters, He answers our cries and revives what's dead.

God still sends signs and wonders through resurrections, a miracle as powerful as a person can experience. I believe we'll see more occurring in these end times. Elijah's oil and meal provision is the first recorded miracle of multiplication of food, but not the last (see Matt. 14:13-21, 15:32-38). Elijah's raising of the son was the first recorded biblical resurrection, though more occurred later. Besides this resurrection, others were as follows:

- The Shunammite son by Elisha (see 2 Kings 4:32-35)
- A man by Elisha's bones (see 2 Kings 13:21)
- Jairus's daughter by Jesus (see Matt. 9:23-26)
- Graves opened as Jesus died (see Matt. 27:51-53)
- The widow's son by Jesus (see Luke 7:12-15)
- Jesus (see Luke 24:1-35)
- Lazarus by Jesus (see John 11:43-44)
- Tabitha by Peter (see Acts 9:36-41)
- Eutychus by Paul (see Acts 20:9-12)

Common elements occur in these resurrections. All were accomplished through a person of great faith. Elijah's, Elisha's, and some of Jesus's examples already had established relationships. The widow's compliance when Elijah said to "Give me your son" (1 Kings 17:19) shows trust, as did Elisha and the Shunammite woman. Jairus trusted Jesus could lay His hand on his daughter, and she would live (see Matt. 9:18). Elijah didn't speak negative words, nor did Elisha or the Shunammite woman, Jesus with Jairus's daughter and Lazarus, or Paul. Too often nonbelievers' words can negate our promise and change God's plan as they head into the heavenlies to create reality on earth. Jesus and Peter made others leave the room, presumably to avoid lack of faith, distraction from grieving, or ridicule like when Jesus said the dead girl was sleeping (see Matt. 9:24). Elijah separated the boy from his mother (see 1 Kings 17:19) as Elisha did with the Shunammite boy, and Peter with Tabitha. Then, he laid his body upon the child like Elisha and Paul did. Jesus took the dead girl's hand. Physical contact was probably to impart power from their own bodies into the dead one. Once, as a point of contact, Jesus touched a coffin and the boy arose (see Luke 7:14). He mentioned this Holy Spirit ability to transfer power when he spoke of virtue, power, leaving his body and going into another (see Mark 5:30). Since Jesus transferred power to heal when virtue left His body, why can't a human, enabled by Holy Spirit, transfer life back into a body? That's not too big a leap for me.

Though elements were different among resurrections, similarities should tell us resurrections aren't outside the prophet's realm. Like any other Holy Spirit work, we prophets should study what these people did if we desire to operate in that miracle. God's calling His Holy Spirit operators to greater levels and raising the dead should be a natural part of our walk. Biblical resurrections should build our faith to know this can and will occur. Like Elijah understood how to be translated, we can comprehend how to do mighty signs and wonders on purpose. Holy Spirit in a prophet's life is God's agent on earth to do the amazing, even resurrect life. Because of His dwelling in us, we can have abilities as powerful as resurrections because Holy Spirit dwells in us and brings life into bodies (Rom. 8:11). The same Holy Spirit Who gave life back to all these people, lives in us to work through us.

A PROPHET'S REWARD

Yet, miracles like resurrections don't suddenly happen one day. The resurrection of the widow's son had been determined years earlier when Elijah came to a foreign place. The widow sowed her seed by taking the prophet into her home and sacrificially feeding him. If we want to be blessed by God, we must take care of prophets, for "He who receives a prophet in the name of a prophet shall receive a prophet's reward" (Matt. 10:41). What's a prophet's reward? Provision and resurrection. If you do that charge, you can expect God will provide a resurrection when you need one. Just ask the widow, the Shunammite woman, and Mary and Martha, who all blessed the prophet and subsequently received the prophet's reward. What do you need resurrected that's as dead to you? An addicted child? A broken marriage? A sick body? A prophet's reward gives confidence to believe even for impossible answers. God elevates His prophets and says to "believe in His prophets, and you shall prosper" (see 2 Chron. 20:20). That sounds easy.

During the drought, Jezebel and Ahab supported 450 Baal prophets and 400 Asherah prophets (see 1 Kings 18:19). While others starved and Jezebel killed God's prophets, the palace supported 850 pagan prophets. We Christians could learn something from these evil people about how to care for our own men and women of God. Like the Widow of Zarephath, we're responsible for those doing God's work. A friend of mine works full time in the ministry, travelling and speaking. Once, someone invited her to speak at a church. After she'd booked a date, the lady said to my friend, "Do you charge, or do you do this because you love the Lord?" We're willing to pay our plumber, doctor, auto mechanic, and restaurant server, yet we don't feel those working for God deserve financial assistance. Scripture says not to neglect supporting those who work for us (see 1 Tim. 5:18). Those dedicating their lives to the ministry are doing a job we can't always fulfill—OUR obligation to take Jesus to a lost world. Besides, again, sowing and reaping are involved. God takes care of those who take care of His workmen, so we can expect a prophet's reward when we need one.

THE PURPOSE

This death and resurrection also show another aspect of receiving from God. Because Elijah had an upstairs room in that widow's house (see 1 Kings 17:19), he was elevated to see that negative report from a different angle. If we change our perspective to view from a heavenly vantage point, we see miraculous events occurring though they haven't yet manifested on earth (see Eph. 2:6). The widow, though, still looked at Elijah and his ministry from ground level. Trusting a God Who could create provision for maintaining their lives should have engaged her faith forever. However, humans possess short memories. Although each morning as she dipped into her meal barrel and oil jar she recalled that Elijah had given life to her and her son, this resurrection was necessary for the widow to know that Elijah was a "man of God, and that the word of the Lord in [his] mouth [was] the truth" (1 Kings 17:24). She reaped benefits of obedience to God's words through unending oil and meal, but in part, she still didn't believe or understand Elijah's call. Does this describe us? Do we forget the lesson of the miracle?

Jesus's first miracle spoke to others in Cana too, when He spared a bride's family the embarrassment of running out of wine at her wedding. Although His disciples had already been walking with Him, this miracle made them believe in Him (see John 2:11). We don't know what will speak to others, but God does. When prayers or efforts don't go like we thought, God's bigger purpose may be to show Himself mighty to a sinner and, in the process, validate us as His mighty men and women. Crises allow others to see God's might and Holy Spirit's gifts working through us. God will bring fulfillment of our words authored by Him.

A few years ago, we started weekly meetings and God came in a great way. Time and again we'd see healings and miracles which became so commonplace that those attending expected them. A friend of mine from another town, Loree, listened to my excited testimonies, but it never seemed to register. One day, she said, "I wonder why God isn't doing miracles anymore."

I looked at her, frustrated that nothing I'd shared had touched her. "He is!" I responded. "He's doing mighty things." I again told her a specific, recent story. Again, she politely listened. However, it was God's job, not mine, to make her hear.

A few weeks later, one Sunday morning, she was going into her church. That morning, she met Sandra. Loree knew about Sandra's physical problems and asked sympathetically how she'd been doing.

"I'm healed!" Sandra blurted. "Didn't Connie tell you?" As Loree listened to Sandra's story, this time she heard. A couple weeks before, Sandra had called for me to put her on our prayer list. As she explained her maladies, I realized we'd be visiting her town in a couple days and asked if she wanted us to come by to anoint and lay hands on her. She'd excitedly agreed and waited expectantly that day as minutes ticked by until our arrival.

Lying on the couch when we walked in, she eagerly awaited God's touch to change the illness which had adversely affected her. God met and exceeded her expectations. As we ministered in her living room, Holy Spirit responded with His glory. Before we left, she was well enough to get up, walk around on her own, raise her arms, and make plans to go to church. The times I'd tried to reach my friend with examples of God's might had been punctuated by a life lesson demonstrating Holy Spirit's power. When she told me this testimony, her words were simple:

"God's still accomplishing miracles." Miracles change our way of thinking, whether healing, wine, loaves and fishes, oil and flour, or a resurrection.

CONCLUSION

Sometimes we blame God for bad circumstances, yet often, they're His tool to accomplish something bigger and bring good instead of bad. When the widow told Elijah about her limited food supply and her plan to eat it and die, God showed her another alternative. Droughts and resurrections give God an opportunity to demonstrate His might and teach many lessons, from reliance to obedience. Those experiences create memorial pillars to allow us to pass the next test more easily and bring us deeper into God's calling. Seasons change, and so does how God works as He moves us to the next assignment. Oh, what great riches each season brings!

We're not told what built Elijah into his mighty prophet status during his three-and-a-half-year stay in Cherith and Zarephath. He probably matured the same way operators in the gifts develop—experiences, one day at a time. This stay shows another aspect of Elijah and the prophetic. Those who operate in any level of prophecy are enabled through Holy Spirit not only to speak His word, but also to bring miracles into being. Elijah's ability didn't stop at pronouncing words about the upcoming drought. He also put the miraculous into practice as he appropriated God's heavenly wonders into this earth realm. Paul said that through us God's promises come into this world (see 2 Cor. 1:20). Like Elijah, we're Holy Spirit's transfer agents to bring those things into the earth. Can we learn from Elijah that God wants us to be His tool to speak and create great things?

ELIJAH AND
THE PROPHETS OF BAAL

1 Kings 18:1-40

Principles:
Calling to Repentance, Trusting and Obeying God,
Bringing Fire, Understanding Your Gifts

Holy Spirit's Role:
Consuming Fire (Heb. 12:29, Luke 3:16);
Convicter of Sin (John 16:8); Creator of Signs and Wonders
(Gen. 1:2); The Spirit of Truth (John 14:17);
The Spirit of Knowledge (Isa. 11:2)

My ex-husband, daughters, and I used to live on a farm outside Brookville, Indiana. Around our graveled-road community, everyone knew everyone; and except for an occasional minor crime, the worst event that occurred was when a cow or pig on the road necessitated a chase back to the barn. That's why we reacted in horror when news stations reported a terrible discovery in a historic church at the southwest end of my road: a pair of human legs belonging to a missing girl from Hamilton, Ohio. The town talked of nothing else. As the story unfolded, we learned the death was a satanic ritual, and the horrific stories made fear mount inside me. The murderers had probably passed by our house. Maybe someone we knew had committed it. Should we let the girls play in the yard anymore? The more stories I heard, the more fear I felt. I realized one morning I needed someone to help me get back to my faith and not fear walk.

My mother had sage words. We Christians live in light. When we're plunged into utter darkness, we're overwhelmed, and the darkness seems much blacker. If we stay in darkness, our eyes will adjust and we won't think the blackness is so bad anymore. The only way to overpower darkness is to stay in light. What a great analogy! We light dwellers see darkness and our spirits grow sorrowful. I was experiencing what Isaiah saw when he said "Darkness shall cover the earth, and deep darkness the people" (Isa. 60:2). Christians have difficulty fathoming "deep darkness"—murders, sexual perversion, killing one's own children, mass denial of God, and persecution. Though that list sounds like today's news, it's the darkness which fell on Israel because of Baal worship. It surrounded Elijah when the nation had descended to such evil that God had to bring forth light again. Though Elijah later felt alone and wasn't, this day he truly was. Hundreds of God's prophets were in the land, but that day at Mt. Carmel, those other prophets were hiding for their lives. Though alone by human measures, Elijah knew God counted differently.

SETTING INTO MOTION

For three and a half years, Elijah was in a season of hiding. Now, his Zarephath season came to an end as God said to "Go present yourself to Ahab, and I will send rain on the earth" (1 Kings 18:1). When God directs, we can speak to any situation and it will be healed, even a drought. God's promises are initiated with a command we must follow to set His will into motion. Naaman would be whole after he dipped in the Jordan (see 2 Kings 5:14). The lame man would be healed if he took up his bed and walked (see Matt. 9:6). We're in partnership with Holy Spirit. If He tells us to twirl, act like a chicken, or stand on our heads, obedience is crucial for the promise's fulfillment. Before Elijah's promise of rain could come to pass, he had two assignments: "go" and "present [himself] to Ahab." Why? He set events into motion by presenting himself so the enemy knew Whose power he came in. The main reason though, to heed those edicts was because God said so.

I had lunch with a friend and another lady who wanted advice regarding a work situation. We chatted for a while before she related her story. Forced from a job, she now drove many miles to her new one. God had promised her she'd be reinstated, but she didn't see anything happening. As I listened, God dealt with me.

"What has God told you to do?" I asked.

At first, she was taken aback but thought for a few seconds before she said, "To write about this."

"Have you done that?"

"No, it didn't seem important." As we talked, I explained how often our answer comes because we obey or doesn't come because we don't obey small things, our own commands to "go." His hand doesn't do His part until we do ours. The last time I saw that lady, she still hadn't received her promise of reinstatement. She still, however, hadn't written. People miss answers because they don't respond to God's word. Trust and obey. Those words had been daily lessons for Elijah during the drought. To "go" and "present" himself to the king who'd dedicated these last years to Elijah's demise wasn't a simple act of faith but a life-death decision to entrust to God. In Zarephath, he must have heard stories of God's prophets' persecutions and deaths by Ahab and his wife, yet Elijah still did what God said. Sometimes we just announce the Lord is in the camp then let Him do the rest. Can you obey God's commands, whether simple or vital?

DIVINE ENCOUNTERS

Elijah made the fifty-mile journey from Zarephath to Mt. Carmel to see Ahab (see 1 Kings 18:2). Before he found him, Elijah met Obadiah on the road and Elijah confirmed his identity. Obadiah, meaning "servant of the Lord,"[1] functioned as messenger between Elijah and Ahab. Though he was Ahab's servant in charge of the house, he also was God's diligent "Servant [who] feared the Lord from [his] youth" (1 Kings 18:12) and thwarted the enemies' plans by saving a number of God's prophets. While Jezebel massacred prophets, he hid one hundred in caves (see 1 Kings 18:4). Obadiah represents those who must work in ungodly places but remain godly and diligent despite surroundings. They're positioned as intercessors to save frontline prophets. God had him on that road that day to bring something to Elijah—encouragement, safety from Ahab, identification of God's remnant. I like Obadiah. Many seek an Elijah calling but may actually be assigned an Obadiah anointing. Perhaps God has positioned you in the enemy's camp to intercede when you become aware of his plans.

Elijah didn't meet Obadiah by accident. On this particular day, at that particular time, Ahab had divided the land between him and Obadiah to find springs, brooks, and grass to keep horses and mules alive (see 1 Kings 18:5-6). As Obadiah went to find the water and grass, he "coincidentally" met Elijah (see 1 Kings 18:7). This "chance" meeting shows an important principle to us Spirit-filled believers. Divine encounters are crucial. The more intimacy you foster with God as you acknowledge His wisdom, the more He'll lead your every footstep (see Prov. 3:6). This exchange shows two ways He makes this happens. Elijah met Obadiah because God said to go to Ahab. He's spoken to me often and sent me somewhere when someone desperately needed me.

God also directs our paths through circumstances. Obadiah was on that road because Ahab had sent him there. Even the enemy's plans can bring divine intersections. Often even nuisance occurrences are God's hand to position us at a certain place and time. We leave our keys in the house and those couple extra minutes make the difference. Traffic is rerouted because of construction, so we go to a store we usually don't shop in and someone needs healing. Jesus once instructed disciples to find a man carrying water in the city and follow him. Then, whatever house he entered would determine where their Upper Room celebration would occur (see Mark 14:13). What if that man had neglected to follow his God-ordained path that day when Jesus tapped him as a divine encounter for their anointed meal celebrating His last night before the crucifixion? When Jesus says to go, we can be sure divine encounters will affect our destiny.

When we pastored, Wade and I were once guests on an Indiana TBN show. The night before we aired live, I dreamt I was standing before a group with my hand outstretched, praying, "And, Lord, for this person awaiting test results...." During the morning, as we were interviewed, I couldn't get that dream from my mind. The interview grew long, so it left no time for me to share. Then, as the host read call-in requests, no one's were for test results. I realized, though, I was supposed to say those words, so right before we went off the air, I prayed how the Lord had shown. A lady in another state had come home for lunch that day and sat in front of the TV to eat and watch the program. She rarely did either, but she had a doctor's appointment for test results about her cancer's potential return. That day, armed with knowledge she'd be okay, she felt at peace. Her results were fine. God encounters accomplish much.

RESPECT

At their encounter, Obadiah "recognized him, [and] fell on his face," asking, "Is that you, my lord Elijah?" (1 Kings 18:7). Calling him "my lord" and falling prostrate show signs of respect. Part of the definition for "recognized" is *nakar*, to "care for, respect, revere."[2] This exchange speaks to me. Like Obadiah acted toward

Elijah, often believers recognize prophets' callings and respect and revere them wherever they travel. What a contrast to those Elijah would meet in Carmel—the king of his nation and 100 percent of his countrymen who rejected his offer to get right with God. Prophets encounter both these groups on their journey but can't let either faction deter them from fulfilling their assignments. Both those who denigrate and those who elevate can influence us, so we must stay grounded when we meet them. Don't get discouraged or prideful. It's part of our prophetic journey.

Jesus had been honored and pursued everywhere. Then he went to Nazareth, His own country. There, he was treated differently. When He taught in that synagogue, they were astonished. They wondered where He received His anointing and wisdom since they'd always known Him and He was, after all, just Jesus, Mary and Joseph's son. He responded that, "A prophet is not without honor except in his own country, among his own relatives, and in his own house" (Mark 6:4). How sad that those who should have supported His ministry lambasted it instead. The tragedy is how much *they* missed since because of their lack of faith, He didn't perform mighty miracles in Nazareth (see Mark 6:5-6). He had life to give, yet those whom He'd loved from childhood rejected Him, and their lives suffered because of their disdain. Like me, you've probably felt discouragement because of those who should have supported your ministry but didn't: "I knew her when she was a bratty kid." "I remember all those bad choices she made when she was a sinner." Jesus knew that sorrow too, and said not to feel discouraged but to "shake off the dust under your feet" (Mark 6:11), grow thick skin, and don't let others' lack of support discourage you. Israel's reaction could have devastated Elijah, but he persevered.

TRANSLATIONS

Elijah told Obadiah, "Go, tell your master, 'Elijah is here'" (1 Kings 18:8). His asking Obadiah to tell the king he wanted to speak to him was a tall order when Ahab had spent three and a half years searching every kingdom for Elijah (see 1 Kings 18:10). Could we make that pronouncement to an enemy who'd scoured the earth to assure our demise? When Elijah gave this request, Obadiah balked because "it shall come to pass, as soon as I am gone from you, that the Spirit of the Lord will carry you to a place I do not know; so when I go and tell Ahab, and he cannot find you, he will kill me" (1 Kings 18:12). Initially, Obadiah reacted in fear because he'd seen firsthand Ahab's hatred for Elijah and other prophets. When Elijah spoke, though, like the Widow of Zarephath, Obadiah believed and obeyed. Obedience to God's word is the key to stepping into His blessings, though that word comes through the mouth of a politically unpopular prophet. For Obadiah, Elijah, and us, though the enemy commits his resources toward our destruction, we're safe as long as we're where God sent us.

Obadiah's misgivings say something else too. He feared if he went to Ahab with Elijah's message, Elijah may be carried away (translated). Ahab would then kill Obadiah when he unsuccessfully went to meet Elijah, who had been translated to an unknown place. His words show Elijah had mastered translations so well he'd gained a reputation. This statement implies that he had been translated during the drought, and apparently he was still learning about and doing the Lord's work. This exchange with Obadiah says even more. When the drought started, Elijah went to Cherith and then to Zarephath at God's command. We don't know how Elijah traveled to those places, whether from a translation or just plain ol' foot power, but by the end of drought, he'd become adept at being translated at will from one place to another. However, even if he trudged every step of those long journeys, much of the expedition's blessing comes as a result of what God teaches during that trip toward our destinies. We don't see how much he used his gifts before that, but he had obviously learned to operate in them prolifically by the end of the drought.

Refinement in the gifts comes by doing. He probably grew deeper like we do—by trial and error, Holy Spirit's or a mentor's tutelage, or creating memorial pillars.

The Hebrew word for "carry" (translation) is *nasa*, to "accept, advance, arise…take (away, up)."[3] I like each of these meanings. Holy Spirit's gifts and results are ours if we accept them. They're to advance us to rise spiritually, but also literally as Elijah went up and away multiple times. We don't see translations actually happen until his ascension, but his comments say a lot. To relieve Obadiah's fears, Elijah tells him to fetch Ahab because he would certainly be there today to meet with the king (see 1 Kings 18:15). His gift not only had earned him a translation reputation, but he'd also become so knowledgeable about how it worked, that he understood how to be translated or not to be translated on purpose. He knew he'd see Ahab that day because he wouldn't be translated.

That statement should get into our spirits. We should intimately understand our gifts' operation. My husband calls some miracles "faith accidents," which happen when we go to God, but don't realize how to appropriate a miracle on purpose. Like Elijah, we should be so in tune with our gifts we know how to bring the miraculous into fruition. On purpose! As we operate in those gifts, we learn how results will be manifested and how to take limits off God. Yes, flying through the air to another location is strange, but is that any weirder than a talking donkey (see Num. 22:28)? Is that any weirder than Holy Spirit coming upon a virgin and her conceiving (see Luke 1:35) or the earth slowing its rotation for military advantage (see Josh. 10:13)? We know God's Word is true, but we often shy away from the miraculous when those wonders take us from our comfort zones. Do we dare believe His Word to expect anything? That should be normal for us, and we too should understand exactly how and when Holy Spirit's manifestations will come or not come.

OTHERS

I don't know how translations occur because I've never experienced one, but I personally know three ladies from my childhood who were translated. First was Alice. One night, angels flew into her house and took her through the sky while they sang praise songs. They deposited her in the refrigerator of a house where church members were plotting against her and another lady. She heard their conversation, which was confirmed when she confronted them the next weekend. Plus, some around that area said they'd heard angelic singing in the heavenlies and knew the song Alice had sung with the angels. Wow!

Another lady, Donna, told of her childhood when she and her sister cut through a woods on their way home and suddenly were past the woods and at their house without making the journey. Neither little girl knew even into adulthood what danger lurked in that woods, but they knew God had protected them through supernatural means. A third lady, Rose, had an experience as an adult when her sister was hospitalized. In church on the praise team one Sunday, she raised her hands in worship and suddenly wasn't in front of that congregation but in her sister's hospital room, three thousand miles away. She could describe the room and hallway, heard conversations, and witnessed a brilliant light outside the door. She worshiped and spoke words of protection and healing over her sister. Remarkably, in a short time, someone called to report that her sister had asked when Rose had been in the hall because she'd heard those words spoken at the time of the translation. Rose's prayers were answered too. Wonders are still happening. God has a reason for everything and may just use a translation to accomplish His purpose.

Elijah's a good example of the extraordinary being commonplace, but he wasn't alone in biblical translations. The spirit of the Lord lifted Ezekiel, he heard a great voice behind him praising God, and he was taken away (see Ezek. 3:12-14). Because of his intimacy with the Father, "Enoch walked with

God; and he was not, for God took him" (Gen. 5:24). Enoch was the first prophet to foretell of Jesus (see Jude 14-15). Interestingly, the two Old Testament men who never tasted death were prophets who experienced translations. We know little else about Enoch except these things: He walked with God, heard from God, and believed God. Paul adds that before he was translated, he pleased God because of his faith (see Heb. 11:5). Could those be requirements if we want to experience amazing wonders like translations or not tasting death?

FORCE

New Testament examples of translations also exist. When Jesus walked across the water and entered the boat with His disciples they were immediately on land (see John 6:21). Paul tells of one caught away into the Third Heaven (see 2 Cor. 12:2-4) and says we shall be caught up into the sky at Jesus's return (see 1 Thes. 4:17). Twice, after His resurrection, Jesus appeared to His disciples then was translated from among them (see Luke 24:31, 51). Philip ministered to the Ethiopian eunuch. Then Holy Spirit "caught Philip away" (Acts 8:39), and he was translated over twenty miles to Azotus. These references are *harpazo*, "to seize (in various applications):—catch (away, up), pluck, pull, take (by force)."[4] This word is interpreted as "force" when they were to take Jesus by force (see John 6:15) and when the commander feared Paul would be taken by force (see Acts 23:10).

Jesus used this word when He told disciples, "From the days of John the Baptist until now the kingdom of heaven suffers violence, and the violent take it by force" (Matt. 11:12). The kingdom of heaven, an allusion to Holy Spirit, responds to the violence of our unrelenting search for Him. Not only John the Baptist but his Old Testament parallel, Elijah, took the kingdom by force—drought, famine, fire, a deluge of rain, translations, and a resurrection. If we want to operate in Holy Spirit's tools, we must be willing to go into the realm of holy violence to seize and hold onto what God has. Elijah invested in knowing his gifts, so he experienced translations in life and in his departure. Again, it's sowing and reaping.

I understand this concept of grabbing hold and not letting go because early on my stubbornness earned me the name "Hammerhead." In second grade, I was sent to the hall for talking. I was innocent, and when my teacher whom I idolized so unfairly accused and punished me, my Hammerhead gene kicked in. Though a polite, respectful little girl lest I be disciplined at home, I dug my feet in because I'd been wronged, and I refused to go back to class when summoned. I stayed out there a long time, arms folded across my chest, my jaw set; and I fought angry, innocent tears. That's the same determination I feel now when I know what I know in the Spirit, and I'm not backing down. It's the angry force which says Satan *must* let go of God's children or that nothing but a healing or deliverance can happen. Putting our Hammerhead mentality into action is dynamic faith which allows us to know more than God *can* do it. This holy violence knows He *will* do it! Elijah was a Hammerhead too, who knew what he knew and forcefully and regularly laid hold of what was rightfully his.

When we dig in and don't let go, things happen others can't deny. Not only had Obadiah heard about the translations, but before his ascension, Elisha and sons of the prophets at Bethel and Jericho knew Elijah would be taken as if that were common (see 2 Kings 2). Also, after Elijah left, children taunted Elisha to "go up" (2 Kings 2:23) like Elijah had done. If even children can see signs and wonders which follow us, why aren't we all acknowledging and embracing what God can do? What could be withheld from us if we treated extreme manifestations as so commonplace kids could recognize God's hand and ability in and through us?

THE TROUBLER

Though he had fear, Obadiah obeyed the prophet and told Ahab that Elijah wanted to meet with him (see 1 Kings 18:16). Unlike the first appearance when we don't know if they've met before, at this second meeting, Ahab knew Elijah and what God could do through him. At their first encounter, Elijah went to Ahab, but at the second meeting at the end of three and a half long, dry years, Ahab came to him. God knows how to capture the ungodly's attention. At this meeting, Ahab called Elijah "troubler of Israel" (1 Kings 18:17). He used "trouble" as a negative word *akar*, "to roil water; fig. to disturb or afflict."[5] Scripture thus far had applied that strong word only to Achan when Joshua asked, "Why have you troubled us?" (Josh. 7:25) when the battle had gone badly against Israel because of Achan's sin. When Ahab leveled this negative word against him, Elijah's faith could have faltered as he recalled Achan's fate. However, instead of cowering, Elijah retorted, "I have not troubled Israel, but you and your father's house have, in that you have forsaken the commandments of the Lord and have followed the Baals" (1 Kings 18:18). Ahab had forsaken God and brought evil to Israel with his idolatry. God responds to evil.

The word *roil* means "to render (water, wine, etc.) turbid [not clear] by stirring up sediment."[6] I love the picture of roiling water. My sister Anita tells how our grandfather used to take her and our brother Jason panning for gold in the Arizona mountains. They held the pan with their arms extended and roiled water around and around until sediment separated from gold. With less substance than gold, dirt would float to the top to be poured off. This left gold. We're God's gold, which sometimes gets mixed in with the world's debris when we stop living as if we have value. Then, God, not Elijah or Ahab, must become the Troubler to roil our lives' waters. Ahab had drawn God's people away as sediment. Drought had come to stir waters and separate idolatry's dirt which had infected them. God roiled the water so they could be

His gold again. Sometimes famine and drought make us wonder if God sees our circumstances, but maybe He's roiling our waters to remove dirt and bring forth gold. Could your time of drought be the Great Troubler's message to turn around?

MT. CARMEL

Elijah followed his pronouncement to Ahab with an order to assemble Baal's prophets for a showdown. Ahab didn't return a negative comment but rather complied and gathered the prophets and all the people of Israel on Mount Carmel. When we come in the authority of the living God, the enemy has no choice but to follow the plan. This exchange set the stage for the challenge between Baal's prophets and Elijah, representing God. One man stood in God's corner against many heathens. If both Baal's and Asherah's prophets were there, he could have stood against as many as 850 pagan prophets!

The time of the Mt. Carmel showdown must have been laughable to Ahab and others as his champions gathered on their side to call on their gods while a little, oddly dressed prophet stood on the other side to call on his God (see 1 Kings 18:20). Carmel means "circumcised lamb; harvest; full of ears of corn."[7] It represented where God's harvest occurred and judgment was fulfilled. Carmel is where Elisha went after he called bears on the children in Bethel (see 2 Kings 2:25). At Carmel, Samuel met Saul to tell him God was tearing the kingdom from him after he'd spared the spoils of war (see 1 Sam. 15:26-28). At Carmel, the Shunammite woman sought Elisha for her son's resurrection (see 2 Kings 4:25). Carmel is a place of judgment but also of mercy. Evil is judged, but God brings grace and renewal; for at Carmel, His people received another chance.

Elijah asked "all the people…, 'How long will you falter between two opinions? If the Lord is God, follow Him; but if Baal, follow him.' But the people answered him not a word" (1 Kings 18:21). What a sad passage! These people felt the drought and heard the man of God's words but didn't speak up for Him. After years of drought, their hearts were still hardened. Christians today also have hardened hearts and have compromised their levels of commitment as they ignore the call to righteousness God gives His separated people. The same question about faltering still applies today. How long will His mercy continue as many waver between right and wrong, straddling the fence? Yet, although no one stepped out for Him at Carmel, God still had mercy by not killing those backsliders. Elijah's purpose was to defeat Baal and rid the land of idolatry to show God's superiority to heathens and win back His lost. God knew what would melt their cold hearts—His fire.

THE SHOWDOWN

As not one person stood beside him, Elijah's emotions must have stirred in him: sadness, hurt, disbelief. Prophetic people often feel these emotions as they look at others' apathy in contrast to their own total commitment to and steadfast heart for God (see Psalm 57:7). He probably also felt anger that they refused to step forward though they'd seen God's power in the drought. Elijah stood against Baal's prophets and reminded them that he was God's lone prophet (see 1 Kings 18:22). God had ordained drought and brought it at Elijah's word. God, not Baal, reigned supreme. Not having rain was especially bitter for Ahab, Jezebel, and Baal's prophets because Baal was considered the rain god. Each day of those long years as the prophets awoke to more scorching heat with no break in sight, they most likely grew angrier and more frustrated. Plus, Ahab and Jezebel were used to getting their way; they probably threatened them with bodily harm if they didn't find relief. The false prophets were ready for a chance to show up Elijah and his God as they showed off Baal and regained respect and clout they'd lost as drought and famine lingered.

Elijah had a plan from the Throne Room to turn things back to God. He said to get two bulls which he and Baal's prophets would cut up, lay on wood, and wait for their respective G(g) od(s) to answer by fire. Baal's prophets would go first. The people responded positively to his proposal (see 1 Kings 18:24), because when we're pleasing to God, He'll cause even our enemies to be at peace with us and our plans (see Prov. 16:7). Then, the showdown commenced. Baal's prophets prepared their sacrifice, called on him, and leaped around the altar from morning until noon (see 1 Kings 18:26). Nothing happened; so Elijah mocked them, saying maybe Baal was meditating, busy, on a journey, or sleeping (see 1 Kings 18:27). He used their own religion to deride Baal since heathen gods supposedly did all these actions.[8] The upset prophets cried aloud and cut themselves with swords and lances until their own blood gushed out. This shedding of blood was also part of their belief that human blood pleased the gods.[9] What a contrast to Jehovah Who required animal blood as a sacrifice until His Son's blood became sin's remedy! Those priests tried until after midday and prophesied until the evening sacrifice, but "there was no voice; no one answered, no one paid attention" (1 Kings 18:29).

People today desire all those: a voice to speak to them, an answer to their calls, and attention paid to them. We look to that formula for direction but too often search in the wrong places— in whatever makes us temporarily feel good or call on gods which cannot answer or save (see Isa. 45:20). Even many of today's churches have ineffectively looked for God's fire to come into their midst, but they're looking to the wrong source. Holy Spirit's fire will come when He's ignited to burn up traditions that have become as idols. If we want fire, we can't lay our sacrifice on the altar of dead religion that no longer looks to God as its source of unlimited power. Jesus declared He came to send fire upon earth and He "wish[ed] it were already kindled" (Luke 12:49). What an amazing prophetic pronouncement our Savior gave about Holy Spirit and His desire for fire to be ignited on earth. How sad His children view that Gift with such ambivalence! People need a voice, an answer, and attention which come through Holy Spirit. He longs for us to be in His presence regularly and let Him take care of His people's needs, but that won't be accomplished if we're satisfied holding onto what doesn't work.

Both camps offered blood as a sacrifice, but priests' blood gushing from their bodies proved a sacrifice is nothing unless it's done God's way. The prophet knows how to get God's fire. As Elijah and God's turn neared, he drew people around before he began (see 1 Kings 18:30). We work in partnership with God, but to build faith, we should bring others into the alliance to see up close and personal what God can do. Witnessing His miracles for oneself creates memorial pillars to Jehovah's ability. I've often heard that those with a true experience with God are never at the mercy of those with just a doctrine. We should stand on the front row of God's tabernacle and see what He's doing in these days. Then, that experience gives victory even if the odds are 850 to one.

THE PROCESS

Elijah delineated a specific procedure for sacrifice, and that's how we get God's fire. God isn't haphazard. When He set up requirements for worship, He specified everything from the tabernacle's dimensions to the priests' garments (see Ex. 25-31; 37-40). For his worship to God, Elijah repaired the ancient broken-down altar of God (see 1 Kings 18:30). Biblical men like Abraham, Isaac, Samuel, Noah, David, and Jacob heard from God and received an answer by building an altar and calling upon God's name. Elijah's altar was probably a high place built in the Judges' or Kings' time then torn down by Baal's worshipers. High places represent areas where people do their own thing and judge actions by what's right to them and not necessarily to God. They can represent doctrines which exalt manmade ways. We can't live by our own idols, but must put God first and sacrifice our ways of doing things on the altar.

An altar was built for several reasons: sacrifice, worship, or great events. This altar, a *mizbeach*, served to "kill, offer, (do) sacrifice, slay"[10] and was to be made only of dust or uncut stones (see Exod. 20:24-26) because other materials indicated man's work. In worship, God doesn't want our effort, pomp, or ornament. Elijah meticulously followed requirements for this altar. He set up twelve (represents divine governmental order) smaller stones (represent tribes of Israel) and built the altar in God's name (see 1 Kings 18:31-2), thus dedicating it to His service. God wants all His tribes, even those who turned away from Him, to come to unity as His prophets woo those not in fellowship with Him. This altar would draw the tribes to God like when Joshua had each tribe choose a stone from the Jordan when they entered the Promised Land (see Josh. 4:3). Those stones became the memorial pillar to remember God's might. Elijah was building a memorial pillar, so everyone could see that altar after this event and remember God was powerful and Baal was impotent.

Elijah built his altar on the old place, and we also bring in a new move built upon the old. Something new is coming in the Spirit realm, but that doesn't mean we discard the Lord's old ways because He does everything for a purpose. We need to build on the foundation of ancient altars that have been torn down—faith healers, signs and wonders, and other concepts this generation hasn't experienced—so the new move can integrate with the older generation's knowledge. Both the old and new generations can find purpose on God's altar.

THE WATER

After he rebuilt the altar, Elijah made a trench around it large enough to hold two seahs of seed. One seah contains about three gallons,[11] so the trench held around six gallons. That trench was made of dirt, just like man. Sometimes God must cut through flesh so we become that trench created to hold water (Holy Spirit). We should ready ourselves for the flood of His water that will flow into us. A trench is *t'alah*, a "conduit, cured, healing, little river."[12] We're the conduit which allows Holy Spirit to flow through us to others, often as healing. As we obey requirements for sacrifice, we set the stage for God to show up. Obedience brings His fire into fruition. Want wonders to happen? Obey.

After that, Elijah laid the wood in order, cut the bull into pieces, and put it upon the wood (see 1 Kings 18:33). Wood represents our humanity and the bull represents carnal strength. We must put our humanness in order, cut up our carnality and strength in ourselves, and sacrifice them on the altar to God before His fire will fall. We cut into our flesh (dirt) so Holy Spirit can flow and God can saturate then burn it all with Holy Spirit's fire. As we surrender carnality, we present our bodies as living sacrifices (see Rom. 12:1). Sacrifices come with a cost—friendships, possessions, an only Son on a cross. Are we giving all?

Elijah sent for four pots of water to pour on the sacrifice. He didn't stop with one dousing though, but used three (see 1 Kings 18:33-34). Putting extra water on the sacrifice accomplished several purposes. First, the miracle would be oh, so much greater when fire consumed the wood, drenched with extra water. Secondly, sometimes pagan prophets hid fire beneath their sacrifices so they would appear to ignite miraculously when it was actually a farce. Extra water would quiet duplicitous claims.[13] Third, dry dust absorbs water quickly. The drought of water and dew had created exceptionally dry ground. Because Elijah saturated the ground, detractors couldn't say the miracle occurred because of dryness. Finally, since water often represents Holy Spirit, the sacrifice would be enhanced by the addition of Holy Spirit, and the more the better.

As men filled pots and poured them on the wood, water ran around the altar then filled the trench, which ensured no water escaped when it fell from the sacrifice. That promise extends to the prophet's words too: "Nothing shall fall to the earth of the word of the Lord, which the Lord spoke concerning the house of Ahab; for the Lord has done what He spoke by His servant Elijah" (2 Kings 10:10). Whatever Elijah spoke, God let it come to fruition even after he was gone. With Samuel too, He gave revelations then allowed none to fall fruitless to the ground (see 1 Sam. 3:19) but kept them in His treasure trove of precious words. Knowing God protects His words is encouraging because many don't give prophetic words for fear of saying something that doesn't happen then being labeled as a false prophet. God guards our words like that trench guarded the water. Holy Spirit will run to overflowing and not a drop will be lost.

FIRE

Elijah didn't consider his job finished although He'd obeyed and set up the sacrifice as God instructed. At evening sacrifice time (3:00 p.m.), this intercessor prayed. He called to the "Lord God of Abraham, Isaac, and Israel" (1 Kings 18:36), the same God Who had sent fire to Moses in the burning bush (see Exod. 3:15). God was true to His word through His prophet, but He let it happen more supernaturally than imaginable. Fire fell and consumed everything: sacrifice, wood, stones, and dust. Then, for good measure, fire "licked up the water that was in the trench" (1 Kings 18:38). Isn't that picture thrilling? All day, those prophets of Baal had been unsuccessfully crying, leaping, praying, and cutting. Oh, but then came the Master's turn. His touch made fire consume everything from the top down. Fire starts with God. Then leaders need to get the vision and let fire flow on down to the people. Revelations, prophecies, and power demonstrations begin with Him then catch us on fire. However, His consuming fire won't come until we're ready with our sacrifice offered His way and not halfway. God commanded that all the sacrifice be used (see Num. 19:5), and nothing of our sacrifice is wasted on God.

Like the Widow of Zarephath needed a resurrection to prove God's prophet, what drought and famine couldn't accomplish, God's fire did. Israel hadn't repented after the drought, but when they saw

God consume it all, they fell on their faces in true contrition, saying, "The Lord, He is God! The Lord, He is God" (1 Kings 18:39)! They stepped forward to stop being the majority, silently approving evil, and came back to their *Elohiym*. However, when we turn or return to God, we must then get rid of idols that led us away from Him, so Elijah said to utterly destroy Baal's prophets. The people obeyed Elijah's command and slew all of them. If they killed both Baal's and Asherah's prophets, they executed 850 prophets in the Brook Kishon. Meaning "hard or sore,"[14] Kishon is where God promised then delivered Sisera into the Hebrews' hands as a torrent swept his army away (see Judg. 4:13-14). At Elijah's command, these people killed the pagan prophets and let Kishon's torrent carry them away too. God is calling for that majority to step forward again today in repentance and slay the evil that has turned them from Him. Sometimes our job is hard as we annihilate the enemy's army, but when we do things God's way, what can stand?

CONCLUSION

During their history when Israel sinned, though prophets preached repentance, the people often didn't repent (see 2 Chron. 24:19). Today we have much availability to hear truth: many preachers, unlimited access to the Bible, worldwide Christian television, spiritual books, churches on every corner, but people still aren't heeding God's word. Many long for His fire to bring repentance, revival, and renewal. But like Elijah showed, it takes a prophet to bring revival. God knows exactly how to reach the backslider, those on the fence, and just plain heathens. The message of hellfire and damnation may reach a soul or a word of knowledge like when Jesus told the Samaritan woman about her past indiscretions (see John 4:29). Signs and wonders like fire on a sacrifice or even our experiencing hard times are God's extreme love, which brings repentance (see 2 Cor. 7:10). Holy Spirit draws the lost and proves Himself and our gifts through our obeying from start to finish. Revival will come, and maybe drought is preparing hearts to receive that fire.

ELIJAH AND THE DROUGHT'S END

1 Kings 18:41-46

Principles:
Bringing Prophecies to Fruition, Using God's Supernatural Ability, Receiving Abundance, Recognizing the Fivefold Ministry, Seeing Answers from God's Eyes

Holy Spirit's Role:
Spirit of Prophecy (Rev. 19:10);
Power of the Highest (Luke 1:35); Intercessor (Rom. 8:26)

Julie slipped into the service where I was speaking. She'd gone through drought for several years since she'd lost her husband. Finances were erratic, even for necessities like food and rent. Her barren, spiritual plane made even studying her Bible or operating in her gifts difficult while she was hurting so badly. Yet, when I saw her that morning, she glowed. A weight had lifted because her drought had also ended. Finances were coming in. She'd found a body of believers who needed what she could offer spiritually and who fed her too. She felt joy, happiness, and peace again. In that dry season, she'd sought God in a deeper way. Her drought had refined her in unimaginable ways. God had shaken her from her place of comfort and forced her to go after more of Him than she'd settled for before. Her drought had been difficult, but she'd discovered much wealth during that season. Elijah's drought had refined him too. Though it had been brought on as punishment for Israel's disobedience, Elijah had grown. God's children repented as a result of the showdown and false prophets' destruction. Then, by God's word, Elijah knew the drought's end was imminent. Like us, we don't speak opinions but rather God's decrees, in His time. Now His words would come to pass.

NOT ALONE

The beginning of Chapter 18 records God's specific assignment and promise: "Go, present yourself to Ahab, and I will send rain on the earth" (1 Kings 18:1). We often must go to the enemy's territory and take back what he stole, but that isn't easy. As operators in the prophetic, attacks could come against our physical safety; or someone could just speak hurtful, unkind words against us like when Ahab called Elijah names at their meetings. One of the enemy's tricks is to ignore his responsibility while shifting the blame to us. His job is "to steal, and to kill, and to destroy. [But God comes that we] may have life, and…have it more abundantly" (John 10:10). Words hurt, and Satan uses whatever ploy he can to discourage or intimidate. We can't fall into that trap which allows the enemy's words to steal our abundance.

Ahab and Elijah's relationship began for the first time in Scripture when he told Ahab of the drought (see 1 Kings 17:1), but something had changed for Elijah when the two met again at Mt. Carmel. Before the drought, he'd told Ahab, "As the Lord God of Israel lives, before whom I stand" (1 Kings 17:1) then proclaimed drought. We don't know God's exact words to Elijah to start the drought, but Elijah's oath was the same when he later met Obadiah on the road. "Before whom I stand" denotes a present tense knowledge of the Lord. Elijah is out in front, risking all, making God's pronouncements as His mouthpiece and partner. He was Elijah's judge, and no matter how Ahab, Jezebel, or any heathen tried to overcome him, he stood before God alone.

Identification of God's name differs in the two statements. Both times, Elijah referred to "Lord" as Jehovah. However, before the drought, Elijah had come in the Lord of Israel's name. After his drought time, he represented the Lord of Hosts. "Hosts" is *tsaba*, "a mass of persons, organized for war (an army), company, host, soldiers."[1] Wow! Sometime during those three and a half years, Elijah had come to know the Lord as more than the God of his nation. He'd become the victorious God, warring for and through Him. He sent Elijah on his new assignment at this appointed time to face the enemy alone, but Elijah knew an army stood at his back. Drought time had taught Him more reliance on his Jehovah's ability in all situations. When our God sends us on a mission, we go with a host to war for us.

THE SOUND

Immediately after the prophets' slaughter, Elijah again had a message for Ahab: "Go up, eat and drink; for there is the sound of abundance of rain" (1 Kings 18:41). This word for "sound" is *qowl*, which can be loud or quiet. As as a gentle sound, it means "to call aloud; a voice or sound:—+ aloud, bleating, crackling, cry (+ out), fame, lightness, lowing."[2] However, as a boisterous sound, it means: a "proclamation, ... thunder(ing), voice, + yell"[3] as Holy Spirit "called out in [Ezekiel's] hearing with a loud voice" (see Ezek. 9:1) when He lifted Ezekiel to show revelation. God spoke once to my friend Theresa that God's new move will come in as a tornado but speak like a whisper. That's *qowl*. The word translated here as a "sound," would be the quiet "voice" Elijah would hear on the mountain (see 1 Kings 19:12). God chooses what He uses, and His sound varies from time to time. But however it comes, as a tornado or whisper, His *qowl* always changes circumstances.

Elijah heard a *qowl* which said rain was coming, but it wasn't thunder or lightning which announced a deluge in the physical world, but rather a mighty stirring in the Spirit realm where answers exist though we don't yet see them. God's sound is undeniable. That sound says fulfillment of the promise is coming. A prophet's job is to declare not what he sees in the natural realm, but what he hears God say, and thus knows it will happen. When we hear that sound from the Lord, we must visualize our answer through faith. Elijah was so sure God would perform His word that he relayed God's instructions to his worst enemy.

A feast was probably already prepared since a celebration always accompanied a sacrifice.[4] Ahab acted on Elijah's words and feasted despite his prophets' slaughter. That food surely went down hard for Ahab though. When they'd cooked it that morning, they had no idea that instead of a celebration of Baal's prophets' successful sacrifice of a bull, Israel would be celebrating the sacrifice of those false prophets in Kishon. Ahab's compliance is a lesson. The ungodly know God is Lord, and even Satan fears God (see Job 1:9) sometimes more than we do. Too often Christians say they hear and believe but don't put that belief into action like Ahab did when he obeyed the prophet. Detractors will know that what we prophesy is of the Lord and will act on it too, like Ahab.

PRAYER

Elijah could approach and speak with confidence to Ahab because he'd spent time in prayer. I love how Elijah prayed: "Elijah was a man with a nature like ours, and he prayed earnestly that it would not rain; and it did not rain on the land for three years and six months" (James 5:17). Can you get that into your spirit? Elijah was just like us yet he knew the answer came through serious prayer, so he affected nature itself with his prayers. He influenced earth's atmosphere by his prayers and knowledge of Holy Spirit. We do too when we come to God in sincere prayer. As a prayer warrior, an intercessor, Elijah heard from God then acted on that. Jeremiah taught about the connection between the prophet and intercession (see Jer. 27:18). A prophet receives his/her revelation through intercession; then it comes to pass the same way. Prayer is the key.

Too often when we get a promise, we believe and then stop seeking God with all our hearts. That's not how Elijah or Jesus did it. Remember when Jesus scolded His disciples because they didn't pray with Him in the Garden? Their neglect made them unprepared for what they'd later endure (see Matt. 26:41). Another time, with multitudes approaching, He withdrew to the wilderness and prayed (see Luke 5:16). How can we operate in our gifts properly if we neglect prayer time? As soon as Elijah prayed then stepped up to proclaim God's judgment of drought, God responded by giving direction for where to go and what to do next. That instruction followed, not preceded, Elijah's intercession and obedience. Many await the fruition of God's promises, but He's not holding us back from our destiny. He's waiting for us, and our answer is often delayed because of our disobedience or neglect to seek Him through prayer.

Elijah's God was on display at the sacrifice. Elijah had prayed to "let it be known this day that You are God in Israel and I am Your servant, and that I have done all these things at Your word" (1 Kings 18:36). His prayer wasn't for self-promotion but rather exaltation of the Father as his prophecy brought about God's results. Often, we think our prayers' answer needs to come yesterday, but God has a purpose for our waiting. Mary and Martha called for Jesus to heal their brother; but when He didn't come, Lazarus died (see John 11). How they must have been confused and bitter because they'd pleaded for healing from Someone with Whom they'd had intimacy, Who had sat at their table. When they needed Him though, He didn't answer. Don't we also call to Jesus and can't understand why He doesn't come and answer our desperate need? But I've often heard that God's delays aren't His denials. Jesus had a grander purpose than just healing His good friend; so maybe He has a reason for His delays in answering our prayers too. Through Lazarus's resurrection, God showed Himself and His Son's majesty.

He approached the cave where Lazarus's body lay and ordered the stone removed. Then He prayed similarly to Elijah: "I know that You always hear Me, but because of the people who are standing by I said this, that they may believe that You sent Me" (John 11:42). He'd always known Lazarus would be raised from the dead (see John 11:11), so He told God that He didn't have to prove anything to Him. When I see God's miraculous answer or when He chooses to be silent, I still know Who He is. Jesus wanted the resurrection so others would see God's power, and in the process the miracle would validate Him too. We aren't responsible for proving our gifts. God is. Solomon says, "A man's gift makes room for him, and brings him before great men" (Prov. 18:16). God validates us just like He did Jesus by Lazarus's resurrection or Elijah by the drought and resurrection. Letting Him confirm us by His results takes pressure off us prophets. In our own might, we can do nothing, so His job is to prove He's speaking and thus show Himself to others by actions Holy Spirit accomplishes through us. When we move at God's word, what He promises *must* happen. And He proves us to others in the process.

TRAVAIL

Yet, Jesus and Elijah both show that after receiving the promise, we don't quit seeking the Lord. Although we've heard directly from Him, prayer brings the answer, renewal, and preparation for trials ahead. James says the "effective, fervent prayer of a righteous man avails much" (James 5:16). The drought started because Elijah had "prayed earnestly." Unfortunately, most of us aren't fervent pray-ers of effectual, earnest prayers but rather are microwave pray-ers. Short and sweet. To bring His nation back to

Him, God chose an extraordinary prayer warrior who understood how to pray. Elijah ascended to the top of Mt. Carmel, bowed on the ground, and placed his face between his knees (see 1 Kings 18:42). Throwing himself upon the ground and positioning his face between his knees was "effective, fervent" praying. He'd heard from God, yet Elijah prayed again with intensity, but that wasn't all. Ahab could feast but not Elijah. A prophet needs to pray constantly then push back his plate because more must occur in the Spirit realm to bring the promise to pass. Our answer often comes through prayer combined with fasting. Jesus delineated the process of intense intercession as He told the parable of the persistent friend who received his answer because of importunity: asking, seeking, and knocking (see Luke 11:9). Asking is part of the equation. Then, we dig in to seek and knock until the answer comes.

Putting his face between his knees represented even more. Knees symbolize our place of prayer, and Elijah took that stance often. His face is mentioned another place—when he covered it in reverence to God (see 1 King 19:13). Prayer is our extreme place of reverence. A face could mean other things too. It demonstrates our heart, and when God sees contrition, He responds. We're also recognized by our faces. As we come into a place of intimacy, He knows our face; and we recognize His face too. As we seek and learn about Him, we know what He can and will do. David said, "This is Jacob, the generation of those who seek Him, Who seek Your face" (Psalm 24:6). David was prophesying that this generation will seek God like Jacob did when God was his only choice as his estranged brother, Esau, loomed in the distance (see Gen. 32). For us to see God's face, we must bury our face in prayer. Elijah's stance with his face covered or between his knees demonstrates both extreme humility and reverence to the Prayer Answerer.

This position also emulated childbirth, travail, a stance for extreme breakthrough to birth God's child of promise. That powerful tool is described: "My little children, of whom I travail in birth again until Christ be formed in you" (Gal. 4:19 KJV). Paul compared travail to the groaning and laboring of childbirth because the pain of travail precedes the birthing of our answer (see Rom. 8:22). Travail is powerful and earth-shattering, breaking through when nothing else can. I once saw a vision of a man I know who travails mightily. He was a jackhammer breaking concrete. That describes travail, an amazing tool, breaking the unbreakable. For an impossible situation, like ending a long drought, a travailer brings victory. It's not a pretty gift—sobs are loud and boisterous—but it's powerful for getting answers.

One night several years ago, a lady stopped by our Bible study on her way to the hospital bedside of her aunt, admitted for kidney failure. As she told us about it, travail entered the room. Sobs erupted, and mine were so intense, my stomach contracted like with birth pains. Another lady felt led to kneel beside me and put her arms beneath my shoulders and knees like a midwife. That prophetic action created breakthrough. At the hospital, before Bible study finished, our friend called to report doctors said her aunt's kidneys were operating again. She was released the next day and has never needed dialysis or had other serious kidney issues. That's exactly how travail works as we birth something through the Spirit.

Travail is part of the prophetic task of intercession and often misunderstood. When we pastored, a preteen girl who attended our church was a travailer. She sat in the front pew; and often from my seat at the keyboard, I'd see her go into travail. Some tried to console her, but her mother would tell them to leave her alone because even a child's travail has an important purpose. While I was writing this chapter, a lady e-mailed and asked if we could talk. When I called to set a time, she was crying then and still crying when she arrived at my house. As she described what was happening to her, I told her that sounded like travail. While I explained how it worked, illumination filled her eyes as she realized God had dropped that special gift into her. When

I saw her two days later, she was a new person. Knowing you're armed with a weapon so powerful it can make a deluge of rain hit a hurting nation is liberating. Often after travail, you're exhausted from what your spirit's been battling. Oh, but just wait and see those babies that are birthed!

God accomplishes great breakthrough on earth, but it must be done through someone who will birth it, who will remain in the position of travail until it comes forth. Travail will bring forth desperately needed answers. You may have been praying for years; but when travail comes in, the answer comes quickly because something happens in the heavenly realm (see Isa. 66:8). Often these tools—travail, fasting, and effectual prayer—are the key to God's answer coming to fruition. Where are the midwives to bring forth God's babies?

WORSHIP

Though God's spoken, we still should seek Him with desperation in our secret place until the answer arrives. Elijah gave Ahab the command to "go up" and eat and drink because even though he had yet to see that first cloud, "an abundance of" rain loomed in the distance. Then, again, he told his servant to "go up" to tell Ahab to leave before the storm arrived. Afterwards, Elijah went to the mountain and put legs to his prayers when he told his servant to "go up and look toward the sea" (1 Kings 18:43). Like when he went to the upper room to receive the resurrection at Zarephath, "go[ing] up" to God's perspective let him see his answer coming to pass. We look above our own earth vision when we "go up" with our Holy Spirit eyes. That's accomplished through worship.

That Hebrew phrase when Ahab went up is 'alah, meaning "to ascend."[5] Another Hebrew word, 'olah, is a derivative referring to smoke which goes up to God after a sacrifice.[6] That sacrifice and smoke represent our worship. What a message! He answers prayers and lets us go higher, but we must proceed in the right order as Elijah did—first things first. Elijah's sacrifice to God with the bull and the heathen prophets became the smoke of worship to God. When Elisha had musicians play before he sought God's wisdom (see 2 Kings 3:15), he put worship in its proper place. He probably learned that on his journey with Elijah because the practice of worship rubs off. Before the Children in the Wilderness entered a battle, the tribe of Judah, which means "praise of the Lord,"[7] preceded others because worship precedes victory. Abraham worshipped as he walked "yonder and worship[ped]" God (Gen 22:5) by preparing Isaac as a sacrifice. What a lesson. Our sacrifice is worship which goes up to God, and it brings answers.

Worship takes us away from our own thoughts and hopes as we submit to Him and His will and acknowledge His majesty. As we worship, fragrant smoke fills our tabernacle and pleases God as our sacrifice rises to Him. Then, just as that worship rises, He allows us to go up to higher levels and see our answers coming to pass. We can also see signs and wonders, healings and miracles, translations and resurrections. We witness faith results because God hears worshipers (see John 9:31). When we allow smoke of our worship to go up first, we see results from His perspective. We worship because we love God, and then we "go up" into His presence.

THE CLOUD

After seven trips, the servant returned and said he saw a small cloud like a man's hand coming from the sea (see 1 Kings 18:44). That servant, by tradition, was the Widow of Zarephath's son,[8] who received life in Elijah's upper room. He knew God uses small things like a little oil and flour or a hand-sized cloud to bring great miracles. A hand is small compared to other body parts, but we can't despise small beginnings (see Zech. 4:10) which grow into divine manifestations. God can create substance from something meaningless—a man from dust or eyes from mud. His hand creates answers.

How often do we need God to rise up in our situations—the sea of hopelessness, the sea of iniquity, the depths of despair, an ocean of troubles, or the ocean of our tears? All of us at some time are drowning in those seas from which escape seems impossible. We've looked for something to change our plight but have seen nothing. We need, however, to look through Holy Spirit's realm. That cloud was God's hand on the horizon, His presence, His ability to create much-needed rain. His hand reaches to the earth's lowest parts or sails to the highest heavens to bring His children's promises to pass. God was stretching out His hand on the great waters to deliver Israel from drought.

FIVEFOLD MINISTRY

The servant saw the cloud which looked like a hand. A hand has five fingers: fivefold ministry operating in the church will end drought. Jesus gave the fivefold ministry—apostles, prophets, evangelists, pastors, and teachers (see Eph. 4:11)—to refresh the body. The prophet is part of that ministry and should operate in each body. Unfortunately, the office of a prophet is often underused and underappreciated for a variety of reasons: others may be intimidated, misunderstand, or misjudge because of past charlatans. However, the problem with acceptance may lie with the prophet himself. Many with gifts think their revelation from God makes them more valuable than the other four ministries. That list is five long, and prophecy isn't first.

Many prophetic people have told us they're not affiliated with a church because leadership doesn't understand them or allow them to use their gifts. Rejection happens to everyone, but our gifts don't operate in a vacuum or work properly without other ones, so we must submit to leadership's authority. Pastors leery of our gifts are part of the prophetic territory. Those gifts will eventually prove themselves; but in the meantime, faithfulness makes us grow and brings favor with God and man. Too often those with prophetic callings leave churches because of offense or because they can't be in charge. Leaving a church because we're offended changes our ability to hear properly from God because offense is part of our carnal nature. God said not to stop getting together with a body made up of other Christians (see Heb. 10:25) for seasoned believers', new converts', and prophets' fellowship and accountability. Like the church isn't complete without the prophet, neither is the prophet complete without the church. Rain didn't fall only on the prophet but the king, the servant, and everyone else in the land. We hold a part in the ministry, but ours is just a piece. How can we prophets be in the equipping business and be absent from the church?

HOPE AND FAITH

Before that cloud showed up, Elijah had his servant go up and look seven times. Seven means "completion," and that seventh time, God completed the answer. Sometimes, fulfillment comes not the first, second, or sixth time we ask, but the seventh time. What if Naaman had given up when he saw no change the sixth time (see 2 Kings 5:14)? What if Joshua had stopped short of their seventh inning victory? How often do we get a promise from God but give up before that seventh dip into the water, journey around the city on the seventh day, or trip up the mountain? Many stop too soon and say God had misspoken or they'd misunderstood. We lose much because we don't understand that God's answers may be down the road, around the wall, or up the hill a ways.

Persistent faith which produces results starts with hope. Joshua hoped as they marched silently around Jericho for all of those trips. Why was silence important? Too often we negate God's purpose by grumbling or speaking words which lack faith. Jericho was six acres, probably a nine- to ten-acre trip including its walls.[9] Estimates are that to walk one acre usually takes about ten minutes,[10] so each of the preceding six days had been a ninety-minute trip. Then, the last day, they trudged in silence seven times around those acres for a total of ten and a half hours of desert walking, each trip in silent obedience to God. How hard was that! But Israel kept on in hope that God's word would come to pass; and sometime during those seven days, their acting on hope became faith. That last trip was filled not with silence, but shouting to proclaim evidence of their faith journey.

Rahab wasn't afraid to ask the Hebrew spies for hers and her family's salvation then hope and believe her petition would come to pass. We can come boldly to God and not think our request is too big. We don't get our needs met because we don't ask (see James 4:2). But asking is the start; the second part is obeying and believing. Rahab's faith grew as she hung her red cord out the window in hopeful obedience to God's words. That cord was a *tiqvah*, meaning "hope."[11] Until Rahab hung her hope out, the Hebrews couldn't fulfill her request because that was how they identified her. Does God recognize our need too, and where to send our answer by the hope we hang out? When Rahab put her hope out, it was her own trip up the mountain to find a hand-shaped cloud. Deliverance hadn't come yet, but it set salvation into motion, for hope and faith start it all. Hope's outcome is faith, and faith brings results. She had faith that this Hebrew God could save; so on the seventh time, that seventh day, her faith answer came. Excavations confirmed Jericho's walls actually did fall down, and only one short section on the north end of the wall didn't fall like everything else.[12] We know who lived there, don't we?

As the writer of Hebrews lists men and women of faith (see Heb. 11), he starts with acknowledging their faith but follows each with an action that proved that faith—they hid, obeyed, refused. They proceeded in faith with actions that said the answer was coming though they didn't see it yet. For Joshua, it was marching. For Rahab, it was hanging. For Elijah, each trip up that mountain was his putting hope and faith into action so God would bring His word to fruition. He believed God's answer was on the horizon long before the first cloud blew in. He performed the ultimate cloud seeding, a process by which chemicals are put into clouds to produce precipitation. He planted seeds of faith and knew that cloud would produce faith results. On that seventh trip up the mountain, evidence of Elijah's faith answer came. Our hope must also be expressed for all to see, hung out our own window. Prayers, persistence, and action show our hope and faith which touch God.

Then, "the sky became black with clouds and wind" (1 Kings 18:45) at Carmel. How often does darkness come before your answer? When that happens, many don't recognize God's provision on the horizon. When your own skies grow dark, you can bet that's one more sign that the answer is imminent. But we still can't forget to pray. Elijah "prayed again, and the heaven gave rain, and the earth produced its fruit" (James 5:18). As we pray in every situation, the answer comes to refresh what has become dry and nonproductive. Then, the fulfillment of the promise brings fruit.

THE JEZREEL JOURNEY

Elijah sent his servant to tell Ahab to prepare his chariot to get back to the palace before rain erupted (see 1 Kings 18:44). As Ahab rode toward his Jezreel home in his fine, fast chariot, "the hand of the Lord came upon Elijah" (1 Kings 18:46). In Old Testament references, this phrase, "the hand of the Lord," not only alludes to Holy Spirit, but also that something miraculous will happen. When Moab rebelled against Israel, after seven days, the army had no water for people or livestock. When they asked Elisha for a word from God, the Lord's hand came upon him and he prophesied that they should make ditches to hold the next day's deluge (see 2 Kings 3:16-17). It happened. His hand causes amazing, supernatural feats. Can we trust His hand, whether in a cloud or coming upon us to do wonders?

Elijah's miraculous event occurred when he "girded up his loins" (1 Kings 18:46), ran ahead of Ahab's chariots, and beat him back to Jezreel, a journey of around twenty-five miles.[13] Girding of the loins meant tucking his robe into his belt to run more easily without the robe hindering him. Peter said we should "gird up the loins of [our] mind" (1 Pet. 1:13). The addition of "mind" brings a picture of stuff flapping around inside there to make us fall during our journey. We're limited by what our minds conceive, but God's plan is often accomplished by foolish things like a foot race with chariots and horses. When we raise expectations, we can step into this faith walk, or should I say, faith run, and anything is possible. Jeremiah also said to "gird up thy loins" (Jer. 1:17, KJV), translated as "prepare yourself and arise" (NKJV). The word for "gird" or "prepare" is *chagar*, "to gird on (as a belt or armor)."[14] Preparation is always necessary before a journey, especially for frontline prophetic warriors. Preparation may include eating the Word to sustain us, suiting up in our armor, girding up our loins, or arming ourselves with the *rhema* of battle. As we prepare, we get ready for the footrace God's sending us on after our own rain starts.

God has spoken to me often in the past to tell me I was unprepared. As I sought His mind, at times He was telling me I was neglecting to study, pray, or get alone with Him consistently. Once, though, He kept giving me that message about lack of preparedness. For months, He gave another dream or scripture with the same message. I tried everything I could think of, yet I didn't discover His meaning. Then, I found out what He was telling me when several months later, I was asked to speak at a conference and needed brochures, a flier, business cards, a website, and CDs for a table. Yesterday. While I was preparing my sermon and doing my normal ministry duties, I was also putting hours into getting the other things ready. If I had pressed harder to find what He was saying to me about my lack of preparation, life would have been easier while I studied to speak at that conference, which turned out to be life-changing for Wade and me.

Another time, He spoke to me that He was sending me into a season of preparation. That time, I immediately discovered what

He was saying. Many mornings as I did devotions, He dropped something from that passage into my spirit and told me to prepare it for speaking. Those sermons were necessary and were fresh manna to people who heard them as my speaking schedule became more intense. Girding is necessary because the journey may happen quickly, so we should be instant in and out of season (see 2 Tim. 4:2). I've often heard preparation precedes blessing. Maybe God can't send you on your journey because you're not prepared with your garments girded. Like Elijah, we should gird our own loins, or reproductive areas, so the miraculous can be birthed. Once we remove delaying obstructions, progress isn't hindered. Our drought will end, and God will accomplish much in the process. Are you ready for the deluge *after* the drought when you'll be heading toward your next assignment?

However, don't be surprised if your newfound faith run is met with opposition, but God will allow you to meet and supersede the wickeds' abilities. Wade and I started a Bible study in our home at God's direction. We'd been teaching on the gifts for several months when manifestations showed up. We had read books and watched videos about amazing worldwide wonders; but like many in the Bible, when they happened to us, we were astonished. This first experience excited those involved, but not everyone felt that way. When word got out, some shunned and criticized us, but we didn't care. Those wonders were God's kisses blown to us, affirming we were on the right road. After we outgrew our house and held bi-monthly services elsewhere, we continued to see wondrous occurrences because we chose God's presence rather than man's approval. They became that fast-paced event for which we'd girded up our loins. Extreme glory manifestations will be Holy Spirit's way of drawing a line in the sand, and you must choose whether or not to be on the side of the miraculous. Once you've elected to believe, the signs will follow like a puppy.

They followed Elijah, even in pouring rain as he raced toward Jezreel. God had brought drought on Elijah's word, dropped miraculous fire to consume the soaked sacrifice, sent torrential rain to beat down upon dried land, and allowed him to win the footrace. Now, He would further trouble Ahab and Jezebel. Their sanctuary was their palace at Jezreel, but God would change that. In Jezreel, Naboth would be killed for his vineyard (see 1 Kings 21:1). There, Elijah's prophecy concerning Jezebel's death (see 1 Kings 21:23) materialized when Jehu had her thrown off the tower at Jezreel (see 2 Kings 9:33). King Joram, Ahab and Jezebel's son, retreated to Jezreel to recover from an injury (see 2 Kings 8:29) and was killed by Jehu (see 2 Kings 9:25). Sometimes where the evil are ensconced ultimately becomes their place of doom.

WISDOM

When Elijah arrived at Jezreel, he stayed at the entrance. Sometimes, we must make decisions based on more than the prophetic. Common sense and wisdom are crucial. Once, a great crowd followed Jesus. He withdrew to the sea, but that multitude pursued because they knew where words of life and deliverance existed. Jesus instructed disciples to keep a boat behind them in case the crowd pressed Him so hard that they crushed Him (see Mark 3:9). I don't believe this was Holy Spirit's revelation but rather His using wisdom when he saw the throng and knew His human body could be hurt by their fervor for His touch. Nothing says God told Elijah to stay outside Jezreel's gates, but sometimes wisdom dictates we don't enter the ungodly's lair. No matter how many signs and wonders we've witnessed or how much we trust God, wisdom often says when we go or when we stay, when we speak or when we be still, when we share answers or when we allow others to discover God's message for themselves.

However, sometimes, that wisdom is Holy Spirit's revelation (see Prov. 1:23). His wisdom whispers His words in our ears. Hearing the Spirit of God is *qwol*, that Spirit-authored wisdom and sound which presents as a hurricane or a quiet voice. It speaks to us that this is the road we should walk on (see Isa.

30:21). We know the right path because of His whispers into our spirits. We understand that through Holy Spirit we *could* storm the gates, but sometimes we *shouldn't*. We know that whether our assignment is a drought, the evil prophets' slaughter, or rain that brings renewal, we comply in obedience and humility. We don't need acknowledgement by the palace to know the King is pleased with us.

CONCLUSION

Certain signs tell of events to come. As Jesus explained the parable of the fig tree, He said that we recognize that summer is approaching by a tree's leaves (see Matt. 24:32). We recognize weather signs, yet many can't discern this time in which we're living (see Luke 12:54-56). How sad we've better tuned our visual perception than our spiritual. Today, signs say God's getting ready to move powerfully. When his servant returned with news of a distant cloud and Elijah sent him to tell Ahab to get back to Jezreel, Ahab was probably still reeling from the prophets' deaths. But he left on Elijah's word. God's consideration to tell Ahab of impending rains showed not only His kindness to Ahab but one more way of demonstrating His love for the Israeli king who'd wandered so far. In one day, Ahab witnessed the sacrifice's fire, fulfillment of rain, and Holy Spirit's enabling Elijah to beat his horses and chariot. Though these miracles weren't enough to cause him to repent, a seed was planted which grew until Ahab did repent later. God is all about wooing the unbeliever.

ELIJAH AND DEPRESSION

1 Kings 19:1-18

Principles:
Dealing with Emotions, Following God's
Will, Gaining Profound Revelations From
Simple Events, Hearing God's Voice

Holy Spirit's Role:
Comforter (John 14:16); Counselor (Isa. 11:2);
Helper (John 16:7)

Having a book published changed my life. I was travelling for book signings, sermons, and television and radio interviews. People were e-mailing and calling from around the country to tell how the book's message had touched them. I met amazing Christians as I spoke or set up a book table at conferences. At churches, God showed up mightily, and miracles occurred regularly. Every little Christian girl dreams of growing up to this scenario—at least in our house. Then, one day, I woke up and felt different. Instead of being excited about what God had allowed to happen to Wade and me in our most thrilling season ever, I focused on the negative. I rarely get dejected or take offense, but then, my attitude of gratitude was gone. I wasn't getting invited to speak enough. I wasn't selling books as quickly as I wanted. My clothes weren't appropriate for speaking. My family didn't seem excited. Somehow while living my dream of regularly doing three of my passions—writing, speaking, and operating in the Spirit—I'd let something slip in like Elijah did. I was depressed.

Some don't understand how prophetic people experience the miraculous only to end up in desperate straits. After God gives great victories, Satan often comes along with great trials. Lows come from different sources—a boss, teacher, neighbor, beloved friend, family member. God worked mightily through Elijah: calling the drought on then off again, defeating Baal's prophets with consuming fire, outrunning a chariot for twenty-five miles before the deluge of rain. Then discouragement arrived. Elijah's trials through Jezebel were part of his Holy Spirit journey. However, Elijah made mistakes from which we can learn.

JEZEBEL

Though he was wicked, Ahab's evil paled next to Jezebel's. Her father, Ethbaal, meaning "with Baal"[1] was the Sidonian king (see 1 Kings 16:31) and Asherah's (Baal's wife's) priest. When he allied with Israel through the marriage of King Ahab to his daughter, she brought Baal worship officially into God's nation[2] and likely followed her dad's example as a Baal high priestess. Though she's often linked with sexual promiscuity and heavy makeup, that stereotype is probably inaccurate. Baal worship entailed both of those, but we're never told about her sexual practices except in an allusion to a woman named Jezebel committing sexual acts (see Rev. 2:20). Her makeup was mentioned only when she descended for her death at Jehu's command and was arrayed in her high priestess garment and makeup (see 2 Kings 9:30). Her evil was both outward as inward. Ruthless and wicked, she had a relentless single-minded goal of persecuting and martyring God's prophets.

We see no personal interaction between her and Elijah though she goes after him multiple times. After Baal's prophets were slain, Ahab informed Jezebel of the confrontation at Mt. Carmel. His story didn't make her turn to Israel's superior God, but to seek further vengeance against Elijah. She sent a messenger to tell him "Let the gods do to me, and more also, if I do not make your life as the life of one of [the slain prophets] by tomorrow about this time" (1 Kings 19:2). She must have known Elijah's location since she realized where to send the messenger. That may have made Elijah nervous; but Satan isn't omniscient, so when Elijah ran, she couldn't find him, either during and after the drought. Satan presents himself as a lion roaring while seeking his prey (see 1 Pet. 5:8). Though he has *dunamis* power, his might is ineffective against even the *exousia* power of Jesus's name against serpents, scorpions (see Luke 10:19), and even lions. Add Holy Spirit's *dunamis*, and dynamite—true power! Once, the Lord showed me a vision of a roaring lion. His ferocious sound shook his surroundings; but when he opened his mouth, he was toothless. Satan's typical reaction when his plans are thwarted is to roar in anger and make you think he'll destroy you. That's when you should realize he can't harm you because a greater One is within you (see 1 John 4:4). Ungodly pronouncements aren't God's decrees.

Often, your grueling journey is fraught with Satan's multiple threats because he wants you destroyed. After a great victory, he'll attempt spiritual and physical destruction. That's happened to many plagued with physical, marital, emotional, or other problems he uses to exact retribution and discouragement. Victory comes if we stand and fight, but running away in fear opens us up to emotions which leave us powerless. Dealing with issues in the carnal brings death while dealing in the Spirit brings peace and life (see Rom. 8:6). Jezebel's vow didn't come to pass because God protects His prophets from the evil one for the sake of His word.

BEERSHEBA

Elijah left Jezreel and went to Beersheba, meaning "well of an oath."[3] It received that name when Abraham and Abimelech made a covenant that the well would be unstopped. Abraham dwelt at Beersheba (see Gen. 22:19), and his son and grandson found God's will there. His father's promise became personal to Isaac when God appeared to him and promised He'd multiply him and descendants. He built an altar, dug, and found water (see Gen. 26:23-32). There, God told Isaac not to go to Egypt (see Gen. 26:2) while at the same spot He told Isaac's son Jacob to go down to Egypt to preserve the nation of Israel (see Gen 46:1-4). Beersheba was a place of covenant and divine direction for these men. We too must find where we hear God's will directly from Him. Elijah didn't do that.

Elijah's reaction to Jezebel's threat is interesting. Usually, strong warriors stand, but this time as Satan roared through Jezebel, "when [Elijah] saw that, he arose and ran for his life" (1 Kings 19:3). "Saw" is a strange choice of words when "heard" seems more appropriate. Jesus said that what our eye takes in, whether good or bad, determines the direction of our whole body (see Luke 11:34). When we let our physical eye see the world's report and not God's, we live through our senses rather than through faith in God's overcoming report. Eve sinned when the fruit was "pleasant to the eyes" (Gen. 3:6). David also created problems for him and his descendants when his eye rested on the woman bathing across the way (see 2 Sam. 11:2). Some interpret "saw" as "feared."[4] When Elijah heard the news, he responded in fear: he saw, he rose, and he ran (see 1 Kings 19:3). Whether we look at what we shouldn't or respond in fear, when we see from natural rather than spiritual eyes, we don't see ourselves as defeaters but as defeated and "like grasshoppers in our own sight" (Num. 13:33). Our viewpoint has to change to God's viewpoint.

THE WILDERNESS

Could Elijah have seen in the Spirit his potential destruction by Jezebel? If so, he should have reacted in his Spirit man rather than emotions. Because Elijah sank into fear instead of faith, he didn't find God's direction, but acted presumptuously and journeyed toward the wilderness. This gives another message. Many wilderness experiences are God's plan, but some occur because we strike out on our own. Elijah dealt with problems on *his* own and didn't wait upon the Lord. He tried to outrun what Satan had in store for him instead of standing against him. Doesn't that describe us when we run instead of staying and conquering issues? We cause ourselves many problems when we don't consult God about choices.

Elijah left his servant, went a day's journey into the wilderness, and sat under a broom tree. No one, no matter who, is an island. Humans need others' companionship. God said this as far back as the Garden when He gave Adam a companion because it's "not good that man should be alone" (Gen. 2:18). Jesus sent out the seventy, by twos (see Luke 10:1). Apostle Paul had an open door to preach in Troas but admitted he "had no rest in [his] spirit, because [he] did not find Titus [his] brother" (2 Cor. 2:13). We visit the mountaintop of the miraculous, but most of our existence happens day-to-day with our brothers. We should fellowship in a Christian body because we need each other—to hear a pleasant voice, give or receive godly counsel, nurse others through crises, mentor or be mentored, and oh so many other treasures we provide and are provided. There, alone and in the desert, Elijah fell into extreme depression.

Operating in our gifts, making decisions, or just living in the HALT stance—Hungry, Angry, Lonely, Tired—is dangerous. We're humans with physical and emotional needs, and sometimes handling one more battle is difficult. Elijah was lonely without his servant. He was hungry and tired from his journey of a day and night. He'd also done extreme ministry and travail. From experience, I can say both drain you so you need recharging. He was stressed and probably angry about Jezebel's quest once again to kill him and because Israel hadn't turned back to God until the sacrifice was consumed. Many reasons brought him to this emotional position. We all can journey there when we forget who and Whose we are.

Jesus understands our weaknesses and hard times because He's been there, done that (see Heb. 4:1). When He did His wilderness time, He suffered the same types of temptations Elijah did. Satan enticed Him with bread while He was fasting (see Matt. 4:3). Elijah too was hungry. Satan told Jesus to throw Himself off a rock to test God (see Matt. 4:6). Elijah had wanted to die. Satan offered Jesus success in worldly kingdoms (see Matt. 4:9). Elijah questioned his success in the prophetic realm. Wilderness lows are part of this journey, but the difference between Jesus's success and Elijah's failure was that Jesus had gone for His wilderness testing by the Spirit's leading (see Matt. 4:1). When we take off on our own and not let the Spirit lead, we open ourselves up to dealing with temptations through our own might. Satan tempts so we will to fail, but God's tests are for promotion.

ATTACKS

In that mental state, Elijah questioned his gifts saying, "I am no better than my Fathers" (1 Kings 19:4). Though he'd dedicated his life to God's service, during the time when he was down, he perceived that his life was no more fulfilled than his fathers, ordinary men and not the prophetic, chosen being that he was. Depression tainted his view, so he thought he'd done nothing discernible to change the landscape of the prophetic world. Self doubt often follows great victories. As a matter of fact, Satan brings uncertainty to operators in the gifts each time they move in the Spirit. When Holy Spirit gives me a word of knowledge, even after all these years, I sometimes muse, *What if no one responds?* Then after a confirmation, other thoughts come. *Did I pray right? Did they receive it?* Holy Spirit's arsenal does damage to the enemy's kingdom, so he tries to keep us from operating effectively, often by attacking the mind.

Elijah pleaded to die (see 1 Kings 19:4). Jonah also prayed to die after his great victory (see Jon. 4:3), and Moses told God to let him die because the burden of the people's dissatisfaction was too great (see Num. 11:15). It's hard to believe these generals of God prayed for death, but that's how powerful discouragement and satanic attacks are. When you make waves in the spirit world by wounding Satan's kingdom, be prepared for an attack to make you question yourself, your call, and maybe your existence. How sad this man of prayer was so temporarily deluded that he used his powerful prayer tool to ask for his own death. Though at this time Elijah saw death as a good way out, ironically, he never did die. What a blessing God doesn't answer our prayers of fear and doubt. He knows humans are subject to emotions, yet despite what they pray at the time, He still has their future in His hands. How encouraging that even great prophets are human and go through emotional lows, but God doesn't give up on them. Many reasons brought Elijah here, or maybe, God allowed him to dip so low he prayed for death because He wanted to show how strongly the Jezebel spirit still works against prophets.

I can relate to attacks. Wade and I felt led to call others to serious corporate intercession. We met one night and planned prayer and fasting, tore shirts as a sign of grief, and put on sackcloth and ashes. We determined to teach on warfare before we went on the offense with intense prayer against principalities. Attacks began immediately—five stitches in my finger, a swollen ankle, extreme weariness, a persistent cough. I fell off the platform one night while I was speaking. The worst thing, though, was the depression which settled onto me and made me question everything I did. People told me they didn't like my writing style. I could see some didn't like my worship. People stayed away in droves from where I spoke. Unlike my spirit's reaction, my flesh took it personally. I became devastated and stayed that way several days. Then as other attacks crept in, suddenly enough was enough. Satan had roared and discouraged me. He'd won territory because

I'd allowed emotions to rule over the Spirit. I'd interpreted events with Satan's spin, not God's. Elijah too miserably failed his Beersheba and Horeb faith tests. Like when he thought he alone was left serving God, we may think no one else goes through trials. A prophet, though, must combat emotions and see by faith from his/her elevated position, seated right by Jesus. God's on His throne, and emotional attacks are from Satan's bag of tricks.

MINISTRY OF ANGELS

There, in the wilderness, in depression's throes, Elijah fell asleep and was awakened by an angel who said, "Arise and eat" (1 Kings 19:5). This is a three-fold message: God will send help, get up, and do something your body needs. God provides ways to restore us, and we don't always know what that will be—an unexpected phone call, scripture, television show, or encouraging testimony. Or it might be an angel bearing a cake and jar of water. Holy Spirit's water is cool and sweet before and after a journey, even into an emotional abyss. When we're about the Father's business, we should understand our minds' and bodies' limits and replenish them when needed.

The topic of angels has long intrigued man. Throughout my life, I've heard a myriad of stories of angelic sightings. Though I've seen an angel with my physical eyes only four times, I've seen them with my spiritual eyes and felt their presence often. I've also heard accounts from others who "unwittingly entertained angels" (Heb. 13:2). Our pastor tells of a time in 1989-90 when he was driving home from college. A family in a beaten-up old blue station wagon sat at a rest area, stranded for lack of money. The old man said his son had been hurt in the military, and they were trying to go south to see him. My pastor knew he had enough gas to get home and wouldn't need food, so he gave that family all he had. They said their good-byes and both cars drove up the ramp and onto the interstate. However, before the car in front of my pastor merged onto the freeway, it disappeared. These stories aren't unusual.

The ministry of angels is demonstrated often in the Bible: Gideon, Daniel, Jacob, Balaam, Abraham, Adam, Elisha, and others were visited by celestial beings. They appeared generally for great purposes: guarding the Garden, saving lives, giving direction or assignments. We prophets should realize these amazing creations are sent to help, and we should cherish rather than be intimidated by them. After all, Paul says someday we'll judge them (see 1 Cor. 6:3). Angelic intercession for Elijah occurred when he wanted to die. The angel's touch gave what he required (see 1 Kings 19:5). How often do we need an angelic touch during our times of great despair? That touch changed him and will change us too, as the angel helps us get our flesh under control.

Elijah ate the cake which the angel baked on coals, drank water from a jar by his head, then lay down to rest. Oh, what a difference when the Lord intervenes. After a while, an angel again touched him and brought more food, but this angel is called the angel of the Lord. When an angel is identified this way, the Bible is referring to Jesus. These appearances at important times are called theophanies, "a manifestation or appearance of God or a god to a person."[5] An angel of the Lord appeared to Hagar to tell her to return for Ishmael would be a mighty nation (see Gen. 16:9-10). He appeared to Sarah and Abraham to say Isaac would be born the next year and Sodom and Gomorrah would be destroyed (see Gen. 18). He also appeared as Abraham sacrificed Isaac (see Gen. 22:11) and to his grandson Jacob twice: Genesis 31:11 (in a dream) and 32:30 (when they wrestled). He appeared to declare Himself to Moses at the burning bush (see Exod. 3:2) to tell Joshua he stood on holy ground (see Josh. 5:13-15), to accept Gideon's sacrifice (see Judg. 6:21), and to announce to Samson's parents the impending birth of their mighty man of valor (see Judg. 13:3).

These examples of when Jesus appeared imply this scene with Elijah too was an important event. The angel of the Lord said, "Arise and eat, because the journey is too great for you" (1 Kings 19:7). These words could be interpreted to mean the forty-day journey to Horeb he would undertake on this sustenance alone. It could also mean this journey of deep depression. Sometimes, we need supernatural intervention for both these hard undertakings. As Elijah arose, ate, drank, and travelled on "the strength of that [angelic] food for forty days and forty nights" (see 1 Kings 19:8), so must we arise and go with God's provision. Too many stay sleeping when "now it is high time to awake out of sleep; for now our salvation is nearer than when we first believed" (Rom. 13:11). We can rest for a season and do what our body, spirit, or soul needs to get healthy and strong again, but then a time comes to awaken from our sleep, arise from our circumstances, and go forward because we, like Elijah, have an unfulfilled purpose. Trials and journeys en route to that assignment are too great without God's supernatural help. His prophets are important to Him, and He'll send helpers to take care of them as they awaken.

HOREB

Elijah journeyed forty days and nights to Horeb on angelic food sustenance alone. Forty means probation, testing, and deliverance. Doesn't that remind you of another wilderness journey with heavenly food, but that one took forty years, not days? Often, manna from God sustains us during a trial or long journey for He knows what we'll need. Horeb means "to parch (through drought), to desolate, destroy, kill."[6] Elijah had made a long journey before and after the drought. He was parched, desolate, and running to avoid physical and spiritual destruction. In our own Horebs, we can still hear from God and slay fleshly, carnal motivations in us. Whatever remains must be eliminated because human emotions are counterproductive to moving into God's fullness.

This place was called the Mountain of God, Mt. Horeb, Mt. Sinai or Mt. Paran. Exodus first refers to it in the burning bush story when Moses led his father-in-law's flock to the back side of the desert where he met God at Horeb (see Exod. 3:1). There, he removed his shoes on holy ground (see Exod. 3:5). At Horeb, Hebrews worshipped the golden calf (see Psalm 106:19) and God gave the Law of Moses (see Mal. 4:4). Horeb was where Moses smote the rock which gushed forth with water (see Exod. 17:6), representing Holy Spirit's revelation. Both Moses's and Elijah's Horeb time was a great revelatory experience when God spoke to Elijah and showed Himself to Moses to tell of his coming destiny. Change occurs as we're renewed at the Mountain of God.

Horeb was Elijah's hiding place. When he arrived, he sought sanctuary in a cave. Many in the Bible also found solace in caves. David ran from Saul and hid in a cave (see 1 Sam. 24:3). He and his closest friends and family also sought refuge in the Cave of Adullam (see 1 Sam. 22:1), which provided shelter in a sorrowful, uncertain time. So too we must find our place of refuge as we maneuver through circumstances which drive us to that mountain where we can find God. At Horeb, children of Israel stripped themselves of ornaments (see Exod. 33:6) like we must strip away pride so that God can give us revelation to go further toward our destinies. Why Elijah needed stripped isn't told. Maybe God allowed him to go to Horeb because he'd let pride creep in after the mighty events at Mt. Carmel. That's an easy thing to happen in the prophetic when God chooses us as His hands to perform miracles. I love Peter's response after he and John were elevated by others after the healing at the Gate Beautiful. He asked why they were staring at them as if the miracle had occurred because of them (see Acts 3:12). The issue isn't what *we* can do but how *God's* ability can work through our availability.

GOD'S WILL

Elijah's cave was a sanctuary too. Elijah's problem with going to Horeb was that once he arrived and spent the night in the cave, "the word of the Lord came to him, and He said to him, 'What are you doing here, Elijah?'" (1 Kings 19:9). Was God asking him what he was doing in this state of depression or why he came to Horeb without being led there by the Spirit? The Beersheba to Horeb trip was a grueling forty-day, two-hundred-mile journey.[7] Before his trip, while in the throes of fear and sorrow, Elijah had decided to go to Mt. Horeb, but he didn't ask the Lord before he went. Did he suffer needlessly by not seeking God? Elijah had forgotten an important element of spiritual warfare. We must submit to God; then we can resist the devil and he must flee (see James 4:1). Instead, Elijah was doing the fleeing. When things are lined up and we're in God's will, we can resist; he has to flee.

My daughter in Oklahoma once needed me to make a trip to her house and bring her car she'd left in Indiana. We set a date, but I didn't ask the Lord about it. I ended up with several problems during the trip. I missed the funeral of a person I dearly loved. I became stranded in a Missouri snowstorm. Since I arrived a day later than I'd intended, I wasn't as rested or prepared for a sermon I preached on Sunday night. Then, before I flew home, a death in her husband's family necessitated her return to Indiana. I canceled my nonrefundable flight, and she and I drove her other car home together. Then, she went back to Oklahoma by herself. If her car had still been in Indiana, she could have flown home and taken it back herself. Both of us would have saved time, money, and energy if I'd asked God first. He understood that events would unfold as they did and asking Him first would have avoided my unnecessary inconvenience.

When we operate from our flesh instead of from Holy Spirit's perspective, we open ourselves up to God's asking, "What are you doing here?" Despite Elijah's flesh fit and pity party, God still loved him enough to provide for his journey with angelic sustenance and still met him on that mountain. Although my Oklahoma trip was a Connie thing, God blessed that Sunday service. Emotional focus changes our ability to see God's true plan. Once when I was having marital difficulties, I wallowed in my hurt. I was befriended by a woman who affirmed me. I discovered later her friendship came with an agenda—she operated in the Jezebel spirit and wanted to kill me spiritually because I operated in the prophetic. Prophets, usually strong and perceptive, see differently from their emotions. Elijah's depression, decision to go to Horeb, and way of viewing events were skewed when he interpreted and acted through emotions. We should ask ourselves, "Am I where God wants me to be, or have I gone on my own?" Have we made things hard on ourselves by pursuing avenues we think will accomplish God's purpose when we could complete it more easily and successfully His way?

GOD'S VOICE

Though Elijah had forty days during this journey to put his emotions into perspective, he still answered the Lord's inquiry, feeling sorry for himself. As God questioned why he came, he had news for God: he'd worked for Him zealously; God's other children had forsaken Him; they'd torn down His altars; and they'd killed His prophets. He alone was left and a target (see 1 Kings 19:10). Elijah's answer to God's question showed his position spiritually. These words are like us, focusing on what's wrong and not right. Actually, most of these weren't even true any longer. A little more than a month before, those who forsook God had repented, Elijah had personally rebuilt that Mt. Carmel altar, and Obadiah had told him he'd saved one hundred prophets from Jezebel. The last thing—"they seek to take my life" (1 Kings 19:10)—had colored his perception. How often do we think "everything" is going wrong when actually a few things have attacked us. When we live in emotions, Satan colors viewpoints with a negative spin.

After his response, God sent Elijah to stand before Him on the mountain. Standing "before the Lord" (see 1 Kings 19:11) changes things. When you stand before Him, facades are stripped away and He sees only you—just you. David and all of Israel worshipped on instruments before the Lord (see 2 Sam. 6:5) as they brought His presence back to Jerusalem. As Moses and Aaron entered the tabernacle, God's glory appeared and "fire came out from before the Lord" (Lev. 9:24) to consume the offering and cause people to fall on their faces. But Aaron's sons "offered profane fire before the Lord" (Lev. 10:1) and were devoured. Before the Lord we can't pretend any longer or hide in our caves because all affectation is revealed and stripped away as we're humbled (see James 4:10). Then He accepts our sacrifice and does a work in us.

As Elijah stood before God, "the Lord passed by" (1 Kings 19:11). Oh, when He passes by, He covers us with His hand (see Exod. 33:21-22). He's our Abba Who cradles us there. The Lord's passing by caused multiple manifestations, all describing Holy Spirit. First, a strong wind tore into mountains and broke rocks to pieces. After the wind, an earthquake, and then a fire came. But the Lord wasn't in any of those (see 1 Kings 19:11-12). He can come many ways because Holy Spirit mixes it up. I've witnessed those so zealous for God they ran around the room, or those who shouted until bobby pins fell from their hair as they touched the throne. I've heard others sob loud prayers of travail. I've observed such amazing manifestations that I stood gaping. Yet, those times when Holy Spirit comes with foundation-shaking power aren't His only ways of speaking, for He doesn't always choose the boisterous. We're often awaiting His glory to show up within the box we've made for Him; then, He reveals Himself another way. Those "normal" manifestations weren't how He appeared to Elijah because Holy Spirit is predictably unpredictable and chooses His way.

Elijah thought these obvious signs were the Lord, but God had other plans. Fire, earthquake, and wind could accomplish much, but sometimes it's not in a shout or a holler, but rather in "a still, small voice" (1 Kings 19:12). What an amazing revelation to a man who'd become an expert at hearing from God, but now he learned another way to receive revelation. Often, not God's majesty and grandeur but His kindness and gentleness speak to us. A lady who attended our church years ago initiated great miracles by blowing softly on someone. I've witnessed gentle whispers bring healing to a deaf ear or a hand waved toward the congregation cause people en masse to be slain in the Spirit. Holy Spirit changes it up, and that requires sensitivity. Elijah's response showed he recognized and revered God's speaking, even His gentle voice, His *qowl*. He wrapped his face in his mantle in reverence (see 1 Kings 19:13); for God's word, big or small, loud or boisterous, is to be cherished. Holy Spirit's stillness is louder than anything man can concoct. When His voice speaks audibly or quietly to our innermost being or He comes boldly or gently, He always has a purpose.

In our ministry, we meet many Christians, nearly all of whom are eager to pursue God's will. Often, however, they don't know what that is and expect Him to show up and speak through something rowdy like a marching band. Then, He communicates through a gentle unction into their spirits or from an unexpected source. When God speaks, whether He comes boisterously or quietly or the message is a pat on the back or a smack on the hand, we must revere each revelation. Like Elijah, we wrap our mantle around our faces and rejoice that God has spoken. To us! I can relate to hearing from God in both ways. Often, He comes to me for myself or others, not in a clap of thunder or with a feel-good message; but it's wonderful, all the same. Recently, within two nights, I had dreams with admonitions about several people. One was a friend whom Wade and I love much. The message to him was, "You don't have a leg to stand on." He received that reprimand in the spirit with which I gave it—love. It confirmed something God had been nudging him about but he'd been ignoring. Then, in a simple, quiet dream, God spoke His will clearly to our friend. What an amazing Father we have! When we reverence God's message, no matter what it is or how it's given, then He can move us out of where we are and toward our destinies.

STEPPING OUT

After he wrapped his face, Elijah stood in the cave's entrance. In an entrance, one both comes in and goes out, so Elijah had a decision to make whether he was leaving or staying in that cave. God had asked him first in the cave why he was there. Now, as he stood in the opening where he could leave his gloom, a *qowl* asked the same question. Listening to God's quiet voice brings more of His presence and revelation. But though Elijah answered Him the same way as before (see 1 Kings 19:13-14), this time, Elijah had changed. He wasn't hunkering in the cave; he was coming out. David couldn't have ruled if he stayed in his Adullam. Gideon couldn't fulfill his mighty-man-of-valor calling if he remained behind his winepress security blanket (see Judg. 6:11-12). As the angel told Elijah, we all must "arise" and move away from our hiding place to be God's warrior we were created to be. We can't hear from and comprehend God if we stay in darkness.

This time when Elijah answered God, God answered back that He had a faithful remnant of seven thousand "whose knees have not bowed to Baal, and every mouth that has not kissed him" (1 Kings 19:18). I love God's mentioning a kiss, a show of intimacy. He's referring to our mouth's importance and with whom we experience intimacy. A kiss is *nashaq*, "to kiss, lit. or fig (as a mode of attachment), [but also] to equip with weapons."[8] Whatever we kiss, we become attached to—our marriages, our jobs, our homes. The mouth is our ally or our enemy—when we eat what keeps us alive or makes us sick, when our words speak life or death, or when it kisses the right or wrong G(g)od. Hosea referred to this kiss because heathen priests often worshiped images of calves by kissing them (see Hos. 13:2). Many kiss idols they think will sustain and equip them, but the showdown with Baal's prophets proved kissing Baal's mouth hadn't armed them for victory. No kiss but the Lord's equips us with weapons to handle what will come next on our journey. How far men fall when they have more intimacy with a cow than with the Father.

God's message of His faithful ones thrills me. Yes, sometimes we Holy Spirit operators are seemingly alone, ridiculed, and criticized. Sometimes we wonder if God sees our isolation. Paul too in all his trials must have wondered at times if he stood alone. He alluded to Elijah's conversation with God on Mt. Horeb and spoke of the remnant which still existed in his time (see Rom. 11:5). That remnant was Elijah, Paul, their godly contemporaries, and us too—the faithful who determined to go the distance. As Obadiah's story showed, hundreds more are bearing the standard and just awaiting God's release for them to come forth from their caves. We're the seven thousand who kiss God's lips alone, so He can use us to accomplish this end-time work. That should encourage us, just as it did Elijah.

MORE TO DO

Between Elijah's first and second exchanges with God, nothing changed in the words, but something did in the heavenlies. The second time, God gave Elijah ministry direction and assurances of other armor bearers alongside him. God still had work for him to do, and Elijah's choices hadn't affected that. God could still use a broken vessel like him, and He can use us too. Sorrowful, down times can bring revelation and clarity after God shows up. He's doing a work in us because at our lowest point, Holy Spirit can impart new focus like God spoke to Elijah with new tasks. These assignments were to anoint Hazael as king of Syria, Jehu as king of Israel, and Elisha as his own successor. God told Elijah, "It shall be that whoever escapes the sword of Hazael, Jehu will kill;

and whoever escapes the sword of Jehu, Elisha will kill" (1 Kings 19:17). All these orders had a purpose—to kill the enemy—and were an important revelation and assignment. Actually, Elijah accomplished only one of these—anointing Elisha as his replacement. Then Elisha finished anointing the kings (see 2 Kings 8:12, 9:6). Did Elijah again miss God's will, or was the timing for later to be carried out by others with a call too?

These men to be anointed as kings were very different. Jehu was a man of God, considered a wild man (see 2 Kings 9:20) in his singularity of purpose in ridding Israel of evil (see 2 Kings 10:28). Hazael was a terrible person though. During Elisha's time as prophet, the ailing king of Syria, Ben-Hadad, sent Hazael to inquire about his recovery. Elisha told him to tell the king he would get well, but actually he was dying. When Elisha wept for that prophecy (see 2 Kings 8:11), Hazael asked why he was crying. Elisha said that he would become king in Ben-Hadad's place and treat Israel evilly and viciously (see 2 Kings 8:12). Though Hazael protested, the next day he murdered the king and reigned instead (see 2 Kings 8:15). Why was such an awful person God's choice to be anointed by His prophet? God accomplished vengeance and used both Jehu and Hazael to do that. As God said, Hazael injured Joram, Ahab's son, in a battle (see 2 Kings 8:29), and Jehu finished the job then threw Him onto Naboth's property (see 2 Kings 9:25). God used Israel's Syrian enemy, Hazael, "to cut off parts of Israel" (2 Kings 10:32) and conquer them as judgment. God always accomplishes His purpose.

CONCLUSION

Elijah heard from God and returned to the Wilderness of Damascus (see 1 Kings 19:15), close to where he'd started, for a preparation time. Like Elijah and Jesus (see Matt. 4:11), much of our own journey is in the wilderness. Elijah's trek started and ended in the wilderness, which speaks to me. He made the forty-day journey only to turn around and go back. How often do we too take off to do something good in our own eyes, even admirable, as we trudge toward the mountain where God can be found? How often do we make life harder for ourselves by *good* choices but not *God* choices? If we allow Him to direct our paths, we can still hear from Him and save ourselves the grueling desert journey which draws on our resources and exhausts us in the process. However, even if Elijah unnecessarily travelled two hundred miles to the mountain and two hundred miles back again, his time with God produced revelation and direction. That's a good lesson. Though we make poor choices and reach dead ends, God doesn't give up on us. We don't always get His direction the first time we approach Him, but we will. On Horeb and in the wilderness, He still had work to do, in and through Elijah, and does with us too. God may be getting revelation into us during low times of sorrow, despair, or depression.

ELIJAH AND NABOTH'S VINEYARD

1 Kings 21

Principles:
Observing God's Laws, Wooing the Backslider,
God's Dispensing Justice, Calling Out Sin

Holy Spirit's Role:
Spirit of Judgment (Isa. 4:4); Vindicator (Psalm 17:2)

My dad was born in the twenties and was a typical young man. He was brought up in church as one of ten children. He served in the navy in World War II and attended college for a couple years before he met and married my mother. He worked for the postal service and supported his growing family of two children. That number would eventually expand to six others. My parents were satisfied with their lives until they realized something was missing. My aunt's miraculous healing made him and my mother hungry to know God in a deeper way than his religious upbringing had taught. After his rededication and infilling of Holy Spirit, his and Mom's entire existence was studying the Word, praying, and constantly attending church.

Eventually, he became pastor of our small church and travelled many nights visiting hospitals and jails after his mail route. Then, at sixty-four, he was diagnosed with pancreatic cancer and lived about three years. Sixty-seven is far too young for someone to leave this world, especially when he had dedicated his existence to the Lord, but life isn't always fair. People work to earn money toward retirement then lose it with one extended hospital stay. A baby develops a fatal illness. A faithful spouse loses everything in a divorce. I don't understand why bad things happen to good people or good things happen to bad people. One Elijah story seems unfair too. But through it, God shows His heart and the prophetic's role. Naboth and his vineyard have much to say.

THE BIRTHRIGHT

Naboth is Chapter 21's focus when he had the misfortune of inheriting a vineyard adjoining the Jezreel palace property. Ahab wanted his neighbor's meager possession, the vineyard, for a vegetable garden. Isn't this similar to another vegetable grower, Cain? His envy of God's acceptance of his brother's sacrifice instead of his own made him kill his brother. That action brought the spirit of murder into this world, and Naboth's murder perpetuated that legacy. Ahab's story tells the depths to which he and his wife would go to get their way. It also reminds us that if we allow ungodly lusts to be conceived, they're eventually birthed, and those births bring forth death (see James 1:15). Ahab's lust brought death not only to Naboth and his sons, but also to Ahab and his sons.

Ahab approached Naboth with a logical proposal to acquire the vineyard: he would pay for it or give Naboth a better one. Doesn't that sound like Satan? He suggests schemes with logic and seemingly irrefutable words: You should find another husband who'll appreciate you. You should steal from your boss because he doesn't pay you enough. Naboth heard Ahab's pleasant-sounding words and refused the offer for the same reason we should refuse—his words weren't God's will. Naboth didn't hold onto his vineyard because of stubbornness or lack of respect for the king, but because the land was an inheritance from his fathers. Hebrew law prohibited selling inherited property unless someone was destitute (see Num. 36:7); then the property returned to him during Jubilee. Naboth wouldn't sell out of respect for his father's heritage and God's law. How often do we do what seems right to us without considering God's commands?

Both Ahab's request and Naboth's reaction show their consideration for God's directives. Both were Hebrews. Ahab was king of Israel; yet, as with other issues, he had little respect for God. Naboth valued his father's gift while respecting God's law to keep the inheritance. This scenario reminds me of two other men. Esau also had a birthright from his father, but he cherished it so little that he sold it for a bowl of soup. Romans 9:13 alludes to this in a puzzling statement: "Jacob I have loved but Esau I have hated." Actually, Scripture records many things God hates, including pride, lying, murder, evil, devising wicked plans, sowing discord (Prov. 6:16-19), and others. Unfortunately, as I look over this list, I see characteristics that describe many Christians, including those who operate in the prophetic.

However, though many in the Bible behaved atrociously, I found only one person God hated—Esau. Why? God had established the firstborn's birthright, which Esau would receive. Though a cherished right, he was ambivalent about that birthright and more concerned with fleshly desires (see Gen. 25:30-32). Jacob, on the other hand, took advantage of Esau's hunger to obtain the birthright then deceived Esau and Isaac to receive the father's blessing. How many of us covet carnal lusts more than Holy Spirit's gifts? How often do we pursue what *we* want instead of growing deeper in what *He* has for us? Are we selling or despising our birthright when we treat God's inheritance of His Spirit so cavalierly?

I once knew a man, Joey, who had many gifts and talents from a young age. He played music at church as a teen; then after he married, he and his wife travelled together, preaching and worshipping with music. But like Esau, Joey hadn't conquered fleshly desires which outweighed his love for the Father's inheritance. He lost his ministry and family and never returned to the Lord. His years of drug abuse made him unable to hold jobs and affected his health and mental acuity. Still, after all these years, he hasn't realized how much he lost being an Esau rather than a Jacob.

AHAB'S REACTION

Naboth cherished his birthright and gift from his father, but his refusal to part with it spelled doom for him. Like a petulant child or the emasculated man he was, Ahab went home "sullen and displeased…, lay down on his bed…, turned away his face, and would eat no food" (1 Kings 21:4). When he told Jezebel of Naboth's refusal to part with the vineyard, she took the situation into her own hands and told him to "Arise, eat food, and let your heart be cheerful; I will give you the Vineyard of Naboth" (1 Kings 21:7). I'm certain, since Ahab knew his wife's vicious character, he realized whatever she was suggesting wouldn't be good for Naboth. He knew what was right yet abdicated his integrity. Even Jezebel said he should "exercise authority over Israel!" (1 Kings 19:7). In other words, Ahab should have acted like Israel's king and a strong man. He should have followed God's law, but instead, he pouted to get his way and obtain the property by any unrighteous means necessary. Doesn't his submission to Jezebel's will sound like the powerless Ahab's response after the slaying of Baal's prophets?

This time, though, Jezebel's target was Naboth. She plotted her own deadly intervention since Naboth's death was the only solution which would allow Ahab to get his way. However, the plan may have been hers, but Ahab was just as guilty in God's eyes, for "there was no one like Ahab who sold himself to do wickedness in the sight of the Lord, because Jezebel his wife stirred him up" (1 Kings 21:25). This was the second time in this chapter Elijah told Ahab he'd sold himself to do evil, but this time he added Jezebel's culpability. This sad statement doesn't apply just to Naboth's murder. When Ahab married Jezebel and brought her into God's nation, she "stirred him up" to do evil as they worshipped idols rather than God. That's why God told Moses not to allow intermarriage between Israel's sons and daughters and other nations' inhabitants (see Exod. 34:15) because sin permeates the house and they're led astray. Like Ahab, your wife or husband may do your dirty work, but your part doesn't escape God's judgment. Ahab's silence about his wife's treachery didn't mitigate his guilt. Passive participation in sin is wrong in God's eyes. If you don't believe that, ask Adam.

THE PLAN

Jezebel put her evil plan into effect. She wrote letters in Ahab's name and with his seal and sent them to the city's elders and nobles to propose a plan. The leaders going along with her plan shows how deeply Israeli leadership had sunk in integrity. Idolatry taints even God's chosen. Then, Jezebel had them proclaim a fast to expose Naboth at trial. Two "scoundrels" (1 Kings 21:13) falsely accused him of two types of blasphemy: against God and the king. Satan loves to twist the truth. Often today, those operating in spirits point accusing fingers at others to keep from exposing themselves. The enemy often says that those doing right are committing sins he's actually doing himself. Jezebel cared nothing about God's law of inheritance nor the law of bearing false witness against her literal neighbor. Naboth had no disrespect for the crown but followed God's precepts while the king and queen thumbed their noses at them because Ahab wanted his way. When God's laws collide with man's desires, God's always must win out.

Stephen too was accused of blasphemy (see Acts 6:11, 7:59). His speaking against prevalent religious and political leaders necessitated silencing him, so he was stoned. They stoned Naboth and his sons too (see 2 Kings 9:26). Sometimes, no matter how unfair, evil is in charge for a season. Solomon commented on how unjust life seems: "I have seen servants on horses, while princes walk on the ground like servants" (Ecc. 10:7). In times when evil's on the throne, God seems to have forgotten the righteous, but He never misses inequities nor forgets to exact vengeance. Evil may be in charge now, but God will prevail. I imagine Amos thought of Ahab and "the ivory house which he built and all the cities that he built" (1 Kings 22:39) when Amos prophesied "the houses of ivory shall perish, And the great houses shall have an end" (Amos 3:15). Evil's ivory house is fleeting. The season of the unrighteous will end, for He's a God of justice and judgment.

Jezebel had no remorse for stealing the vineyard nor for killing Naboth and his sons. She marched triumphantly to the palace and announced to Ahab that he could take the vineyard because Naboth was dead. Ahab also felt no shame for the death of a man whose only "crime" was to receive and cherish his inheritance. As a matter of fact, the pouting was over, and Ahab got up from his bed and went to claim his new vineyard (see 1 Kings 21:16). His celebration was short lived, though, because Ahab couldn't enjoy the fruits of his new garden, for he was unworthy of being in that garden. Like Paul said that sinners shouldn't partake of the communion meal's wine unworthily (see 1 Cor. 11:27), so was Ahab unworthy because of the vinekeeper Naboth's blood. Just when we think we've gotten away with sin, God makes a reckoning. We kings, priests, and prophets can't hide behind others to keep from getting our hands dirty. God sees everything, especially the heart.

THE ENEMY

God told Elijah to meet Ahab in Naboth's vineyard (see 1 Kings 21:17-19). Their history had cast them as enemies in roles with opposite commitments to integrity and to God. As he approached, Ahab spoke confrontationally to him, as he had in former meetings, "Have you found me, O my enemy" (1 Kings 21:20). More than other Christians, we're the world's enemy because we can see Satan's plans. It's part of our job description; for if we're friends with the world, we're God's enemy (see James 4:4). When Ahab commented on his enemy's finding him, apparently, the king was hiding in his newly acquired land. Elijah's response showed God was in control: "I have found you, because you have sold yourself to do evil in the sight of the Lord" (1 Kings 21:20). God may permit wrong for a time, but evil is a magnet which draws His attention. He sees everything that happens to His kids, from a baby in a basket in the Nile to an inconsequential vineyard owner. Jesus told us that not being hurt is impossible, but a reckoning awaits those through whom hurts come (see Matt. 18:7). No one escapes judgment.

The history between this king and prophet created a possibility that Elijah wouldn't emerge alive, especially when this evil couple had just killed a man so Ahab could grow carrots and potatoes. Despite the threat to him, however, Elijah handled Ahab with authority. When he was called to vindicate Naboth, he spoke hard words to the king holding life and death power over him. How many of us shy away from giving hard words that could bring ridicule or ostracism? How often do we pick and choose which revelations we'll act on?

IMMATURITY

Sometimes hard words come at a cost. Whenever those with prophetic abilities discover another's sin, that prophet becomes the object of disdain and a target for destruction. Joash became king at seven years old (see 2 Chron. 24:1) after his aunt and uncle, Jehoshabeath and Jehoiada, hid him from Queen Athaliah's murderous purging. Jehoiada became Joash's father figure and mentor. Joash had a heart for the temple and its artifacts' restoration; so unlike previous kings, he did what was right before God "all the days of Jehoiada the priest" (2 Chron. 24:2). How admirable, but this statement should have read, "all *his* days," not Jehoiada's. Joash should have done what pleased God because he had a personal relationship with Him, not an affiliation with Jehoiada alone. Some use prophets as their conscience and covering when God wants repentance and relationship. Our works don't determine our character. The inside of a man must be holy, not his actions alone. Some leaders aren't mature enough to lead because they filled their role as a baby Christian or spiritual teenager and never gained maturity or intimacy with the Father.

Jehoiada died and Joash buried him among the kings. That honor speaks to me. Being respected is awesome; and like Obadiah with Elijah, prophets meet those who honor and exalt them. When someone elevates me, however, he has his eyes in the wrong place. I tell him to take me down from that pedestal because if he doesn't, God will, and that's not fun. We must seek personal relationship with the Father because, eventually, people we honor will disappoint us: our parents will pass away, the pastor may receive an assignment elsewhere, or a person we look up to may make poor choices. If our relationship is with a human, we're left with only memories. Since Joash had relationship with Jehoiada, not God, after his death, Joash didn't have the substance necessary to sustain his God-walk. He followed those who worshipped idols, though God's prophets and priests tried to woo him back to the Lord. One was Jehoiada's son, Zechariah. When he told Joash the Lord had forsaken him because he'd forsaken the Lord (see 2 Chron. 24:20), Joash became so angry they stoned Zechariah "in the court of the house of the Lord" (2 Chron. 24:21).

That murder was wrong on many levels. Zechariah was a priest. He was Joash's cousin and probably brother-in-law. He was his mentor's son. He was killed in God's house. Doesn't that detail resonate with you? Often, we're persecuted or spiritually martyred as prophets not by those in the mean old world but rather right inside God's house. The Jezebel spirit isn't always what goes after prophets, but sometimes just an immature leader who hasn't grown to know God personally. When our gifts don't fit with what the world wants or understands, expect attacks, and sometimes those come from other Christians.

Jesus commented on the slaying of innocent blood:

> I send you prophets, wise men, and scribes: some of them you will kill and crucify, and some of them you will scourge in your synagogues and persecute from city to city, that on you may come all the righteous blood shed on the earth, from the blood of righteous Abel to the blood of Zechariah, son of Berechiah, whom you murdered between the temple and the altar.
>
> Matt. 23:34-35

The Zechariah He mentioned is interpreted three ways: Zechariah, killed by Joash; Zechariah, the prophet; or Zechariah, father of John the Baptist. Whichever man Jesus was indicating, they're believed to all have been martyred, so all were righteous blood spilled. Abel's and the prophets' blood speaks to God. As Zechariah told Joash, God sees it all and will avenge injustices (see 2 Chron. 24:22). Zechariah means "memory of the Lord,"[1] and His memory is long. Joash's subsequent murder by his servants vindicated Zechariah. God also remembered Naboth and others who were killed by Ahab and Jezebel. As Jehu sought retribution, God said to "strike down the house of Ahab...[to] avenge the blood of My servants the prophets, and the blood of all the servants of the Lord, at the hand of Jezebel" (2 Kings 9:7). The blood of Abel, Zechariah, Naboth, and those prophets Jezebel martyred called to God, for "when He avenges blood, He remembers them; He does not forget the cry of the humble" (Psalm 9:12). God never, ever forgets to vindicate His children.

HIS WORDS

Today, we don't physically kill prophets in America, but they're frequently denigrated and persecuted until they're murdered spiritually because Satan wants to kill their words. God guards His words and elevates them even higher than His name (see Psalm 138:2). He protected Joash as a baby because he was the end of David's line through whom Jesus would come (see 2 Chron. 21:7), so God guarded His words spoken through the prophet Nathan about establishing David's kingdom (see 2 Sam. 7:12). Those who try to destroy God's words are treading on dangerous ground. Instead of receiving the prophet's reward, they receive God's vengeance. Joash paid a price. His kingdom was taken by the Syrians, he was killed, and he wasn't buried in the kings' tomb (see 2 Chron. 24:24-25). God didn't allow even an honorable burial for those dishonoring his prophets.

Though God gives leeway to repent, eventually, the sinner faces His judgment. As Judah became increasingly evil, God sent messengers to call them back to Him. Instead of heeding His word, "they mocked the messengers of God, despised His words, and scoffed at His prophets, until the wrath of the Lord arose against His people, till there was no remedy" (2 Chron. 36:16). They were overtaken by the Chaldeans, and Jerusalem fell. Yet another time, Israel had fallen into sin and served Baal, so God punished them by allowing them to be again conquered. Despite His judgment because of sin, His heart toward His wayward children was still tender, and "the Lord was moved to pity by their groaning because of those who oppressed them and harassed them" (Judg. 2:18). He cares so much that even when they suffered for their sins, it hurt His heart. God loves all His kids.

GOD'S JUDGMENT

Though Elijah had experienced Ahab and Jezebel's great power and hatred, he didn't neglect his job. God sent His prophet to walk right into that ill-begotten vegetable garden to prophesy of Ahab's death and God's judgment against him and his house (see 1 Kings 21:21-24):

- God will bring evil upon Ahab and his children (Verse 21).
- He will cut off his house (Verse 22).
- Dogs will eat Jezebel by the wall of Jezreel (Verse 23).
- Ahab's descendants who die in the city, dogs will eat (Verse 24).
- Ahab's descendants who die in the field, birds will eat (Verse 24).
- Where dogs licked Naboth's blood, dogs will also lick Ahab's blood (Verse 19).

Though not all in Elijah's time, these prophecies were fulfilled. Ahab died on the battlefield and dogs licked his blood (see 1 Kings 22:37-38). Jehu shot King Joram with an arrow through his heart and left his body on Naboth's land (see 2 Kings 9). As Jehu prophesied, "'I saw yesterday the blood of Naboth and the blood of his sons,' says the Lord, 'and I will repay you in this plot'" (2 Kings 9:26). We don't sin in a vacuum. Our sins will be visited upon our children unless we repent. Later, as someone washed away Ahab's blood in a pool at Samaria, harlots bathed and dogs licked up his blood to fulfill Elijah's prophecy. Evil's grand ending eventually comes.

This story gives much instruction for the prophetic. Judgment comes full circle, and our words can change destinies. When Elijah spoke God's judgment against Ahab for his part in killing Naboth, Ahab trusted Elijah's words of God's judgment and knew the true prophet of the true God. He mourned, tore his clothes, put on sackcloth, and fasted (see 1 Kings 21:27). Unlike his behavior when he pouted for not getting his way, this time, he repented. Though his contrition evolved from fear of consequences, God changed His mind. Because Ahab humbled himself, He deferred Ahab's judgment until his son's days (see

1 Kings 21:29). What a message that God would love Ahab so much to show mercy and kindness to him. When He should turn His back or give up on us, He loves us all. Even awful Ahab. Even sinning Israel in darkest drought. Even you and me. He loves His children enough to give them drought, to give them a death and resurrection, to give them a hard word.

Ahab had everything but also wanted Naboth's. Doesn't this sound familiar when another Israeli king, David, looked at his neighbor's property and lusted after his sole possession, Uriah's wife (see 2 Sam. 11)? Both wanted it. Both made it happen. Both were accosted by prophets. Both had judgment spoken against them. Both repented. The difference, though, was Ahab repented out of fear of judgment, and David repented because he'd sinned against God (see 2 Sam. 12:13). Another similarity amazes me. Both Naboth and Uriah were killed because they took a principled stand which was contrary to a king not acting in godliness. God loved innocent Naboth and Uriah so much He vindicated them. Naboth's enemies were killed. Uriah received a special place in Jesus's genealogy: "David the king begot Solomon by her who had been the wife of Uriah" (Matt. 1:6). What an honor! God doesn't forget His godly little ones who made the ultimate sacrifice for righteousness. Some things live beyond death, and being included in the great Master's genealogy is an honor that surpasses all. Like these two kings, we too deserve much more punishment than we received for past sins. But God included us too in the great plan His Son brought.

THE SPIRITS

Spirits are powerful and assigned for particular purposes like drawing people into sin or destroying them (see Mark 9:22). Many spirits are mentioned in the Bible: a spirit of bondage (see Rom. 8:15), fear (see 2 Tim. 1:7), deaf and dumb spirit (see Mark 9:25), distressing spirit (see 1 Sam. 16:14), false spirit (see Mic. 2:11), spirit of ill will (see Judg. 9:23), and lying spirit (see 1

Kings 22:22). Besides these, innumerable others are in the Bible and can present themselves in our lives. I know people who've been delivered from spirits of lust, addictions, abuse, perversion, and many others. By sheer numbers of biblical references, much human behavior occurs because of spirits. That should be a revelation to many that undesirable behaviors are often because of spirits. People were pursued by spirits in the Bible and are now too.

The Jezebel and Ahab spirits are alive and well and assigned to families and churches, often to go after the prophetic like much of Elijah's ministry years were spent being pursued to kill his anointing. Naboth's story demonstrates how they work. Naboth, whose name means "fruits,"[2] grew grapes which would become wine (a Holy Spirit symbol) from his vineyard. He represents the Spirit-filled believer whose fruit the enemy wants to obliterate to keep the prophetic from coming forth. We'll come across many who don't cherish prophetic gifts and even denigrate them with attacks motivated by something as simple as the spirit wanting to get its way about an issue or not wanting seers to expose motives.

JEZEBEL

John mentions the Jezebel spirit in his letter to the church at Thyatira:

> Nevertheless I have a few things against you, because you allow that woman Jezebel, who calls herself a prophetess, to teach and seduce My servants to commit sexual immorality and eat things sacrificed to idols. And I gave her time to repent of her sexual immorality, and she did not repent.
>
> Rev. 2:20-21

This passage addresses much. Jezebel's goal was to rid Israel of those following God instead of Baal, so this spirit is interested in promoting the counterfeit while derailing the prophetic. The Jezebel spirit not only goes after prophets but operates as one too, calling herself a prophetess. Jezebel is about control; and today, false prophecy is rampant as many declare themselves to be prophets and speak their own words in God's name to manipulate others. They present their opinions as if the "word" is from God then become irate if someone questions or doesn't follow what they "prophesied." Even true prophets should assess their lives often and motivations for giving words. How much is God-directed and how much from the flesh?

The statement about "commit[ting] sexual immorality" is never shown about Jezebel in Elijah's story as I said before. However, Jezebel had constant love affairs with the world. She seduced Israel to follow other gods and leave their first Love, the God Who established the nation to exalt Himself. I'm saddened about those who straddle the fence with God and dabble in the world. We're impregnated by what's around us, so fornicating with sin won't birth God's children but rather illegitimate ones, evil imitations of His plan. We're sleeping with the world when we gauge our actions by what's socially but not spiritually acceptable. Like that church at Thyatira, many of today's churches have allowed this spirit to operate freely and to teach her heresy. That's dangerous, and we're called to repentance.

We've encountered this spirit several times. Like the woman, the Jezebel spirit is ruthless and wicked. She undermines and verbally attacks those opposing her, often accusing *them* of operating in the Jezebel spirit like she accused Naboth of blasphemy when she and Ahab were actually guilty. Like with Elijah, she assaults the prophetic which can expose her. In our experience, the attacks come against the prophet's character and gifts with the end goal of destroying the prophetic in general. Once, the Lord spoke a warning to me through a dream about a woman operating in the Jezebel spirit. When I told her what God had shown me, she didn't accept it as a word from the Lord, but rather went on the offensive and told others I was putting word curses on her! How like Satan and this spirit to make someone reject a word of life then twist it so prophet and prophecy appear perverted.

This spirit works through fear. Jezebel killed other prophets and threatened then tried to kill Elijah. However, she's the one who died and Elijah never did. She's powerful and intimidating in order to keep God's prophets from speaking *rhema* to bring freedom. The spirit is strong like Jezebel was formidable enough to cause extreme discouragement in an amazing man who'd experienced mighty miracles. Her outliving Elijah's time on earth shows the spirit's staying power. After Jehu had her servants throw her from the wall, her blood splashed on the wall and horses (see 2 Kings 9:33). Blood is a life source, and horses are tools of warfare. We do much warfare against this spirit that's alive and well.

Jehu intended to bury her as a show of honor to a king's daughter, but she not only wasn't honored with a royal tomb but didn't have one anywhere. Her death fulfilled Elijah's prophecy that her corpse would "be as refuse on the surface of the field, in the plot at Jezreel, so that they shall not say, 'Here lies Jezebel'" (2 Kings 9:37). Before Jehu could bury her, dogs ate her and left only her skull, feet, and palms of her hands (see 2 Kings 9:35). Today, those three parts that remained from Jezebel are still affecting people: what they think, where they go, and what they do. Elijah's prophecy—that she would be eaten by dogs by the Jezreel wall (see 1 Kings 21:23) foretold more than just her fate to be dog food. Some manuscripts say "plot of ground" instead of "wall."[3] That's powerful wording because the implication is that she was killed beside Naboth's plot of ground. How amazing that Naboth is mentioned briefly in the Bible, yet just as God guards His prophets and their words, He also watches those who keep His commandments and work in His vineyard.

AHAB

The Jezebel spirit needs a leader to assure she has conferred authority and usually chooses a docile submissive Ahab, who goes along with her wishes rather than asserting himself. The manipulative and aggressive spirit operates unhindered in churches because she makes herself indispensible to leadership, her Ahab. She aims to please leaders like she instigated Naboth's death to please Ahab. We never see face-to-face confrontations between her and Elijah, but rather she pursued him in the background. The spirit too often hides in the shadows and controls those in charge to get her evil way. She concocted the scheme to kill Naboth, then wrote letters in Ahab's name with his seal and sent them to elders and nobles. The spirits operate the same way, hidden behind the scenes but proceeding under leadership's authority.

Like the man, the Ahab spirit is compliant with those operating in the Jezebel spirit and allows evil to continue because of benefits to him. Ahab was also compliant with his enemy Elijah: on Elijah's command, he went to Carmel, gathered the prophets and the people, feasted to celebrate the loss of his prophets, and returned to Jezreel at Elijah's word. Then he tattled to Jezebel about what had happened so she would go on a rampage against Elijah (see 1 Kings 19:1). Ahab played a passive role while Jezebel actively devised the plan for Elijah's and Naboth's executions. Though leaders may see the wrong, they often ignore it because that person operating in the Jezebel spirit contributes greatly to their ministry.

One word of caution. Jezebel and Ahab are spirits, not people. We must separate the person from the spirit for "we do not wrestle against flesh and blood, but against principalities, against powers, against the rulers of the darkness of this age, against spiritual hosts of wickedness in the heavenly places" (Eph. 6:12). Thinking of the spirit when the person is in your face calling you names and undermining you is difficult, but Jesus also dealt with these dynamics. He loved sinners but separated them from their sins. The spirit, whether Jezebel, Ahab, or the religious spirit, is your enemy, not the person through whom the spirit operates.

CONCLUSION

When God has us confront evil, we're obligated to identify sin and proclaim His judgment. We're watchers and can't afford the luxury of not speaking truth, even to kings, like Elijah did to Ahab, Nathan to David, or John the Baptist to Herod (see Mark 6:18). Watchmen must faithfully speak what God gives (see Isa. 62:6), no matter the cost. God desires to woo sinners and is married to the backslider (see Jer. 3:14). Jesus said the shepherd will leave ninety-nine to bring back one who's wandered (see Luke 15:4)—a drug-addicted, wayward child; an adulterous, wandering husband; a murderous, evil king. God cares about them all, wants them back, and uses Holy Spirit's drawing to accomplish that. Our prophetic words can cause repentance in the hardest sinner. I wish I could say each of your revelations will be met with tears of joy, welcoming arms, and spiritual renewal. Often, the opposite is true, and you may never see results. Though Elijah often brought words to Ahab, he didn't repent until now. If you're willing and obedient to fulfill each job you're led to do, His great master plan will fall into place.

ELIJAH AND THE OTHER PROPHETS

1 Kings 20 and 22

Principles:
Training the Next Generation, God's Moving Through Many,
Listening to Wise Counsel, Trusting God for Victory

Holy Spirit's Role:
Teacher (John 14:26); The Spirit of Truth
(John 16:13); Author (2 Tim. 3:16)

The Bureau of Labor Statistics says that in May 2012, forty-four thousand clergy practiced across America.[1] That's a large number officially in God's battlefield, but how many are household names? The number of preachers with name recognition worldwide is small, yet those actually working for the Kingdom is great. When God told Elijah that thousands were still faithful, that indicated a massive number. Though much of God's work is done by Elijahs and Billy Grahams, more often, innumerable prophets and armor bearers with unknown names are God's army. Except for Elisha, Elijah's servants aren't named in the Elijah chapters, and just one other prophet is mentioned by name. God is moving through these types of ministers today. An army of nameless, faceless prophets uphold the Lord's banner. I believe that's why the Elijah narrative is interrupted by two scenarios involving other prophets. Elijah's story begins in 1 Kings 17 and ends in 2 Kings 2—just eight chapters discuss this man with many references throughout the rest of the Bible, even from Jesus. However, in the midst of telling his story come other prophets' brief tales, and Elijah appears to have no role in these men's ministries. However, in my experience, something seemingly misplaced in the Bible has a purpose.

CHAPTER 20: UNNAMED PROPHET

The first interrupting story comes immediately after Elisha's ordination. At the end of Chapter 19, God told Elijah to anoint Jehu, king of Israel (Ahab was king), and Hazael, king over Aham (Ben-Hadad was king). Ben-Hadad's story creates an opportunity for God to speak through prophets other than Elijah. As king of Syria, Ben-Hadad gathered thirty-two other kings for war against Israel. He sent Ahab a message that he wanted his silver, gold, wives, and children. Since the nation had been under siege, Ahab agreed to give him everything he'd asked for (see 1 Kings 20:3-4). Ben-Hadad wasn't satisfied though. He sent word that he wanted more. His servants would search houses the next day and take anything they wanted. Doesn't this speak to us? We can't give the enemy an inch because he's never satisfied.

The Lord once spoke to me that like the secular world, many Christians have fallen into a lifestyle of compromise. We're part of a society where speaking God's truth gets Christians ostracized and ridiculed, but we must remain a separated people. We listen to jokes we shouldn't, watch movies we shouldn't, let our eye look where it shouldn't, cut corners we shouldn't. Righteousness and holiness have faded from style though they're needed more than ever. Those values are especially crucial for prophets because compromise hurts God and our ability to be used by Him. Sin breeds sin. When we give in to Satan, he then desires more. He's a bully who gets what he wants, then lies to get a deeper foothold until we're stripped of what's valuable. Then our testimony and witness are tarnished.

Ahab called his elders together and told them of Ben-Hadad's request to plunder the city. This is a good concept for leaders. Everyone needs a group to give sage godly advice. Even Solomon, the wisest man ever, had advisers. Every king, priest, pastor, and prophet needs a system of elders from whom to ask opinions, especially as we're growing (see 1 Kings 20:7-8). Without that network of counselors, we often blunder; but with them, we have a greater chance of making solid, well-considered choices (see Prov. 15:22). Those men told Ahab to refuse Ben-Hadad's request so he passed along that word (see 1 Kings 20:9). However, Ben-Hadad replied that he would rout Samaria so badly there wouldn't be enough dust for each soldier in his massive army to find a handful. Ahab's answer was good: "Let not the one who puts on his armor boast like the one who takes it off" (1 Kings 20:11). What a message! We become discouraged as battles go badly for us, but we forget the importance is in winning the war. We fight an already-defeated foe because Jesus died and rose again; but as skirmishes rage around us, we forget that. Too often we anticipate a negative outcome because we envision the battle from our own eyes, so the enemy seems stronger than we are. God, however, sees circumstances from a different perspective. What our eye sees and mind conceives can change in an instant.

Ben-Hadad poised for attack; then God spoke His mind through an unnamed prophet historians identify as Micaiah.[2] He told Ahab that God would deliver the Syrians into Israel's hands. This prophet represents those who don't fill a coliseum when they come to town but are still mightily used of God. When Ahab asked by whom victory would come, the prophet said by young leaders of the provinces, but Ahab would set up the battle for them (see 1 Kings 20:14). This message excites me. The pronouncement by this prophet symbolizes what's to happen in God's end-time army. A younger generation is arising to take the army into battle, yet we need each other. A time comes when the older generation passes the baton, or mantle, like Elijah did to Elisha, but our job isn't finished. As seasoned warriors, we mentor in warfare and set the fight in order as God gives the battle plan. This becomes God's method of operation to bring victory. When He reveals His plan, we can rest, assured of triumph. God uses prophets to declare His plan then brings success if we obey His directives.

THE BATTLE

Ahab did obey. At noon, seven thousand children of Israel and 232 young men of princes of the provinces prepared for battle (see 1 Kings 20:15-16). What a disparity against an army of a "great multitude" (1 Kings 20:13), at least eighteen times larger than Israel's army (see 1 Kings 20:29-30). God slanted the odds though. Arrogant about victory, when Ben-Hadad was told Ahab's young men were amassing against them, he again bragged of triumph and told them to take the Hebrews alive whether they came for peace or war (see 1 Kings 20:17-18). Ben-Hadad and the young kings had gotten drunk and gone to battle in that state (see 1 Kings 20:16). The Israelites made a great slaughter, but Ben-Hadad escaped. We're to totally destroy the enemy because letting him live to fight another day multiplies problems. After Samuel anointed Saul as king, he told Saul to totally destroy the Amalekites, everything from men to donkeys (see 1 Sam. 15:3). Saul smote everyone but took the king alive and spared the best of the livestock for a sacrifice. God sent Samuel to tell Saul that because he'd disobeyed, the kingdom would be torn from him. Going our own way has consequences; for as Samuel told Saul, "to obey is better than sacrifice" (1 Sam. 15:22). Doing things God's way the first time saves us from much sorrow later.

After Ben-Hadad's escape, the prophet told Ahab to amass troops because Syrians would attack again in the spring. We may miss the mark on God's battle plan, but that doesn't mean we can't have ultimate victory. When we know the enemy's plan, we must prepare. When Joab led the Mighty Men of Valor against the Syrians during David's reign, they made a plan of attack, prepared as best they could, but realized the battle's outcome was God's (see 2 Sam. 10:11-12). Is that your war plan—preparing to the best of your ability then letting God do the rest? Many don't occupy while awaiting their next assignment. God expects diligence to heed the prophet's words and to work at your current job.

In the spring, the prophecy was proven. Syrians believed various cultures had gods that ruled over geographical areas. They made a plan to attack in the plains where they would be stronger because they thought Israel's God was of the hills only. They probably also thought that militarily their great army of chariots they were reassembling (see 1 Kings 20:25) would provide an advantage on the plains. When Ben-Hadad returned, Israel marched against his army. The Syrians filled the countryside and outnumbered the Hebrews so greatly that "the children of Israel encamped before them like two little flocks of goats" (1 Kings 20:27). God didn't leave His "little flocks" without a battle plan though.

MAN OF GOD

A man of God approached Ahab. That term means a prophet who speaks for God. It's used seventy-five times in Scripture[3] to describe an elite group: Elijah (see 2 Kings 1:9), Moses (see Deut. 33:1), God (see Judg. 13:6), Samuel (see 1 Sam. 9:6), Shemaiah (see 1 Kings 12:22), Elisha (see 2 Kings 4:7), David (see 2 Chron. 8:14), Igdaliah (see Jer. 35:4), and several unknown prophets (see 1 Sam. 2:27; 1 Kings 13:1, 20:28; 2 Chron. 25:7). This name described those who knew Scripture well, were perfect (mature), did good works (see 2 Tim. 3:15-17), and represented Jehovah (see Ezek. 3:17). Men of God were qualified to act as if God

Himself were acting (see Judg. 13:6). What an amazing moniker! Would you qualify to be called a man or woman of God?

This man of God came in His authority to inform Ahab that He would defeat that great Syrian multitude (see 1 Kings 20:28). Ben-Hadad had made strategic errors because those who trust in horses, chariots, and strong horsemen rather than God are doomed (see Isa. 31:1). Ben-Hadad had miscalculated where the Hebrew God ruled. He didn't factor in that Israel's God fought with weapons that could overcome a numerical disadvantage in mountains or valleys and certainly wasn't superior only on the mountains. In addition, he'd bragged twice that the Syrians would be stronger than Israel (see 1 Kings 20:23, 25). God doesn't like being underestimated. The armies encamped across from each other for seven days. Again, that's the number of completeness, and this victory was complete on that day: one hundred thousand Syrian foot soldiers were killed and the rest fled to Aphek where a wall fell and killed twenty-seven thousand more (see 1 Kings 20:29-30). When a prophet or man of God tells of the enemy's plan, that word of wisdom will occur. Men and women of God speak His events into existence; and God accomplishes His word, even with a falling wall.

Ben-Hadad fled and hid in an inner chamber of the city. His servants advised him to dress in sackcloth on his loins and ropes on his head to show contrition. Sometimes, we must be aware, though, of an enemy who acts defeated. Though God is love and Ben-Hadad's servants had heard about the Israelis' mercy (see 1 Kings 20:31), when we battle the enemy, obedience should supersede mercy. When they approached Ahab, Ben-Hadad and his servants shrewdly assessed the king and said what he wanted to hear. Ben-Hadad appealed to Ahab's mercy and vanity and promised to restore cities his father had taken from Ahab's father (see 1 Kings 20:34). Ahab agreed and sent him away with a treaty. The problem with making a treaty with the enemy, though, is that evil doesn't keep its word. When God says to destroy totally, complete destruction is crucial. Though Ben-Hadad made promises, he never kept his word.

SONS OF THE PROPHETS

God's anger was aroused because of Ahab's disobedience, so He sent a son of the prophet to declare judgment. Scripture has many references to sons of the prophets, or prophets-in-training. Samuel headed a school of prophets (see 1 Sam. 19:20). Elisha's miracle of the oil happened to a widow of a son of the prophets (see 2 Kings 4:1). Gehazi ran back to Naaman professing that two sons of the prophets from Ephraim had requested goods (see 2 Kings 5:22). Elijah was master at several schools of prophets— Gilgal, Bethel, near Jordan, Jericho, and others.[4] The total number of sons of the prophets isn't specified in Scripture but seems numerous. Obadiah hid one hundred during the drought. Sons of the prophets stood at Bethel before Elijah left, at Jericho, and on Jordan's banks during Elijah's ascension. Though the chapter doesn't mention them at Gilgal, Scripture later refers to Elisha eating with them there (see 2 Kings 4:38). He also summoned a son of the prophets to go to Ramoth Gilead to anoint Jehu as King of Israel (see 2 Kings 9:1-2).

Many sons of the prophets existed then and now. Examples of these prophets-in-training say much to me. Recently, a lady asked me questions about how her newly acquired gifts of the Spirit worked. I was honored to tell her what I'd learned through my own study and experience because we're "sons of the prophets, and of the covenant which God made with our fathers" (Acts 3:25). We learn as these men did from prophets like Samuel, Elijah, Elisha, or nameless ones. Elijah mentored two kinds of future prophets. A number had the official title of son of the prophets and were formally trained by the great leader. However, Elisha learned by watching and doing at the prophet's feet. Some of today's ministers are modern-day sons of the prophets, educated at seminary, but like David and Abraham, some are simply called by God. The prophet Amos wasn't schooled in the prophetic. He "was no prophet, nor...a son of a prophet, but...a sheepbreeder and a tender of sycamore fruit" (Amos 7:14). Don't you love that? We're teachers, lawyers, electricians, doctors, homemakers, nurses, welders, and tenders of sycamore fruit, not necessarily learned, but learning, nonetheless, while doing dishes or checking out customers at the grocery.

The problem is that too often modern seminaries teach doctrine but don't formally train sons of the prophets about Holy Spirit's gifts. Though many Bible colleges and theology degrees exist, where are schools for prophets? Where are deeper things of God being taught? How can we expect seminary-trained ministers to move into Holy Spirit's depth if we don't provide training centers to bring sons of the prophets along? Occasionally, I'll hear of those marvelously educated at schools like Bill Johnson's Bethel Church in California. Those men and women possess a great advantage, but the rest of us can't lose hope. We're like Amos and received our calls while we were occupying as a "sheepbreeder and a tender of sycamore fruit," and then we proceeded. We find our way in the prophetic because of mentors, books, experiences, Holy Spirit's direction, a hunger to learn more, and digging into the Word.

AHAB'S JUDGMENT

This son of the prophets wanted to present himself to Ahab as if he'd come from battle, so he asked a neighbor to hit him before he approached the king (see 1 Kings 20:35). Since the man of whom he made the request was described as a neighbor, he too was probably a son of the prophets and should have known to respond to that other man's unusual request. When the neighbor refused, the son of the prophets said because he didn't obey God's word, he'd be eaten by a lion. He was. What a hard lesson. When God gives instructions through His mouthpiece, obey! The son of the prophets found another to hit him, so he waited, wounded, for Ahab to come by.

When he did, that son of the prophets cried out and showed himself. He spoke in a parable and claimed to have gone to battle and then was charged with guarding a prisoner. If that prisoner escaped, he would pay with his own life or provide the equivalent of a talent of silver, around one hundred pounds and worth about $660,000 today. Although the cost was high, this man became busy and the prisoner escaped. That parable speaks to me. Christians, especially prophets, are charged with guarding God-given duties. The son of the prophets called it a prisoner, but I think of the charge God birthed in me as my baby. That assignment should be number one on our priority list. However, we get busy—car pools, jobs, dinner, laundry, ministries. None of our busyness should take precedence over our God-given assignment. I fail at that often; then God reminds me once again to put things in order. When the son of the prophets told Ahab he'd allowed his prisoner to escape, Ahab became indignant with the soldier and said the threatened punishment would be his fate. The son of the prophets then took off his disguise and Ahab immediately recognized him. He gave Ahab a word that the same scenario would happen to him because he'd let Ben-Hadad go instead of destroying him as God had instructed. Ahab left displeased, sullen, and unrepentant (see 1 Kings 20:43). That reaction shows Ahab's immaturity and inability to follow through with all God said.

CHAPTER 22: MICAIAH

After Chapter 20 finishes, Chapter 21 tells of Elijah, Naboth, and Ahab. After Naboth's death, Elijah declared God's judgment to Ahab, who heard, believed, and repented. As a result, God changed the judgment so He wouldn't destroy Ahab's family until his sons' days. At the beginning of Chapter 22, three years have passed with peace between Israel and Syria. However, time made Ahab slip into old patterns. Jehoshaphat (king of Judah and Ahab's relative by their children's marriage) visited a distraught Ahab in Samaria. Moses had set aside three cities of refuge east of the Jordan: Bezer, Ramoth Gilead, and Golan. If someone accidentally killed another, he could flee to and live in a city of refuge, safe from retribution from the victim's family. Ramoth Gilead had been taken by the king of Syria during Ahab's dad's reign. Ahab wanted it back, especially since Ben-Hadad had promised to restore it but hadn't. To assure compliance with him, the enemy makes many promises so he can manipulate and control lives. After we do what he wants, he doesn't follow through because he doesn't want to give up his territory.

AHAB'S PROPHETS

Ahab asked Jehoshaphat to go to war as his ally. Jehoshaphat offered his resources to help defeat Syria but with one caveat: he would go to battle only after hearing from God (see 1 Kings 22:5). That request should accompany everything we do—we must hear from God. To appease Jehoshaphat, Ahab gathered his four hundred prophets who told them to go ahead with the battle and the Lord would deliver Ramoth Gilead to him from the Syrians (see 1 Kings 22:6). This group of men is interesting. We're not told if these prophets were Baal's, God's, or a mixture. Since Ahab had repented and Baal's prophets had been killed, they were probably God's prophets, or at least had been originally. Some may have even had legitimate callings but had somehow lost their way and now prophesied what Ahab wanted to hear. Later, the messenger cautioned Micaiah that "the words of the prophets with one accord encourage the king. Please, let your word be like the word of one of them, and speak encouragement" (1 Kings 22:13). What a sad statement that a prophet should feel he must misrepresent God, even to encourage the king. True prophets don't fit in with most others, even with other prophets who've forgotten their godly charge. We can't fear or please man because that ensnares us. That's especially true for God's spokesmen!

This tale was probably included with Elijah's stories because these prophets can teach us about our own gifts. All operators in the gifts should test the spirits of those who claim to be prophets because many false prophets do exist (see 1 John 4:1). Too many "prophets" today crave acknowledgement and a recognized name but have forgotten prophetic integrity. We prophets must speak what God says. Period. Who knows why these prophets had left their calling and spoke only what Ahab wanted to hear. Like the man cautioned Elijah, maybe they wanted simply to encourage rather than hurt the king. Too many fall into that trap when they prefer to speak kind, not hard words. When tough messages are required, speaking anything besides God's heart is wrong. When false prophets speak, those words come from their own heart, not the Father's, and are therefore without worth (see Jer. 23:16). Plus, often the kindest act we can do is to offend someone to save him/her in the long run.

Perhaps, like Baal and Asherah's prophets during the drought, Ahab had given monetary motivation as he supported these four hundred prophets. Many pastors, prophets, and other ministers cater to big tithers and neglect to speak truth to those supporting their ministries. Perhaps Ahab's prophets' motivation to speak lies was plain ol' survival since Ahab and Jezebel had a history of persecuting and killing prophets who spoke against them. Sometimes prophets get sidetracked and forget their job—hearing then speaking God's words. Anything else is false prophecy, wrong, and the spirit of Jezebel. Jehoshaphat, though, didn't buy into prophecy spoken to please Ahab and asked for a true prophet. Ahab told him one prophet existed—Micaiah, whom he hated because all of Micaiah's prophecies to him were bad (see 1 Kings 22:8). He spoke only God's words and not feel-good, ear-tickling messages to Ahab.

TICKLE YOUR EARS

Doesn't Ahab's statement speak volumes? We're told "The time will come when they will not endure sound doctrine, but according to their own desires, because they have itching ears... they will turn their ears away from the truth" (2 Tim. 4:3-4). The Modern Language Bible translates that people will "gather up teachers that will tickle their ears." That time is now when churches don't take stands against sins like homosexuality or abortion because they don't want to offend. Some ministries have become businesses which speak what congregants want to hear lest they leave and take their money with them. Isaiah called those "a rebellious people...Who say to the seers, 'Do not see,' And to the prophets, 'Do not prophesy to us right things; Speak to us smooth things, prophesy deceits'" (Isa. 30:9-10). How sad! These former men of God have lost their way and have become as those Ahab prophets.

A friend used to call me regularly to see if I had a word for her and ask my opinion about situations. In reality, she wanted me to validate what she'd already decided. I couldn't do that although it meant an argument always ensued. She would, without fail, defend her choices, and this constant scenario left me tired and frustrated. I wished she'd stop calling altogether. One day, I complained to my mother, my own mentor and confidant. She said, "She always disagrees with what you say, but she still calls *you* when she needs to hear another's opinion." That statement created perspective about my friend and others who call for advice but actually want positive "Ahab" words. They continue calling because however unpopular, they know godly words. Ahab sought prophecies from those who said what he wanted to hear, but he knew God's true prophet.

When Ahab said he hated Micaiah, Jehoshaphat defended the prophet and scolded Ahab. This shows a fundamental difference between these two men and demonstrates modern-day, contrasting stances—varied respect for the office and person of the prophet. Today, some churches revere and embrace the prophetic while others endure or reject it. As prophets, we must faithfully keep giving what God reveals regardless of the word's popularity. Elijah's and Micaiah's commitment to speak God's true words despite the cost created a stark disparity with Ahab's prophets. While the kings awaited Micaiah's arrival, more words from the false prophets said the venture against the Syrians would go well. One prophet, Zedekiah, gave an elaborate prophecy showing horns of iron to demonstrate they would gore the Syrians (see 1 Kings 22:11). That prophecy probably pleased Ahab since horns often represented power. As others joined in these pronouncements, the hall must have resounded with excited assertions of these prophets whose goal was to please their master. They may have even begun to believe those words themselves.

MICAIAH

When the messenger arrived with Micaiah and warned him to speak good things, Micaiah said "Whatever the Lord says to me, that I will speak" (1 Kings 22:14). Those words should be a prophet's motto. Micaiah means "who is like to God?"[5] He operated in humility, had covenant with the Father, and spoke only His words for no one is "like to God." Could you go authoritatively before the hostile king as Elijah and Micaiah did and speak God's words that could mean your demise? Could you stand against Baal when the entire nation had different religious beliefs? Could you go into a room filled with "prophets" speaking opposite of what you knew to be true and stand in prophetic integrity? When we operate in righteousness, we must judge Him to be faithful and believe that God will reward our stand for integrity (see Psalm 25:21).

When Micaiah first arrived, Jehoshaphat and Ahab sat dressed in royal garments on the threshing floor at the Samarian gate. The Hebrews' threshing floors were important because that was where the harvest was ground. Because of that crushing action, one of their symbolic usages is violent judgment[6] (see Mic. 4:12). Here, violent judgment would be pronounced on Micaiah. Zedekiah, who a short time before had been leading the group with his prophetic play acting, struck Micaiah on the face (see 1 Kings 22:24), a great insult in those times. Since Micaiah had probably been brought from prison (see 1 Kings 22:26) and his hands were still bound, he had no recourse from the slap. Then, when he gave his prophecy, Ahab sent him back to jail. However, man's judgment isn't God's. Ultimately, Micaiah's unheeded prophecies about Ahab would violently come to pass.

Zedekiah's slap wasn't the only time a prophet was treated that way. This same scenario happened to Jeremiah when the temple chief slapped him and put him into stocks after he prophesied negatively (see Jer. 20:2). Jesus too was mocked, spat upon, blindfolded, beaten, and slapped because He spoke God's word without sugarcoating it (see Mark 14:65). Even before Micaiah spoke, as he stood there with the stench of prison still on his clothes and disdainful leers from around the room, he knew there would be a cost. Words of truth don't make God's prophets popular, but we must speak them anyway.

The king asked him if they should go to war to reclaim Ramoth Gilead (see 1 Kings 22:15). Doesn't that sound like my friend who asked my advice when she'd already made up her mind? Micaiah understood that and answered sarcastically: "Go and prosper, for the Lord will deliver it into the hand of the king" (1 Kings 22:15). His mockery reminds me of Elijah's snide comments to the Baal prophets during their sacrificial rituals. Ahab recognized his tone and said, "How many times shall I make you swear that you tell me nothing but the truth in the name of the Lord" (1 Kings 22:16). This statement is ironic when he'd just told Jehoshaphat that he resented Micaiah's negative words. These comments to Micaiah could be interpreted a couple ways. Perhaps Ahab was referring to other times when Micaiah showed disdain for the puppet prophets' words. Perhaps Ahab desired his way but wanted it validated in God's name, and he thought if Micaiah said it, it would become true. That's what Balaam thought as he returned to God multiple times on Balak's behalf (see Num. 23:15). God's words are established, and He doesn't change His mind because we'll gain an advantage.

Micaiah spoke his word from God. He saw Israel scattered as sheep without a shepherd, "And the Lord said, 'these have no master. Let each return to his house in peace'" (1 Kings 22:17). Jesus alluded to this in His analogy of sheep without a Shepherd (see Mark 6:34). What a message—the Great Prophet cherished the words of a minor prophet whose name is mentioned only a few times in the Bible! God's word is gold no matter who delivers it. The second part of the prophecy would literally happen as Ahab lay dying, and at sunset a shout went out for everyone to return home (see 1 Kings 22:36). The prophet's words stand when false words don't, but Ahab didn't heed them. He accused Micaiah of prophesying negatively on purpose. The enemy always questions God's true words.

Micaiah then told another vision which said the Lord would defeat Ahab, and he would be killed at Ramoth Gilead because of the "lying spirit in the mouth of all [Ahab's] prophets" (1 Kings 22:23). The phrase "lying spirit" tells me again that we are fighting a spiritual battle. When we understand that, we're victors. Anything not of God will kill whatever situation we're involved in. God often "will send them strong delusion, that they should believe the lie, that they all may be condemned who did not believe the truth but had pleasure in unrighteousness" (2 Thes. 2:11-12). When "strong delusion" comes, that lie which sounded pretty will be the downfall of those who believed and promoted it. Ahab's belief in the strong delusion sealed his fate.

THE PROPHECIES' FULFILLMENT

By declaring the prophets' lying spirits, Micaiah not only challenged their words but also their integrity. After slapping

Micaiah, Zedekiah refused to concede but rather challenged Micaiah, who didn't back down either. He responded that after Ahab died, the lying prophets would need to hide from those seeking vengeance for sending him to a fatal battle. Ahab tried to show contempt for Micaiah's prophecy by his rearrest and order to be fed with bread and water "of affliction" (1 Kings 22:27), or small portions, until he returned from war and proved Micaiah wrong. Micaiah's last words were that Ahab surely wouldn't return from battle.

Though his anger toward Micaiah said otherwise, Ahab believed the true prophet. He disguised himself on the battlefield while he had Jehoshaphat dress as king. Even after hearing Micaiah's bad report and Ahab's self-serving request, Jehoshaphat didn't withdraw from their alliance. As admirable as his seeking God's will from the true prophet was, the second part of his and our responsibility is then to obey. When Jehoshaphat returned from the battle, his own prophet questioned why he had helped Ahab who was wicked and hated God (see 2 Chron. 19:2). What a profound question which addressed his unholy association with Ahab. We often continue to collaborate with instead of fleeing from those who don't treat God's words or precepts with the same reverence we do. Seeking His will but then ignoring His voice results in consequences. Because of Jehoshaphat's poor judgment, the Lord's wrath (see 2 Chron. 19:2) was spoken on this man who loved the Lord. God mitigated his punishment, though, when Jehoshaphat prepared his heart to seek God.

In battle, the Syrians had one goal: to get Ahab (see 1 Kings 22:31). Thinking the elaborately dressed Jehoshaphat was Ahab, Syrians surrounded him and he "cried out" (1 Kings 22:32). That word is *zaaq*, "to shriek (from anguish or danger)."[7] That strong word was used as men on Jonah's boat cried out to their gods with death imminent on those stormy seas (see Jon. 1:5). Mordecai cried out when he learned of the death plot against the Jews (see Est. 4:1). Don't you imagine this man who loved God "cried out" with everything in him to his Abba, his Daddy? Don't you think he "cried out" fervently to his Jehovah Jireh to provide safety? Don't you think that cry reached El Shaddai, Almighty God? This king "cried out" unashamedly during time of utter danger. How often in our dire circumstances do we cry out to our Lord and an accident is avoided as His hand miraculously steers our car for us? How often do we cry out to our Father when a bad report brings panic into our hearts, and He changes that report? Our Abba hears our cries.

He heard Jehoshaphat's too. As Jehoshaphat "cried out,…the Lord helped him, and God diverted them from him" (2 Chron. 18:31). Though the subterfuge with Jehoshaphat tricked them for a while, suddenly, a captain realized this king wasn't Ahab and stopped pursuing him. Although Ahab had risked Jehoshaphat's life to save his own, God wasn't fooled by his plan for self-survival. A man haphazardly shot an arrow which pierced the joints of Ahab's armor. He left the battle and sat propped up in his chariot until he died in the evening. His fate was sealed by his backsliding into idolatry and turning to false prophets. Lying prophets cause destruction if what they're speaking is for any other purpose but to share God's word.

SO WHAT?

So why interrupt the telling of Elijah's life with these two stories of the prophetic? Perhaps Elijah needed a season of avoiding Jezebel. Maybe he was tired and had gone somewhere to rest. Maybe he needed to become emotionally solid again or God had sent him on another unrecorded assignment. No matter why these chapters are positioned here, I see similarities to Elijah's ministry. All show prophets dealing with matters of warfare and state but also personal to them. Like Elijah, prophets or men of God spoke declaratively to Ahab and pronounced judgment against him. Ahab believed and acted on their words. Chapter 20 referred to all types of seers: an unnamed prophet, a man of

God, and a son of the prophets. Prophets (speak the word), Sons of Prophets (are prophets in training), and Men of God (show God's might and revelation through their character) all engage in Holy Spirit's work. Whether our name is Elijah or Sally, if our word is authored by Holy Spirit, the message is important and will come to pass. Each of these seers had the same goal then as now: to speak God's word. Unnamed or lesser-known prophets, whether men or women, are important to God too.

HIS WRITING

I've been blessed to do extensive travelling for book events. At various conferences, prophetic speakers are amazing at how they so accurately receive revelation. Some have name recognition and some don't, but one thing that has struck me is how each anointing and administration of that anointing are so different. First Corinthians 12:4-6 says Holy Spirit is the author of the variety of gifts—nine in all—but how individual ministries operate is different (see 1 Cor. 12:5). One dynamic woman I heard in Chicago walked through the crowd and gave words about situations. Another lady in Florida heard specific names for whom she prophesied amazingly. A friend of mine gives prolific words, often through worship. She reminds me of Jeduthun's sons who worshipped prophetically with a harp (see 1 Chron. 25:3). For Wade and me, the Lord reveals many words of knowledge which bring healings and miracles, but even the two of us have different ways God reveals needs. Each receives differently and is anointed, yet each has a niche; we can't compare our gifts and administrations with another's.

Like our children are alike yet different, God's hand has crafted a unique prophetic ministry for us like He did for Elijah, Moses, Isaiah, and others. We recognize differences in other five-fold ministries such as a pastor. Some are street pastors, home pastors, prison pastors, youth pastors, and senior pastors. Each is a pastor, yet each demonstrates his heart by what he brings to that ministry. We combine our motivational gifts with our five-fold ministries and create different nuances. If our heart is for teaching, our ministries and gifts reflect teaching. If we have a heart of an encourager, each message we see in the Word speaks encouragement. Joel Osteen is a good example of that because his messages all encourage others. God flavors prophets' gifts too with the motivation within their hearts. If they have a heart of a blessing prophet, their words speak blessings. Serving prophets demonstrate that through their gifts, as do teaching prophets. God put that into their DNA, and they reflect that in what they do, even their prophecies. All are special, whom God made them to be, and should execute their gifts the very best they can.

Like us, Elijah wasn't a "typical" prophet. That term seems inappropriate because God isn't typical. Elijah didn't write a book or prophesy about Messiah like Jeremiah or Isaiah. Only one writing, a letter, is attributed to him. Jehoshaphat, king of Judah, had died, and his son Jehoram reigned. After he settled in, Jehoram killed his brothers and the Israeli princes; reigned for eight years; and was evil like Ahab and Jezebel, his in-laws. He made Judah do evil as he created high places and caused the nation to sin against God. Elijah spoke judgment in his letter:

> Thus says the Lord God of your father David: Because you have not walked in the ways of Jehoshaphat your father, or in the ways of Asa king of Judah, but have walked in the way of the kings of Israel, and have made Judah and the inhabitants of Jerusalem to play the harlot like the harlotry of the house of Ahab, and also have killed your brothers, those of your father's household, who were better than yourself, behold, the Lord will strike your people with a serious affliction—your children, your wives, and all your possessions; and you will become very sick with a disease of your intestines, until your intestines come out by reason of the sickness, day by day.
>
> 2 Chron. 21:12-15

This powerful word came true. Arabians invaded Judah and carried away Jehoram's possessions and family. Then a disease struck his intestines. He lived two years, apparently in excruciating pain, and died when his intestines burst. He wasn't honored as a king upon his death nor buried with the kings (see 2 Chron. 21:17-20).

Elijah's letter speaks to me. Not everyone has gifts and talents as a writer or speaker. However, although God generally uses us in one way, that doesn't mean He won't change His plan. This letter shows how Elijah, though not a writing prophet, could write God's prophetic word when called to. We generally fit into the ministry place God prepared for us, but then He takes us from our comfort zones when Holy Spirit changes it up and assigns us something that's not our forte. We're called to speak what He says and how He chooses for that time. Our forum may change depending on the need. At times we may spread God's word by preaching at churches, yet some Christians use Facebook as an amazing tool to proclaim His word. God may send us to a home; but sometimes an e-mail, text, or phone call does the job. A trip to the grocery allows us to preach to one whom God put in our path while a letter might be what's needed.

Elijah had many platforms. Usually, God sent him face-to-face with the king. But Elijah also sent messages via others like Obadiah, Elisha, and Ahaziah's men. Sometimes, God sends us as a prophet to the nations, but sometimes it could be for a private word like when Elijah met Ahab alone in Naboth's vineyard. All these ways, including writing, are powerful as long as we follow Holy Spirit's directives and realize our gifts' administration is unique and precious. Operators in the gifts should be aware of the prophetic's power through spoken, written, and recorded word, but it should be birthed by God and not so we can say we have a book, CD, or speaking ministry. All His ways are to spread His message in a manner He chooses just for us.

QUESTIONS

Some scholars question inconsistencies in Elijah's letter. Jehoram reigned after the ascension, so people wonder how Elijah wrote the letter. Many possibilities could exist. The Jehorams ruling simultaneously in Judah and Israel certainly contributes to the confusion. Maybe Elijah's letter was a future prophetic word written in advance and passed along by one of his students, or he left this assignment for Elisha as he did other tasks. Also, since Elijah's life is often related by allusion, perhaps unwritten parts of his story would clear up any misunderstanding. Another theory is Elijah stayed somewhere on earth after his ascension and still performed prophetic works through his protégés. Another possibility is that Elijah's ascension wasn't related in chronological order. Explanations have often been proposed for other things that people question in the Bible. No matter how any biblical mystery is explained, like much in our Christian journey, we live by faith. His Word is truth. Period. Even if questions exist, this writing speaks to me. Elijah was who he was. He didn't fit a mold, nor do we. His words, like ours, were powerful, whether written or spoken, for they were authored by Almighty God. Like Elijah, we do what God says, when He says, and how He says. Period.

CONCLUSION

During his depression time, God told Elijah He had a faithful remnant (see 1 Kings 19:18). He still does so the work of the Kingdom doesn't fall to one man. Like when Paul said his work for the Lord was a collaboration between him, Apollos, and God (see 1 Cor. 3:6), one man starts while another continues; then God causes it to all work together. In our gifts, we're not Lone Rangers. We're more like the Texas Rangers—a team. Too often I see dueling prophets try to outdo one another or make negative comments about another's word. That shouldn't be. We're one body made up of many Elijahs, Micaiahs, sons of the prophets, men and women of God, and unnamed prophets. All fight a common enemy who's not our brothers or sisters. God's work is tiring—physically, spiritually, and emotionally. He uses more than one person so we don't get depleted like Elijah during his journey. God's word will be spoken by His seers, big or little, famous or no name. In the battle against Ben-Hadad, that remnant of seven thousand became the small yet powerful army of seven thousand which defeated a multitude that far surpassed it in numbers. Are we training God's remnant to become that powerful army? We're all part of the seven thousand God has reserved for such a time as this.

ELIJAH AND AHAZIAH

2 Kings 1

Principles:
Surviving the Enemy, Employing the
Ministry of Angels, Declaring God's Supremacy,
Embracing the Glory, Seeing God's Fire

Holy's Spirit's Role:
The Fear of the Lord (Isa. 11:2);
As a Guide (John 16:13); As a Consuming Fire (Heb. 12:29);
The Spirit of Power (Acts 1:8); The Spirit of Might (Isa. 11:2)

"Connie!" Wade shouted from downstairs to where I was working upstairs. In his excitement, I couldn't understand his next garbled words. As he talked, he'd reached the bottom of the stairs and was quickly coming up. All I heard as I turned toward him was "Gold!"

He rounded the landing when our gazes locked on one another. His excited expression made me cock my head and ask, "What?"

"Gold!" he repeated. "Gold!" His right index finger pulled his cheek back and with his left he pointed to his tooth. Suddenly, it dawned on me. A few days before, a lady at our Bible study had received a gold filling shaped like a cross, and everyone was still astounded. My excitement grew as I realized why Wade was so excited—he had a filling too.

"You got a gold filling?" I stood and quickly met him in the hall.

"No!" He smiled as big as a finger in his jaw would permit. "No, it's a tooth!" He'd been brushing his teeth when a glint had caught his eye. He not only had an upper gold tooth on the right side; but on the left, he had gold brackets and fillings. I was dumbfounded. I'd come to terms with the lady's filling, but this was something else to wrap my mind around. We stared at each other with unbelieving astonishment. We'd heard stories and had personally seen many signs and wonders. We'd watched videos and read books. But an amazing phenomenon had happened to *us* personally. That day, we were forever changed.

Whether scoffers believe in them or not, signs and wonders occur regularly and are hard to imagine. How does God put a gold tooth into someone's mouth? Skeptics' questions aren't new today. Because of His wonders, Jesus's family and others once thought He'd gone off the deep end and was doing Satan's works (see Mark 3:21-22). Naysayers are part of this prophetic journey, especially when you deal in signs and wonders. All wonders are amazing, and Elijah's ministry demonstrates many: a drought, a resurrection, translations, a deluge, supernatural running ability. Now, those are wonders! Another exciting wonder he understood how to perform was calling down fire from heaven. He'd done it at Mt. Carmel and that wonder was going to happen again.

AHAZIAH

As 2 Kings begins, one story precedes the ascension—a brief tale about Ahaziah, Ahab and Jezebel's son. Like his mother, Ahaziah was a Baal disciple and walked in the evil of his parents (see 1 Kings 22:51-53). He became king of Israel in the seventeenth year of Jehoshaphat's reign in Judah, and friction between the two existed. Ahaziah asked to allow his servants to go with

Jehoshaphat's servants on a merchant ship to get gold (see 1 Kings 22:49). Though he'd complied with Ahab's past requests, when Ahaziah asked, Jehoshaphat refused. If he'd acquiesced to Ahab's evil desires but refused Ahaziah, his son's brother-in-law, Ahaziah must have been far more evil than Ahab.

One day, Ahaziah fell through lattice of his upstairs room and was badly injured (see 2 Kings 1:2). This lattice was probably equivalent to a railing around a deck protruding from a second-story bedroom, and the rail broke and permitted the fall. Ahaziah wanted to ascertain his recovery chances, so he committed a final act which angered God. He sent messengers to inquire of a pagan god, Baal-Zebub, to see if he would recover (see 2 Kings 1:2). Baal-Zebub, meaning "god of the fly,"[1] was the local god of Ekron, which means "barrenness."[2] Ahaziah didn't turn to his nation's God but rather turned to a barren useless god of one of earth's lowest creatures. Doesn't that describe the world today? Sadly, even religion has devolved into what's low, barren, and nonproductive. Like in Jesus's time, religion has in large part become dead, drawing flies to its carcass instead of being alive and productive to feed people. As religion observes its rituals, it creates a stench by "making the word of God of no effect through your tradition which you have handed down. And many such things you do" (Mark 7:13). God wants His own—especially His nation's king—to come to *Him*, not an earthly or religious counterfeit. Ahaziah discovered what his dad came to know—no Baal is supreme against Jehovah.

Like when God sent angels for divine sustenance, now God sent an angel of the Lord to Elijah (see 2 Kings 1:3, 15) for protection and direction. Angels are "ministering spirits sent forth to minister for those who will inherit salvation" (Heb. 1:14). That tells me angels come to enrich our lives with warnings, sustenance, direction, and proving His word. The angel told Elijah to meet Ahaziah's messengers and ask if they were questioning a pagan god "because there is no God in Israel?" (2 Kings 1:3).

This reminds me of Jehoshaphat's question to Ahaziah's dad: "Is there not still a prophet of the Lord here" (1 Kings 22:7). Hadn't Ahaziah learned anything from his father's mistakes which ended in his death? He surrounded himself with his mother's powerless gods because when evil is your heritage, seeing truth is difficult. Are we letting our children see God through our actions, or are we giving them a heritage of death too by allowing them to repeat our mistakes? Have we turned elsewhere because God has lost His voice? We prophets should be asking, "Is there not a God in America," Who delivers, heals, and gives sought-after answers? Are we letting the next generation know He's the answer to that question?

Like he'd done to Ahab, Elijah brought God's word of judgment of Ahaziah's impending death because he'd inquired of the pagan god so "therefore" he would "surely die" (2 Kings 1:4). Ahaziah's death would "therefore" come because he chose to look toward other sources rather than God. How profound! Do we try everything before we go to God? Are we creating death because of lack of faith and looking to other venues? Though the world seeks answers every other direction, that shouldn't be what God's children do. He has life that doctors, lawyers, friends, counselors, family, and others don't. Satan, a liar by nature, wants us to believe his lies, so he counterfeits Holy Spirit. Remember when Saul sought wisdom from the Witch of Endor (see 1 Sam. 28:7-16)? God was so angry, he was killed the next day. Worldly things are death, but God's are life (see 2 Cor. 7:10).

EVIL

Ahaziah turned to Satan like some still trust him today. A young mother came to my book signing one day. She told me she was a Christian but had a Wiccan symbol dangling from her necklace. She proudly pointed to it, then spouted new age dogma about how they believed similarly to Christianity. I was saddened and sickened by lies she'd swallowed. I told her bitter and sweet water can't come from the same fountain. No matter how innocent or good something seems, if Satan's the author, it's evil. When we believe in something not from God's fountain, a cost ensues. Incidentally, I didn't sell her a book. God sends us to proclaim His word but sometimes, that means calling evil, evil.

Susan, whom I met on Facebook, messaged or called me occasionally whenever her life was falling apart. Often she'd go away from our conversation with renewed clarity. Once, though, she called agitated. Things had gone badly that week. As she related what had happened, she also spoke negatively about how God had treated her unfairly. I listened for about five seconds before her words hurt and sickened me so much I could no longer stand it.

"Wait right there," I interrupted. "What's goin' wrong for you is because of your choices, not God's choices for you." As she began to rant again, again I interrupted. "My whole life, God's always had my back. I've gotta have His now. I can't listen to that awful stuff you're saying about Him. If you ever talk like that to me again, I won't take your calls." She stopped, then changed her tone. By the time she hung up, she too spoke of God's faithfulness and her choices which brought her to where she was. Elijah too had God's back when he asked Ahaziah if he'd gone to Baal because no God lived in Israel. Like Susan, Ahaziah had brought himself to this point by his actions—first with his accident, then by seeking ungodly advice.

AHAZIAH'S RESPONSE

After Elijah sent the messengers to give Ahaziah the message, they described the shaggy garment, skin, hair, and beard. Ahaziah recognized him as Elijah, a hairy man with a leather belt around his waist (see 2 Kings 1:8). Scholars speculate that the hairiness referred to his long hair, body hair, beard, or an animal (sheep, goat, or camel) skin garment. His appearance must have been unique, though, since Ahaziah recognized him by the description alone.

Unlike his dad who repented when God delivered judgment, Ahaziah went after Elijah by sending fifty men and one captain to kill him. That often happens—Satan tries to kill the messenger because of God's message.

After delivering God's word, Elijah had departed, maybe by a translation or by just leaving. When Ahaziah sent his men back to kill him, he was sitting on a hill. When God gives an assignment, you must victoriously occupy high ground in the face of the enemy, speak from your elevated perspective, and continue until God says to move. Like at Mt. Carmel, higher ground allows you to see God's plan from His perspective. This time, when Ahaziah threatened, Elijah didn't run like when Jezebel had pursued him. When the king's men arrived, the captain said, "Man of God, the king has said, 'Come down'" (1 Kings 1:9)! He probably used "Man of God" mockingly, for prophets and their words are often objects of scorn, even today. However, when you know God's sent you, you can withstand persecution or scoffing. Though the captain spoke sarcastically, God showed up to prove Elijah and Himself in a real way. Again, let God confirm your gift. When you speak from His authority, people recognize you're men and women of God. Once, when the Syrian king wondered who informed the enemy of their battle plans, his servant told him that Elisha heard what the king spoke in the privacy of his bedroom then passed that information along to the king of Israel (see 2 Kings 6:12). Sinners don't want you to read their mail, and Satan certainly doesn't want his battle plan discovered, so they'll try to discount your words in any way possible.

Elijah didn't go down from the hill. Obedience says you can't move until God permits. Elijah's answer to the captain showed his utter confidence in who he was and what God could do: "If I am a man of God, then let fire come down from heaven and consume you and your fifty men" (2 Kings 1:10). Like when he called down fire on the sacrifice, this time the fire killed the captain and fifty men (see 2 Kings 1:10, 12). Fifty represents Holy Spirit's anointing and Year of Jubilee, the return of possessions (see Lev. 25:8-10). Right now, it may seem Christians aren't prospering, but Jubilee's coming. God "will restore to you the years that the swarming locust has eaten" (Joel 2:25) in your own circumstances. At Jubilee, Satan has to give it all back.

That fire is *esh* "burning, fiery, fire, flaming, hot."[3] Great men have known God's fiery hot flame and its power: for example, Moses's burning bush (see Exod. 3:2) and fire in the wilderness by night (see Exod. 40:38). Esh was the all-consuming fire Elijah had called down on the sacrifice (see 1 Kings 18:38), seen on the Mountain of God (see 1 Kings 19:12), and would experience in the chariot which would take him to his journey where he wouldn't taste death (see 2 Kings 2:11). Holy Spirit's fire consumes it all, even soldiers and captains sent for your demise.

SIGNS

This fire is a type of amazing wonders—like resurrections and translations. For much of my life as a child and then as an adult, I attended a church with a banner above the pulpit—"These signs shall follow them that believe" (Mark 16:17). I read that terminology and saw a multitude of miracles in that church but didn't understand those signs' purpose. Basically, a spiritual sign is like a road sign. It gives information or points to something. Fifty miles to Indianapolis. Speed limit: thirty. Next exit: eleven miles. By receiving information, you can determine where that sign points and then you follow. You recognize signs indicating an impending occurrence too—a darkened sky, whispers before Christmas, a rickety banister on a staircase. God's signs are the same. He gives them for spiritual awareness that something is coming.

Just like Jesus told His disciples that they would see signs and recognize them like leaves on a tree which show summer is nearly here (see Matt. 24:32), spiritual signs are recognizable and point toward a destination—God. They're God's call to anticipate His great wonders to come, yet we don't always pay attention to those signs. The Old Testament word for sign is *owth*, "a signal, evidence, mark."[4] Amen. Those signs are evidence, a mark, of what's to come and point to a deeper spiritual reality. New Testament signs, especially when used with the word wonders, are usually *semeion*, adding the detail that signs are "especially… supernatural."[5] These supernatural signs create much excitement.

SIGNS AND WONDERS

Though signs and wonders are often used synonymously, wonders are God's manifestation of power and usually what a sign points to. Wonders draw people, for "the whole earth is filled with awe at your wonders" (Psalm 65:8, NIV). Doesn't that describe your reaction to wonders—awe? Old Testament usage is usually *mowpheth*, a "miracle, sign, wonder."[6] New Testament *teras* is "a prodigy or omen—wonder,"[7] which indicates "extraordinary occurrences, supernatural prodigies, omens, unusual manifestations, miraculous incidents…, and acts…so unusual they cause the observer to marvel or be in awe."[8] There's that word "awe" again. Awe is that feeling when you can't believe what you just saw—a blind man healed, legs lengthened, a fire which consumed the bad guys. If you respond to those with awe, not unbelief, then wonders will take you deeper. After Paul resurrected the boy Eutychus, "they brought the young man in alive, and they were not a little comforted" (Acts 20:12). Don't you love how that's worded? They were all probably high-fiving and doing some Holy Ghost shouting, and not just a little bit either. It's okay to respond with awe and rejoicing because wonders are miracles and supernatural events to which signs are pointing and validating the Father, Son, and Holy Spirit.

The raising of Eutychus wasn't the only time those who witnessed and experienced wonders were awestruck. I can relate because Wade's gold tooth is still hard to fathom. Twice, the

Spirit set Ezekiel up on his feet (Ezek. 2:2, 3:24); and after his translation, he "sat where they sat, and remained there astonished among them for seven days" (Ezek. 3:15). That scripture makes me smile as I visualize Ezekiel sitting with the people, probably speechless, eyes wide in astonishment as he reflected upon the heavenly journey he'd experienced. Jesus's disciples reacted that way also. As He walked across the water to the boat and the storm was calmed, they were greatly "amazed...and marveled" (Mark 6:51). Daniel too was "afraid and fell on [his] face" when an angel touched him in his sleep and stood him up (Dan. 8:17-18). Habakkuk said to watch for bizarre happenings: "Look among the nations and watch—Be utterly astounded! For I will work a work in your days Which you would not believe, though it were told you" (Hab. 1:5). Work a work you couldn't believe? Sounds familiar.

In Acts, Peter quotes Joel who spoke of signs and wonders. In the last days, God will

> pour out [His] spirit on all flesh....[He] will show wonders in heaven above And signs in the earth beneath: Blood and fire and vapor of smoke. The sun shall be turned into darkness, And the moon into blood, Before the coming of the great and awesome day of the LORD.
>
> Acts 2:17, 19, 20

This scripture thrills me. As much as today's signs bring amazement and disbelief, wouldn't "blood and fire and vapor of smoke... [and] the sun [turning] into darkness, and the moon into blood" be so intense that people would be dumbfounded? In awe. Now those are wonders! This scripture also differentiates between signs and wonders in Heaven and Earth. That tells me signs must be what He gives us on earth because of wonders generated in Heaven. As we spend time in His presence, they manifest as wonders here too.

A GENTLE EBBING

One day, the Lord whispered to me, "A gentle ebbing." I understood His meaning. My spirit had been disquieted about comments I'd heard of Christians berating others who experienced supernatural glory manifestations. Maybe the Bible doesn't mention specifically that Jesus experienced today's signs, or maybe it does, but we don't understand Scripture correctly. Saying something doesn't exist is pretty hard when your hands are covered with gold dust or the glint of a gold tooth smiles when you do. That day, God was telling me the tide in the Spirit has brought amazing manifestations, but now the ebb is gentle compared to what's to come. Just wait for the tsunami. Current manifestations are quiet reminders God is on His throne. You should embrace those signs then brace yourself. If He's pouring His Spirit out like a flood in the end times, what's happening now is just a drizzle. How will earth respond to God's Spirit outpouring?

God's time is "at the doors" (see Mark 13:29). The cloud of not-so-gentle signs, God's deluge of rain, is on the horizon. If you can't accept or comprehend gentle ones, how will you react to fire falling, jet-less air travel, abundant rain, and resurrections? Now, *those* are signs! Current manifestations are overwhelming because of their power and might but we've had just a little, gentle taste. If you can't believe this, how will you accept that storm to come? After Peter quoted Joel, he said Jesus brought "miracles, wonders, and signs which God did through Him in your midst," and they not only didn't believe but crucified Him (see Acts 2:22-23). Are we still crucifying Him today as we dishonor His signs and wonders' power? Miracles happen today as Holy Spirit takes us into new magnitudes. In our meetings, heat or oil has come into hands to bring miracles. We've felt tingling, an inability to move limbs, and glory zones where people couldn't walk without falling. At times, the *kabod* has been a heavy blanket, thick fog, or bright light. We've witnessed people struck mute and not able to preach or blinded to sermon notes. Sometimes God sends a whirlwind to stir up or destroy what's not of Him and take us to a new level, like Elijah. A spiritual tropical storm's coming, and we'd better watch out. Those waves may be gentle now, but what we've yet to see is unimaginable!

However, we must keep signs and wonders in perspective. The "signs shall follow them that believe," but many believers mistakenly have it the other way around. We often follow the signs. We shouldn't look toward signs as the end result, or we're as Simon the sorcerer wanting to purchase Holy Spirit because of what came with Him (see Acts 8:18-19). As awesome as experiencing signs and wonders is, no one should make that his/her goal. They point to the Lord, Who alone is worthy to follow. Apostles didn't preach in the early church so that signs and wonders would follow. They preached Jesus and Holy Spirit's arrival, then wonders automatically followed. That tells me if we're preaching Jesus but nothing's happening in the signs and wonders realm, something's wrong. The first century church operated in and taught about being filled with Holy Spirit as a crucial element of salvation. Their actions demonstrated miracles, signs, and wonders as reality. Through and because of Him, we see signs and wonders, but He's the purpose. We should want Holy Spirit's gifts because they're part of Him, and because of His person, we should seek those gifts and "covet" (1 Cor. 12:31, kjv) them. Covet. What a strong word to show the importance of our Spirit-filled walk and gifts. As we get excited when jewels or manna falls from the sky or gold dust covers our bodies, remember it's all about Him.

HARDENED HEARTS

Wonders abounded for Jesus. He and His disciples were so busy meeting needs they didn't have time to eat, so once, they left to rest and eat in a boat (see Mark 6:31-32). When the crowd saw them going, they followed and arrived there before Jesus's boat. He was moved with compassion and taught all day. At day's end came the great event of five loaves and two fish which fed five thousand men plus women and children. Then, He sent His disciples away so He could disperse the others and pray. In the evening, He saw those disciples straining to row against the wind. Before dawn, He walked to them on the water. Disciples thought He was a ghost and cried out in fear. They struggled with the wonders He'd performed, "For they had not understood about the loaves, because their heart was hardened" (Mark 6:52). They'd seen the wonder of feeding the multitude yet didn't apply that to their own needs.

God calms waves, brings the Master across waters, and expands a food supply. Is He doing mighty acts which increase your faith, or is your "heart...hardened" to what He's doing? Some say they want signs and wonders but want to pick which ones to experience personally. The Pharisees sought a sign from Jesus (see Mark 8:11). He'd already fed the multitudes, healed the deaf mute, and delivered the Greek woman's demon-possessed daughter. He'd already healed by the touch of His garment and raised the dead. He'd already taught knowledgeably and authoritatively. He'd done all this, but they hadn't seen, so He said, "No sign would be given to [that] generation" (Mark 8:12) because they'd ignored what He'd already done. Much of today's church resembles the Pharisees who see God's works but still search for something to convince them. If we want what God has, looking at Elijah can change our thinking. His life was all about signs and wonders, and he didn't care what others thought, from the king to the popular religious sect. His desire was to be about his Father's business and grow adept at whatever it took to accomplish that. And wonders abounded.

LOVE

Who knows what God will use to promote Jesus and our ministries if we do things His way. His purpose may be fulfilled by wonders: meals from birds' beaks or a widow's hand or maybe an all-consuming fire. Ahaziah had an opportunity to change and saw consequences of coming against God's prophet when fifty-one of his men were burned. But instead of repenting, he sent another fifty men and one captain to kill Elijah. Again, they called him a man of God. Again, Elijah utilized his fire wonder. Again, fire consumed them. Then, Ahaziah sent a third group. Obviously, this king not only thought little of God but also his own soldiers' lives. Satan's not in the business of building but rather destroying. In contrast, God cares about all His creations. Even little prophets and heathens. The fire not only spared the prophet but also spoke to those king's men because when the Lord's word spoken through His prophet comes to pass, they'll acknowledge the prophet (see Ezek. 33:33). This time they obviously did know God was real. When the captain called Elijah a man of God, he meant it and pled for their lives. As the angel gave permission to descend, Elijah came down from the mountain and boldly approached the king to give God's message personally. Ahaziah would die.

Jesus's disciples alluded to this incident. They were rebuffed by Samarian residents disliking Jews. James and John desired retribution and asked Jesus if like Elijah, they should call fire down from heaven to consume them (see Luke 9:54). Jesus rebuked them because "the Son of Man did not come to destroy men's lives but to save them" (Luke 9:56). Was Elijah wrong to call down fire to destroy 102 people? No! The difference between Elijah's and Jesus's reactions was the difference between a life-death situation or simple ridicule. If you've never encountered others' scorn, you will and should take it with grace. God's grace. Another difference between Elijah and the disciples was he was in a defensive position while disciples were on the offense. It's also the difference between Old Testament law and Jesus's grace. Elijah responded this way for survival and compliance with the law's judgment.

Jesus ushered in such love that He died for sinners, even those who mocked Him. Although Elijah spoke God's words confidently, Jesus's authority hinged on His character of love which demonstrated His Father's heart. Though we prophets know God's vengeance will come on those who hurt us, we don't take delight in their destruction. Our gifts operate through Holy Spirit by love—for God, for each other, for the sinner. Jesus demonstrated that commandment, and those in the prophetic are called to a higher level of love (see Luke 12:48). Too often, like Jonah, we want to see the wickeds' destruction rather than God's mercy.

Seeking vindication isn't why Jesus gave His life or why we received our powerful gifts. When Paul describes those gifts, he discusses them in 1 Corinthians 12. Then in 1 Corinthians 14, he describes how they operate. The chapter in between—1 Corinthians 13—is about love. He says though amazing wonders occur through our gifts, they're nothing without love. Love wants our fellow man to find salvation, God's will, and an overcoming lifestyle. Love doesn't call down fire to destroy them, but rather fire to draw them and allow Jesus to take up abode in their hearts. Our gifts operate for ours and others' good, and love is right in the middle.

CONCLUSION

Think of the faith required for Elijah to go to the man who'd committed 153 of his men's lives to killing his two-generational sworn enemy. Though he tried three times, Ahaziah died instead of Elijah. God doesn't send you into danger without a plan. Holy Spirit's fire will consume your worst enemy if you trust, listen, and obey. Hold your ground where God placed you. Then God will direct you when to move from your position to a different plane. You can survive the enemy if you obey God. Evil Ahaziah's sins gave God a chance to shine while He protected Elijah. When God commanded not to touch His anointed ones or harm His prophets (see Psalm 105:15), He was talking about Elijah, Isaiah, Zechariah, Nathan, the unnamed prophets, and us. We speak God's truth to change situations and know He has our backs. He knows when to send fire as judgment or as cloven tongues to sit upon His people (see Acts 2:3). Despite current circumstances, judgment is coming to the wicked. In the meantime, His goal is to bring repentance. Our job, like Elijah's, is to speak His words in love and let His goodness lead others to repentance (see Rom. 2:4).

ELIJAH AND
ELISHA'S JOURNEY

1 Kings 19:19-21, 2 Kings 2:1-18

Principles:
**Making of a Protégé, Learning Single-Minded Focus on
the Goal, Experiencing the Impossible, Stepping into
Our Holy Spirit Destiny, Cherishing Servanthood**

Holy Spirit's Role:
The Empowerer (Zech. 4:6);
The Spirit of Wisdom and Understanding (Isa. 11:2);
The Spirit of Sonship/Adoption (Rom. 8:15)

Sara grew up in a Christian home and was born to pursue God's destiny. She was called, and that calling was confirmed often. Right after high school, she married and longed to work in the Lord's battlefield with her husband. She'd work as anything—missionary, worship leader, preacher. She didn't understand why God didn't plunge her into ministry though. Then as years went by, she wondered what she'd missed being reared by parents sold out to God. She tried many things—alcohol, drugs, promiscuity—and ended up divorced, alcohol dependent, and unstable. In her fifties, she finally recommitted to God, sought Him with all her heart, and turned loose of what she'd held onto. This time, she was serious about the Lord. Then, God used that woman who'd thought she was ready decades before. God can't entrust His kingdom to us until we've matured, so He had to get rid of things inside her that made her unstable. Scars from past choices still exist, but now she's finally making her way toward her destiny.

Receiving our calling is an amazing event, powerful and priceless. Like with Jacob and his ladder dream (see Gen. 28:12-17) or Moses and his burning bush (see Exod. 3:2-6), those calls change us and our lives' direction. However, "many are called, but few are chosen" (Matt. 22:14) because much transpires between promise and fulfillment. As a child, prophets would confirm my own calling, and I was thrilled. For a while. Then, unfortunately, I didn't always live like that call was number one on my list. When I became single-minded about it, things happened. In contrast, determination was Elisha's response to his call from the beginning. Like us, God handpicked Elisha, son of Shaphat, but forging ahead into his preparation season was his choice. Elisha's focus should speak to us. God calls us, but the journey to our destiny takes single-mindedness, time, and mentoring.

THE CALLING

In Chapter 19, Elijah experienced extreme depression. Afterward, God gave direction, and one of those jobs was to anoint Elisha to take over his ministry. That trip from Mt. Horeb to Abel Meholah where Elisha lived was 160 long, hard, hot miles.[1] Elijah went immediately after God gave him the directive to find Elisha (see 1 Kings 19:19) because not only did he need companionship, but God's desire is for us to train prophetic protégés to step into the ministry He's built through us. This assignment was important for Elijah and Elisha. I've often heard that our ceiling should be the next generation's floor. In other words, we should pass our knowledge of Holy Spirit on to the next generation so they don't start from scratch. Elijah and Elisha demonstrated that, but so do others—Moses and Joshua, David and Solomon. The Psalmist said, "Now also when I am old and grayheaded, O God, do not forsake me, Until I declare Your strength to this generation, Your power to everyone who is to come" (Psalm 71:18). What an important role for those of us who think we're too old to work for God. We've gained a wealth of knowledge to be dispersed to others so they can exceed what we learned.

God knows what He's doing when He pairs up mentors and protégés. These two men were similar yet different. Doesn't that describe all of us? We're similar in our giftings, yet we're different in other ways, from personalities to our gifts' modes of operation. God doesn't make cookie-cutter Christians, nor did He want Elisha to be a replica of Elijah. Similar, yet different. When Elijah approached, Elisha was plowing with one of his yokes of oxen. This demonstrated one contrast between the two. Elijah seemed to have had no earthly possessions while Elisha was a man of means since he had twelve yokes of oxen when most had one. Twelve means divine order. Elisha lived an orderly life, plowing in straight rows while Elijah's days were filled with zigs and zags pursuing God's direction. Elisha had family, and Scripture never mentions Elijah's. Elisha had stability, settled in one location, while Elijah seemed content living in the desert or in caves. God doesn't match up mentor and mentee because they're the same but rather because the protégé needs what his mentor speaks into him to qualify him to step into that role.

Oxen represent human effort. Letting go of worldly possessions and our own might is difficult, but that's what God calls His prophets to. As a wealthy man, Elisha could have bemoaned what he would lose like the rich man was saddened when Jesus told him to sell his possessions and follow Him (see Matt. 19:21). We're often glad to get that call to follow unless it means giving up what's important to us because we're keepers of stuff—clothes, shoes, knickknacks, oxen. We want ministry, but many won't turn loose of what God requires to step into that calling. Elisha was different about his priorities though. When he received his call, he left his oxen and *"ran"* after Elijah (see 1 Kings 19:20). That's how Rebekah answered the call to water Abraham's servant's camels (see Gen. 24:20) and Philip when God said to speak to the Ethiopian eunuch (see Acts 8:30). They "ran" to do God's bidding. Will we answer our own call like them and Elisha or like the rich young man?

I love this plowing picture and Elisha's response. When I was young, a good portion of our property was dedicated to a garden. Each year our farmer neighbor drove his tractor across the road and plowed then disked our garden. Then, Dad did his magic. With his old hand plow, he laboriously cut rows into the chocolate-colored, smooth earth which would soon hold a plethora of seeds. I loved to wiggle my bare toes in that soft ground while observing Dad's skill. One year, I watched his progress from the very first row as he trudged from the edge of the garden to the lane on the other side of us. Working meticulously and systematically, he eventually got closer to where I was sitting in front of the old, yellow shed.

I gathered my courage and asked if I could plow one row. He ignored me. Undeterred, I waited for a couple more rows to be cut before I again broached the subject. "Dad, can I do that?" He just looked at me for a moment, shrugged slightly, and held the hand grips my way. Ecstatically, I jumped up and took them.

He put the plow's blade in the place where I should start; and I took off, merrily cutting my own row which would soon be planted with corn or beans or maybe yummy peas. When I proudly got to the end of my swatch, though, and turned around expecting to see Dad's approving nod, I was startled. He was still standing on the other side of the garden, arms folded across his chest, and lips curved slightly in a half-smile. Between us, instead of the parallel, arrow-straight rows that marked Dad's handiwork, my row meandered across the garden without purpose or direction. He didn't say anything but walked toward me, kicking my ambling row back into flat dirt. Then, he took the plow from my hands and went back over that stretch of ground, making another straight, deep row.

I walked back to my spot beside the shed and watched as his next two rows turned out perfectly. As he turned the corner and set up for his next pass, I asked, "Why are all your rows straight and mine was so crooked." He just looked at me.

"You have to get your eye on something over there and never take it off." Elisha knew that lesson, too. Once God gives that call, you focus on the prize off in the distance and never take your eye off. Looking away changes the landscape of your own fertile garden, so you can't realize the potential God has for you. Lack of a focal point always ends up in failure and defeat. God's call isn't just an arbitrary, unimportant decree. He's calling an Elisha, a Samuel, a David, a you, a me. That call is perfect and important, but it comes with choices. Do you go single-mindedly toward that prize or let life's distractions keep you from your destiny?

THE MANTLE

As a symbol of Elisha's calling, Elijah threw his mantle over him (see 1 Kings 19:19). Mantles are used in Scripture as a covering, like when the Witch of Endor saw Samuel, clothed with a mantle (see 1 Sam. 28:14). Tearing another's garment represents removal from power as when Saul grabbed and tore Samuel's mantle, symbolizing God's tearing the kingdom from him (see 1 Sam. 15:27). Ripping one's own garment represents grief and humility as Ezra tore his garment then plucked hair from his head and beard (see Ezra 9:3). It also represents brokenness as when Job tore his robe (mantle), shaved his head, fell to the ground, and worshiped (see Job 1:20). Elijah's mantle was an *addereth*, meaning "something ample, wide or large, excellent, glorious, mighty, noble, worthy."[2] Doesn't that describe Elijah's ministry? His mantle was ample enough to be a covering when he stood in great despair in the cave's entrance (see 1 Kings 19:13) but represented a calling as he threw the mantle on Elisha. It became the symbol of "electing Elisha to receive the authority and power of his office,"[3] both in the initial calling and at the Jordan (see 2 Kings 2:13-14). Like Moses's rod symbolized his authority, this also signified Elijah's and Elisha's authority through Holy Spirit.

God has a plan to throw that mantle on us, but before He takes us into our destiny, an equipping must occur. I love the analogy of our developing into our calling and how a pearl evolves. Its growth begins with an irritant, a grain of sand or debris, inside the oyster. The oyster secretes a substance—nacre—which created the shell of that oyster. Then, to protect the incipient pearl, nacre also lines its shell. That lining, the protector, is called the mantle. During that time of the pearl's growth, the mantle protects and nurtures it, just like our mantle protects and nurtures us. As our calling comes, God's mantle is spread upon us to protect the potential of His pearl-in-progress. If we leave where He's positioned us to grow into our destiny, we step away from the mantle's protection. Aaron was protected by God until he was stripped of his priest's garments (covering), which were passed along to his son. When that mantle of anointing left, he died (see Num. 20:28). The anointing of our mantle protects and builds. Each layer upon layer is molding us into that jewel of extreme value in the Lord's treasure box. The mantle thrown on Elisha was just the beginning of his pearl journey.

After the call, a process ensues before the destiny's fulfillment. During that time, you grow to understand your calling and its authority. In the meantime, like Elisha with his oxen, you occupy. I love Solomon's words: "Whatever your hand finds to do, do it with your might" (Ecc. 9:10). As a child, I saw men receive a call to preach, quit their jobs, leave to evangelize, and create hardship for their families. We receive our call and our lives are changed, but we don't usually go into our destinies immediately. Biblical men prepared for their ministries for years—David, Joseph,

Moses, Abraham, Jesus. In the meantime, how they occupied was crucial to what they became.

TO FOLLOW

As Elijah threw the mantle on Elisha (see 1 Kings 19:19), he didn't need words to understand his calling. When your anointing comes, it doesn't need to be spelled out; you'll know as you go. God had probably already told Elisha. Usually, He confirms it after He's put it into your own spirit. Then He unfolds bits and pieces to direct you through your journey. To follow God's call though, you must be willing to leave your current situation. Elisha had one request: to go back to kiss his parents (see 1 Kings 19:20). How ironic that God had just told Elijah about seven thousand who hadn't kissed Baal. Elisha was part of those faithful ones, but whose mouth kissed his parents. Many who've been called don't follow other gods but still kiss what they cherish. They're tied to family, jobs, and possessions, so they don't want to move when God says to because they yearn for what they'll lose. They desire to go back to kiss them one more time and long for what's familiar. When they can't let go, those things or people become their Baals, their idols, which they worship more than God. Not Elisha. From the beginning, he was willing to give up whatever God required to follow his calling into his destiny. Even what he kissed. That's what God desires—total abandonment in Him.

Elisha wanted to kiss his parents, and Elijah responded— "Go back again, for what have I done to you" (1 Kings 19:20), showing his approval of Elisha's request to cut family ties before he left. This seems like a contradiction since when one of Jesus's disciples wanted to bury his father before he followed Jesus, He said to "Follow Me, and let the dead bury their own dead" (Matt. 8:22). Elijah and Jesus probably responded differently to the same question because of motivations. Elisha's going back to kiss his father signaled an end to that earthly father relationship. Elijah became his spiritual father, mentoring him in Holy Spirit, like his earthly father had mentored him in how to be a godly, industrious man.

Just like He knows us, Jesus knew His disciples and so perhaps knew the one who asked wasn't as determined as Elisha. If His disciple had gone back to his family, he may never have returned or stepped into his God-ordained destiny with the Master. We don't know who this disciple was, but imagine if Peter or John had missed his amazing call because emotions and love for family hindered his destiny. That easily happens to us humans. Elisha's purpose for returning wasn't to cry over his loss. He wanted to go back to throw a party—slay his oxen and burn his plows (see 1 Kings 19:21). Then he fed the people (see 1 Kings 19:21). What a lesson for him to learn immediately that a prophet's job is to feed others with fresh meat from God. However, this celebration wasn't to bemoan lost family and friends or to boast that he would be the next Elijah. He went back to eliminate his safety net, just in case. We humans crave security. Once we step into the path toward our destiny, the enemy fights to keep us from fulfilling it. Yet, Jesus said, "No one, having put his hand to the plow, and looking back, is fit for the kingdom of God" (Luke 9:62). Elisha and my dad would understand that plowing analogy and what happens when we dwell on what's behind.

Once, Wade and I were in leadership in a church. I felt led to call a meeting with other leaders to resolve misunderstandings. That didn't happen. Instead, the meeting ended terribly after I was called a liar and my motives questioned. I left, sobbing so hard I could barely catch my breath.

"Why, Lord?" I asked. "You knew how bad this meeting would be. Why'd You tell me to go?" I told Him how unfair their accusations were and repeated a litany of unjust comments.

As I paused, Holy Spirit whispered gently into my heart with that quiet voice He'd used with Elijah on the mountain. "Connie, dust off your feet. I have bigger plans for you. I wanted you to slay your oxen and burn your plows so you wouldn't have this to come back to when times got rough." My broken heart still ached from hurtful, untrue words my supposed Christian friends had said to and about me, but my tears were sweeter knowing God would work this devastating circumstance to my good. Since then, He's been true to His word as He led Wade and me into paths we never dreamt of in those days. And I couldn't go back during down times. God's allowing me to go through such a painful experience was His absolute love for me. He knew me and that I would opt for security. When circumstances didn't seem like my promised destiny was coming, I may have gone back to that other situation instead of forging ahead. As it happened, I had neither oxen nor plows to return to.

When we're called into ministry, we should get rid of what could draw us back, for a rearview mirror mentality brings a distorted view of what was rather than God's view of what is to be. Elisha probably knew human nature wants to hold onto the familiar. As he followed Elijah during the ensuing years, he most likely had days when times became hard in Elijah's then in his own ministry, but he didn't have his oxen safety net either. Sacrificing his oxen showed how all of us should proceed toward ministry. Before we step into our calling, we should surrender everything. We learned to be living sacrifices to God when we first came into the kingdom. Now, as we head toward our destiny, more sacrifice is required. We focus on the calling and "press toward the goal for the prize of the upward call of God in Christ Jesus" (Phil 3:14). Then, no matter what comes along, we don't move our eye from God's plan for us. Following the call must be paired with leaving behind what was familiar and comfortable—our homes, our fishing nets, our oxen. Can we answer that call like Elisha did?

SERVANTHOOD

In his ministry Elijah lived simply, as prophets were wont to do. For menial chores, they usually had a servant who functioned as the prophet's protégé, like Elisha. When Elisha eliminated his safety net, he "followed Elijah, and became his servant" (1 Kings 19:21). What a lesson! God told Elijah to "anoint [Elisha] as prophet in [Elijah's] place" (1 Kings 19:16), but the anointing's fulfillment couldn't come without preparation. Before we can become Elisha the prophet, we must complete our season as Elisha, the servant. We can't reach our ministry's fullness unless we learn servanthood's lessons. Elisha's and Elijah's ministries show two kinds of servants: those who are helpers, and those who can learn and eventually step into ministry. The first servant is a *naar*, "a boy from the age of infancy to adolescence."[4] This servant doesn't mature into spiritual adulthood, so he can't be a prophet's protégé. Elijah's servant who saw the cloud was a *naar* (see 1 Kings 18:43). After he left Elijah, we don't hear from him again because this servant didn't grow into a mature prophet.

Other servants, though, are protégés who eventually become the prophet. A *sharath* means "to attend as a menial or worshipper, minister, wait on."[5] This servant is a protégé who understands ministry starts with menial serving. A *sharath* performs tasks "to which the closest servants of God or the king are assigned… [and] conveys yieldedness, servanthood, and obedience."[6] This word was used for Elisha and also Joshua when he was called Moses's assistant (see Num. 11:28). Elisha became that close assistant to Elijah and ultimately stepped into the prophet's role. As we *sharaths* move toward our callings, important changes take place as we learn how our prophetic gifts work and understand faith's operation. When Elisha faced the Syrians with confidence unlike his frightened servant (see 2 Kings 6:15), Elisha asked the Lord to reveal to his servant what he couldn't see with his own eyes. When God opened his eyes, he saw legions of angels encamped around them. Interestingly, before this event, his servant was referred as a *sharath*. Then, when he didn't look with faith's eyes, he became a boy, *naar* (see 2 Kings 6:15). We could miss our destiny because of not becoming the man or woman of faith we're called to be.

Whatever our servant's job is, we should execute it intensely. We don't know what duties Elisha performed and don't see his progression daily as he learned by serving Elijah. As a *sharath*, he didn't promote himself but followed in the background. Perhaps he was the ministry secretary or massaged Elijah's aching feet, stinky from dirty roads. He might have swept up or dealt with students from the schools of the prophets. His later description of having "poured water on the hands of Elijah" (2 Kings 3:11) showed his job wasn't glamorous and didn't earn accolades, but that servanthood season produced much wealth. As we submit to leaders, or even our bosses or husbands, we learn about our own relationship with God. We learn to prefer others and perfect our love for them and the Father. We become like Jesus. Servanthood is our Father's gift to us.

That became clear once when I visited my daughter in Oklahoma City. When travelling to various cities around the country, I scheduled book events. Those few days in Oklahoma were blessed in those events and in my visit with Jill. Sunday night, I spoke at a church where multiple miracles occurred. Afterwards, the church bought a whole box of my books to teach in their ladies' group. The next morning, I got up, still excited from the night before. I leisurely got ready to start back to Indiana. As I sat in Jill's kitchen, sipping my coffee and eating the Word in my devotions, the Lord spoke to me—"You're halfway to Bisbee." I knew what He meant.

My youngest sister Anita lived in Bisbee, Arizona, and had inundated the technological airwaves that weekend with prayer requests for her husband, hospitalized with a supposed blood clot. That morning, God was saying she needed help. After a call to her and to Wade, I headed west for the extra one thousand miles. I spent nearly two weeks helping after her husband's release. One morning, as I walked down the hall after taking Tony his breakfast, God spoke to me, "In Oklahoma, you were a servant." I understood that concept. Our gifts of the Spirit, even healings, are to be used to serve others. As Jesus saw the multitude, "He was moved with compassion for them, and healed their sick" (see Matt. 14:14). That word "healed" is *therapeuo*, "to wait upon menially."[7] Jesus's gift of healing was as a menial servant. In Oklahoma as Holy Spirit gave revelation and healed many, I was a servant, like Jesus.

Then, the Lord continued, "That servanthood was no more important than this servanthood." The Arizona jaunt wasn't just to help my brother-in-law and sister, desperate like that Zarephath widow, but also to do something in me during my own Elijah journey. The Lord blessed me even after Wade flew out to drive back with me, and the Lord again sent us out of the way through Mississippi to hold a service at the home of a couple, desperate for deliverance. They ended that weekend with a renewed sense of hope that their family would be protected during their own drought. When the Lord orders our steps (see Psalm 37:23), we're both blessed and a blessing. That long trip added 5,300 miles to my car and insights, direction, and opportunities to see God's hand on mine and Wade's Elijah journey. But that gift of servanthood was greater than I realized at the time. Three months later, my brother-in-law went home to be with God. Through servanthood, God had given me a two-week gift of being with him. What a lovely privilege God bestows when we learn to serve.

Whatever his duties, I'm sure Elisha did them gladly though at times he wondered if God and Elijah would ever consider him ready. Everyone thinks that at times. God has a plan though, and knows when we're ready to step into our calling. We may become discouraged as we fill our role, but whatever servant's work we do ushers us toward our destiny. Even Jesus "did not come to be served, but to serve, and to give His life as a ransom for many" (Mark 10:45). Why would we think we should travel any other route but the servant road? Plus, if we're mentored by another who's prophetic, our prophetic tools are also sharpened (see Prov. 27:17). In other words, we mirror those we hang out with. Servanthood was a gift to Elisha and is to us too.

THE ASCENSION

GILGAL

From calling to ascension, we don't see Elisha again until 2 Kings 2, so we don't see the developing relationship between prophet and servant until God was about to take Elijah (see 2 Kings 2:1). The two men interacted on ascension day when they journeyed to several towns. It's assumed they started their trip in Samaria and ended at the Jordan, a thirty-eight mile trek.[8] Some believe Elijah was going there because Mt. Nebo was located on the other side of the Jordan. That mountain was Moses's burial plot (see Deut. 34:5), and some propose Elijah wanted to stay with Moses until they saw Jesus at the Transfiguration.[9] Though many interpretations exist for the Jude 9 scripture when Satan argued with Michael the archangel for Moses's body, maybe Satan knew God's plan was for Moses to meet up with Elijah and Jesus at the Transfiguration before the crucifixion and end-time plans were fulfilled.

The places they visited that day represent Elisha's growth and our own Holy Spirit maturation toward our prophetic destiny: Gilgal is salvation, Bethel is building relationship with God, Jericho is being Spirit-filled and learning about our gifts, and Jordan is stepping into Holy Spirit abandonment and our destinies. The men knew of the upcoming wonder though we don't know how this event was predicted, but Elijah's understanding of his gift of translation surely made this foretelling easy. In 2 Kings 2:1, Elijah and Elisha came from Gilgal, meaning "whirlwind; also dust (as whirled)—heaven, rolling thing, wheel."[10] What an appropriate name for what was to come! Gilgal's being the first stop tells me this also represents our first stop in the Promised Land experience: salvation, crucial to receiving Holy Spirit. Some are satisfied staying in their salvation encounter until they go to Heaven, but not Elisha. In Gilgal, Elijah told Elisha to stay, but he didn't. He's like those who go higher and move through their own Nehemiah's gates' journey toward their destinies.

Elijah's motives for why he told Elisha to stay aren't clear. Perhaps he was being humble, not boasting of the upcoming great event. Perhaps, he didn't want anyone to witness what was to happen. Maybe he realized the two men's closeness would cause Elisha to grieve his loss. Maybe this was one last test to prove Elisha's faithfulness. Perhaps he wanted to communicate with God regarding this event, which would be reflected upon for generations to come. None of those possibilities, though, convinced Elisha he should part from his mentor. Since the start, he'd focused on the prize, so why would he lose sight when this last stretch of road would bring him from servant to prophet. No matter what comes along to change your path, focus can't waver. Too many forget their diligence at the eleventh hour. The race is determined by how we finish.

After Elijah gave permission for Elisha to stay at Gilgal, Elisha again showed his unwavering character: "As the Lord lives, and as your soul lives, I will not leave you" (2 Kings 2:2). Elisha's double oath by the Lord and by Elijah that he would stay with his mentor was part of the tenacity and single-mindedness he demonstrated at his calling and which would bring him a double portion. As his resolve was tested three times, each time he refused to leave and repeated these words at Bethel and Jericho. The statement returned to him later. When Elisha told the Shunammite woman to go ahead of him to where her dead son lay, "the mother of the child said, 'As the Lord lives, and as your soul lives, I will not leave you'" (2 Kings 4:30). In a similar manner to Elijah's resurrection of the widow's son, Elisha brought forth the Shunammite woman's son (see 2 Kings 4:34). Words possess staying power, and we should too. Again, it's sowing and reaping. If we want to come into God's fullness and see fulfilled promises, we must stay connected to the source.

BETHEL

Elijah and Elisha next traveled to Bethel, "house of God."[11] In our destiny journey, this place of God's presence is when we enter into deeper relationship with Him. God dwells where people praise Him (see Psalm 22:3), so His house is where we worship. Our prophetic walk must include intimacy with God. Elijah dwelt in His presence and passed that lifestyle to Elisha as they travelled together. Later, when Israel prepared for battle, Elisha called for a musician. When he played, God gave Elisha the battle plan (see 2 Kings 3:15). Samuel demonstrated this concept too. After he anointed Saul, he sent him to find a group of his prophetic students who would be worshiping and prophesying. He told Saul that after worship, he would prophesy and would turn into a different man (see 1 Sam. 10:5-6). Worship changes us as it brings intimacy with the Lord. How can we possibly hear words of life from the Father's lips without getting into His presence? When we stay there, the miraculous happens.

At Bethel, sons of the prophets told Elisha that God would take Elijah "from over [him] today" (see 2 Kings 2:3). That phrase in King James says "from thy head." Elijah was the schools' headmaster, and in those times, the teacher was literally a head above his students as he sat in a chair over them with his feet at the level of their heads.[12] I wonder if Elisha nervously heard these words. He was accustomed to Elijah's being the "head" during their season together. Stepping into his own ministry and being the head himself of sons of the prophets must have made him question his readiness. When I graduated from college and took my first job as a high school teacher, I was filled with insecurities. Barely older than they were, I wondered if they'd respect me, if I'd learned the subject matter well enough, or if they would ask questions outside my expertise. I stepped from my role of student to teacher like Elisha needed to do. These prophets-in-training who had also received the revelation of the ascension might have been men who would become amazing prophets like Ezekiel or

Isaiah; and Elisha, the former farmer, would speak into their lives now as their teacher. Wow!

Elisha was probably inundated with an abundance of thoughts as sons of the prophets at Bethel announced Elijah's leaving, but his response was again that they should be silent (see 2 Kings 2:3)! Many reasons may have prompted him to request silence. Maybe he wanted them to respect this sacred graduation rite he and Elijah would experience. Perhaps Elisha needed focus so he wouldn't miss his own destiny. Perhaps he anticipated his grief when his mentor left. Maybe he didn't want negative words spoken which could change his and Elijah's destinies. Often, God requires silence so our words don't derail His plans as with the Jericho marchers. Sometimes the best advice we can receive or give our own prophets-in-training is to keep words unspoken.

At Bethel, Elijah again told Elisha to stay. Again, he refused. This refusal to leave reminds me of Ruth. No matter how much Naomi gave her permission, she refused (see Ruth 1:16). What if Ruth had turned back during the journey? She would have missed her relationship with Naomi and marriage to Boaz. But most importantly, God had slated her to be the great-grandmother of King David and ancestor of Jesus. If she'd given up, she would have missed the destiny God put her on earth to accomplish, and so would Elisha. Do we settle for less than our God-ordained destiny?

JERICHO

Again, Elijah told Elisha to wait in Bethel, and Elisha again refused. Their next stop was Jericho, which represents stepping into a deeper walk in Holy Spirit as we learn to operate in His gifts. When a person is born again, he/she receives a three-part package—Father, Son, and Holy Spirit. However, most Christians neglect a further aspect of salvation—to become filled with Holy Spirit to activate His gifts (see Acts 9:17) with evidence of speaking in tongues. Israel's first Promised Land victory was

Jericho, called the city of palms (see Deut. 34:3). The word itself means "its month, fragrant."[13] Holy Spirit gives victory and becomes our oasis as He spreads His fragrant, lovely presence by His gifts operating through us (see 2 Cor. 2:14). Like Jericho's walls fell, Holy Spirit breaks down dividing walls. Our common language (tongues) creates oneness in men to accomplish all things (see Zeph. 3:9).

As the two men arrived at Jericho, again sons of the prophets said God would take Elijah that day (see 2 Kings 2:5). Again, Elisha confirmed and told them to be silent. Every town Elijah and Elisha visited was a location of a School of the Prophets. A later reference to Jordan is also associated with prophets in training when students and Elisha were building a replacement dorm (see 2 Kings 6:1-7). Sons of the prophets being part of this ascension thrills me. Though why Elijah wanted to see them isn't specified, these nameless students were important enough to be included in this sacred day. He had precious little time left on earth, but he spent those hours with his protégé and pupils in the prophetic. God's little ones matter.

THE JORDAN

Elijah again told Elisha to stay in Jericho. Again, he refused (see 2 Kings 2:6). They then went to the Jordan, meaning "to descend, cause to bring down, carry down, cast down, subdue, take down."[14] This represents total abandonment in our Holy Spirit glory walk where we enter the dimension of the miraculous through Holy Spirit. Jordan was crossing over into a new land when Joshua entered the Promised Land, and now the two men were going into a different kind of Promised Land of Holy Spirit. Joshua's journey took much the same route as Elijah and Elisha. God had told them forty years before that they would go over the Jordan to possess the land He had given them (see Deut. 11:31). They camped at Gilgal (see Josh. 5:10) where they were circumcised, the manna stopped, and they sent spies to Jericho. They first attacked the land's inhabitants at Ai, an insignificant battle which they lost because of Achan's sin (see Josh. 7:11). They then set up an ambush between Ai and Bethel, and Ai was destroyed (see Josh 8:28). For Joshua, Jordan's rolling back symbolized the reproach of Egypt rolling back to Adam (where the curse started) and off Israel (see Josh 3:16, 5:9). The feet of the priests bearing the ark caused Jordan's waters to roll back, creating that miracle (see Josh 3:15-16). When Moses stretched out his rod, the Red Sea's waters had also rolled back (see Exod. 14:21-22). These men used their symbols of authority, the ark and rod, to accomplish God's purpose as they crossed on dry land.

Elijah and Elisha understood the importance of an authority symbol. When Elisha received his calling, the mantle had been thrown across his shoulders. However, at some point, that symbol of our calling must expand from a covering to a tool which produces miracles. The mantle representing Elisha's anointing and probably Elijah's covering on many a cold, desert night, now meant authority. As fifty (Holy Spirit) sons of the prophets stood and watched by the Jordan (see 2 Kings 2:7), Elijah "took his mantle, rolled it up, and struck the water; and it was divided this way and that, so that the two of them crossed over on dry ground" (2 Kings 2:8). This time, Elijah rolled up that cloak. His attitude was different as he clutched the mantle, probably tattered from years of wear on those Middle Eastern roads. He no longer held it between his fingers as he probably did to anoint Elisha but now grasped it with his hand. He stepped forth in boldness and authority to create that same water-parting miracle Joshua and Moses had performed.

I once attended an educational seminar on authority and attitude. The speaker distributed paper straws and whole unbaked potatoes, then asked us to put the straw through the potato. We tried as hard as we could, yet each potato remained impenetrable. Then, she told us we can accomplish more if we change our approach. As we followed her directions to grasp it in our hand as a weapon and thrust, each of us had immediate success. We carry around our Holy Spirit weapons which do us no good until we grasp them with authority and a winning attitude. Our authority supersedes Satan's on all fronts when Holy Spirit's in the picture. A mantle in the hand of a man or woman of God who knows his/her Holy Spirit authority changes from a tool to a wondrous weapon. Elijah knew how to use his calling tool with confidence.

Our Holy Spirit walk increases exponentially when we cross our own Jordan into the Promised Land. God can't entrust His treasures to us until we prove we can handle them. Jesus said we must learn to be faithful in the little things before we can be entrusted with greater ones (see Luke 16:10). In other words, prophets go through their own prophets-in-training season. Through servanthood, God tests them with little lessons to see faithfulness before He promotes to the greater place of destiny. Have we gone through Nehemiah's Gates of preparation to come into His fullness? Have we stuck with it when we could have turned aside? Have we learned the lessons which took us into the valley and wilderness in the first place? God has a plan, and we can enter our Promised Land if we stay on course.

THE DOUBLE PORTION

When the two men crossed over, Elijah asked, "What may I do for you, before I am taken away from you?" (2 Kings 2:9). I love two things about that exchange. First, although Elijah could have asked that any time during that day, he waited until Elisha had gone the distance. Secondly, Elijah's asking him that question at all thrills me. Our desires, talents, and opinions matter to God. God filled the artisan Bezalel "with the Spirit of God, in wisdom, in understanding, in knowledge, and in all manner of workmanship, to design artistic works" (Exod. 31:3-4). Through Holy Spirit, Bezalel had strengths, gifts, and talents which were important to God, and Holy Spirit used them. David also showed God is interested in what we are. After the Temple's completion,

Solomon told those assembled that David's heart was to build the Temple (see 1 Kings 8:17) to honor God. Because David's heart longed for this, so did God's heart. Our gifts, talents, and desires are Holy Spirit birthed and God loves them.

When Elijah asked what was on Elisha's heart, Elisha responded that he wanted a double portion of Elijah's spirit (see 2 Kings 2:10). Elisha could have asked for anything, but from the beginning, he'd wanted nothing else. Many receive a double portion because they've sought God with abandon. For Elisha, earthly riches paled next to what he could receive in the Spirit. However, Elisha's request wasn't just for more miracles and power. Many prophets and sons of the prophets were there on whom Elijah could have bestowed a blessing, yet Elisha wanted that anointing to fall on him to allow him to step into Elijah's ministry as his firstborn son in the Spirit. He wanted the first son's inheritance, a double portion. Jacob too wanted the first son's double portion so badly that he connived to get it. Are you ravenous for the Father's blessing?

Jesus dealt with double portions in the parable of the talents. He said the kingdom of heaven (usually denotes Holy Spirit) is like a man who gave his three servants talents: one had one, another had two, and the third had five talents (see Matt. 25:14-15). The parable's message is about what each did with his talents. The industrious servants with two and five received a double portion of those talents, but the servant with one talent buried his and therefore lost it. Elisha too had the power to bury or double his anointing. When that mantle of our calling falls on us, our anointing is all potential. We should assess our gifts, talents, and callings. Are we diligently using them to bring wealth into our Master's house, or do we bury and neglect gifts entrusted to us? Many never realize their potential because of buried talents. Jesus said "to everyone who has, more will be given, and he will have abundance; but from him who does not have, even what he has will be taken away" (Matt. 25:29). Elisha wanted abundance.

Too often we're afraid to ask for big requests, but we should take the limits off God. Elijah said a double portion was hard for him to give (see 2 Kings 2:10) but didn't say it was impossible. Just like Elijah stretched himself to resurrect the dead boy, as his ministry on earth was ending, he was asked to give twice as much as he had himself. Doesn't that speak to you? I've often heard the Lord's work has no retirement, so prophets never stop growing. Elijah was still growing and prophesying. He told Elisha that if he saw him leave, his request would be fulfilled. What we see with our eyes gets into our spirits; then we believe and receive. We must see God's glory ourselves to understand His principles because experience is better than head knowledge alone.

THE WHIRLWIND

Elisha stayed, and "they continued on and talked" (2 Kings 2:11). I wonder what that conversation entailed. Perhaps, they spent their last precious moments as mentor and protégé. Maybe Elijah told his charge just how a double portion would work. Elisha may have asked more questions about the prophetic, and Elijah may have had encouraging words about the new role his protégé would soon assume. They may have spent this time as father and son, joking with one another, remembering past experiences. Their journey had been long and sometimes arduous, but Elisha had learned much during his season of training. They were probably talking when that chariot and horses of fire appeared, and Elisha's mentor was taken into the heavens by a whirlwind (see 2 Kings 2:11). This was the ultimate example of translations-being taken from earth in a whirlwind. What if Elijah hadn't experienced the drought which refined the gifts God had given him, including the knowledge of translations? Could he have missed becoming the second man never to taste death, which spoke to believers then and more than three thousand years later? Could he have failed to be part of the most amazing event in history, the crucifixion and resurrection as he, Moses, and Jesus talked at the Transfiguration? Did his drought season allow him to understand a crucial tool that would make him play a vital role even in end-times?

A whirlwind is *ca'ar*, "a hurricane:—storm(y), tempest, whirlwind."[15] One of nature's most powerful forces, it refers to high, tornado-like winds on the ocean or in a thunderstorm.[16] It's compared to chariots because wheels stir up dust like a windstorm (see Isa. 66:15). A whirlwind represents Holy Spirit's extreme power. Isaiah said the whirlwind would take princes away like stubble (see Isa. 40:24) and scatter beaten-down mountains (see Isa. 41:16). Ezekiel saw a great whirlwind coming from the north with raging fire (Holy Spirit symbol) (see Ezek. 1:4). Jeremiah said a great disastrous whirlwind would be raised from earth's farthest parts (see Jer. 25:32), and that the Lord's whirlwind erupts with force to fall violently on the wicked (see Jer. 30:23). There's that word again: force. Holy Spirit's *dunamis* power is a whirlwind beyond our minds' comprehension but is at our disposal. Holy Spirit partnered with Elijah to bring amazing, forceful, violent, whirlwind results. Like the whirlwind separated Elijah and Elisha, Holy Spirit's whirlwind separates us from others. Our gifts and signs and wonders we experience will take us higher and make us unlike the rest of the world, even other Christians.

A SUCCESSOR

Yet, no matter how much he'd witnessed and participated in Elijah's ministry, Elisha had to come into his own faith walk. And he did—a double portion's worth. Prophets are to prepare a new generation to carry on God's work and go on to greater ministry opportunities, their own double portions. If we stay focused like Elisha, double blessings will come. As Elijah rode off in the chariot, Elisha probably stood for a moment in awe of what he was witnessing. Then he grieved, tore his clothes because of his loss of Elijah, and called out "My father" twice (2 Kings 2:12). These words are important. They indicate a closeness that had evolved between the two men. As Christians progress into their destinies, they do their season as a servant, then move from servanthood to sonship. Then we're not a slave but become a son and heir of God (see Gal. 4:7). Elisha had wanted the first son's rights and blessings, and calling Elijah "father" meant he'd stepped into that role, which would take him rightfully into his authority. We should realize we're sons with full rights of the firstborn for all our Father has, including the double portion.

Our job as prophets is open-ended and not complete until we pass along our knowledge to the next generation who must step into the faith walk we vacate. Lester Sumrall said "success is not a success until it produces a successor."[17] Like students sat at the level of the headmaster's feet, we must graduate from protégé to mentor to stand above our own students and pass that on to another generation. A principle God established for man was that everything would produce after its own kind (see Gen. 1:11). If we're a peach tree, that's what we produce. If we're a camel, we produce camels. If we're a prophet, we produce prophets. Whatever gifts we operate in, we should teach others to produce more peach trees, camels, or prophets. As we're mentored then mentor others toward their destinies, we teach what they too must know for their calling. First, though, we must get beyond what we've lost, arise, and go on. Elisha had done that when he gave away the life he knew. Now, he also needed to get beyond the grief of losing his best friend, confidant, example, mentor, and father.

He stepped into that destiny he'd begun back at Abel Meholah. He immediately put his faith into practice, and "he took the mantle of Elijah that had fallen from him" (2 Kings 2:14). He probably held it for a moment and fondly remembered its history. He recalled how he'd felt that day Elijah had come calling, calling him into his ministry. He reflected on each step of his servanthood season when he'd washed Elijah's mantle in the river, or watched when Elijah had used that symbol of authority to perform miracles. Now, as smoke from that chariot and those horses of fire still stung his nostrils, Elisha knew that cloak of calling had become his mantle of authority. He stood by the Jordan, struck the water, and said, "Where is the Lord God of Elijah?" (2 Kings 2:14). His words phrased as a question tell me he felt unsure at first about this inherited gift. A time comes, though, when He isn't only the God of our dad or mom or mentor, but becomes a reality to us. After that first question, he no longer asked, "Where's the Lord?" but made a proclamation of "Thus says the Lord" (2 Kings 2:21). *His* Lord. When we pick up that authority mantle, we change from our servant season to our prophet destiny. Our training and servanthood produces prophetic living word with multiplied power. Elisha's words and actions created the same result Elijah's had: rolling the Jordan back (see 2 Kings 2:14).

We prophets are God's mouthpiece to pass the mantle to the next generation and bring them along in the gifts. This Holy Spirit anointing can be transferred to our own successors. When God instructed Moses to delegate to the seventy elders, He said He would put Moses's spirit upon those elders (see Num. 11:17). After the ascension, sons of the prophets witnessed Elisha stepping into his own anointing and acknowledged "The spirit of Elijah rests on Elisha" (2 Kings 2:15). Zacharias, John the Baptist's father, was told his unborn son would operate in Elijah's spirit and power (see Luke 1:17). This phrase "spirit of Elijah," probably referred to his powerful, miracle-producing anointing. Others recognize when we operate in the anointing as those prophets recognized Elijah's influence on Elisha. Holy Spirit became synonymous with Elijah's, Elisha's, and John's spirits. Is He your essence too?

Elisha still had much work to do to come into God's fullness. He crossed back into Samaria to start his ministry. He and the sons of the prophets had seen the ascension, but some couldn't comprehend the magnitude of what they'd witnessed. Those were probably part of the fifty who stayed off in the distance and just watched (see 2 Kings 2:7) but weren't part of it. Too many miss blessings because they don't get into the thick of things. Those sons of the prophets spent three days searching for Elijah in case the Spirit of the Lord had translated, then deposited him elsewhere like He'd done often (see 2 Kings 2:16). Elisha remained at Jericho (oasis) (see 2 Kings 2:18) in the Father's peace. Instead of resting in Holy Spirit and knowing He's doing something new and mighty, many still look to resurrect past movements rather than seeing the miraculous things He's doing now. Those sons of the prophets sound like many today who want to step into what God has but can see only what He's done in the past instead of how He's working differently in the here and now. We should believe His glorious ways no matter how they stretch us.

CONCLUSION

As Elijah left in the whirlwind, Elisha saw, took up the mantle, and began his double-miracle ministry. Elijah had performed eight recorded miracles during his life. Elisha had performed fifteen at the time of his death.[18] Then, number sixteen happened when a man killed during a battle with the Moabites was thrown into the tomb on Elisha's bones and sprang back to life (see 2 Kings 13:21). Elisha's double portion. This Holy Spirit anointing is so strong that objects like battered mantles and old dried bones can still be powerful and miracle-laden. God guards the prophet's words. Like Elijah didn't taste death, neither does the prophetic because those words don't die, fall barren, or return void because Holy Spirit's words embody life (see John 6:63). When we speak God's words with integrity and diligence, though we may not live to see them come to pass, they're established.

ELIJAH AND THE TRANSFIGURATION

Matthew 17:1-9, Mark 9:1-10, Luke 9:28-36

Principles:
Operating in the Glory, Declaring
Jesus's Majesty, Preparing for the End-Times

Holy Spirit's Role:
Spirit of Glory (1 Pet. 4:14); As a Leader (Rom. 8:14)

Science isn't my forte, so I can't comprehend how nature operates. How can an enormously heavy planet filled with billions of tons of people stay suspended in space? How can the human body repair itself? How can gravity keep objects that weigh thousands of pounds from careening into space? All of these seem to be impossibilities, but they happen. So many amazing unexplainable phenomena exist in the world that the most skeptical must admit Someone smarter than we created inexplicable wonders. In the Spirit realm, the same unexplainable occurrences exist. How can Holy Spirit reveal to His prophets? How can God change an unchangeable man? How do signs and wonders occur that make us catch our breaths? All of these seem to be impossibilities too, but they happen. Elijah's story is filled with unbelievable events that make man wonder, but his journey doesn't end with the books of the Kings. References exist elsewhere, even in the New Testament. Holy Spirit's role for him continued as he participated in the Transfiguration, which preceded the most important event in history—the crucifixion and resurrection of Jesus. Elijah had a front row seat.

THE WRITERS

Jesus had revealed Himself as Lord to His disciples and discussed His death. After this, He told them some wouldn't "taste death till they see the Son of Man coming in His kingdom" (Matt. 16:28), an allusion to the Transfiguration which occurred a few days later. Interestingly, the account of this event shows up in only three gospels—Matthew, Mark, and Luke—but John, who was a firsthand observer, didn't record it. No other author of the gospels witnessed it because Jesus had taken only His Inner Circle. Matthew was a disciple who didn't see it, and we don't know who related his story. Mark probably heard his account from Peter because his gospel came in large part from Peter's eyewitness account of his time with Jesus. As a matter of fact, Mark's called "the interpreter of Peter."[1] We don't know from whom Luke heard his version of that day's events, but much of his gospel was written from Mary's memories and from Paul. Doesn't a mother's sweet recollection speak to you? She probably heard about this event from her Son. Paul, however, wasn't one of Jesus's twelve disciples. He was an adversary until his conversion on the road to Damascus. If he's the one who told Luke, could his version have come straight from Holy Spirit?

The three accounts correspond but also differ because each adds his twist. I love that about the Word, especially the Gospels. The Bible evolved as God moved upon men, but those writers in large part witnessed what happened. They selected details that mattered to them, and each varied detail speaks to me too. What a wondrous way for God to say, once again, our quirks, individual viewpoints, and personal relationships are important to Him. Like eyewitness accounts vary even today, whenever different writers give first-hand accounts, details vary. So, since these accounts of the Transfiguration were from secondary sources, recollections and choices of details vary even more. For example, Matthew and Mark list the Transfiguration as occurring six days after Jesus's proclamation while Luke says it occurred "about eight days after" (Luke 9:28). This inconsistency could also be explained because others may not have included the days of the actual prophecy and Transfiguration or that Luke estimated by using the word "about." Actually, the phrase "eight days" is a Greek idiom that means around a week. That's just one variation in the Gospels about this event.

THE INNER CIRCLE

Matthew and Mark include the detail that this time, the Inner Circle—Peter, James, and John—went "by themselves" (Matt. 17:1) with Jesus. He would often take this intimate group with Him. When he raised Jairus's daughter from the dead, Peter, James, and John were the only ones allowed in the room (see Mark 5:37). This was the same group He would take into Gethsemane (see Matt. 26:37). Though speculation exists about why these three were special, all these men were so devoted to Jesus that they followed Him from the beginning and persevered for Him though ultimately they were persecuted and martyred for the cause of Christ. James was killed by Herod (see Acts 12:2). Tradition says Peter was hanged upside down on a cross. Though John wasn't martyred, history says he survived a boiling in oil and an exile to the Island of Patmos (see Rev. 1:9). After the event that was to occur this day, they all would be even more devoted; but from the beginning, they had separated themselves from the other chosen ones by their intense loyalty to their Lord.

Every prophet has followers, but each needs an intimate group to serve as confidants and friends. Plus, wisdom says not to include everyone as we experience deeper revelations of Holy Spirit. This event wasn't for the faint of heart with little faith who may have spoken fear or unbelief which could have negated God's purpose. One meaning for three is witness. Jewish law required three witnesses to verify events.[2] When Jesus asked them to keep quiet until after His death, the three could confirm this event after He was gone.

PRAYERS

This time, Jesus "led them" (Matt. 17:1) to the mountain. That's how many, including me, live—by the Lord's leading. We even use that terminology: "The Lord led me to do (go, say...)." Those who operate in Holy Spirit's gifts understand Jesus can lead in many ways—through an audible voice, unction, impression, vision, circumstance, dream, or other ways. Even Jesus Himself is an example of how though sometimes He heard God's voice audibly, other times, "Jesus perceived their thoughts" (Luke 5:22). I love one example in Acts of how others heard from God. Disciples were trying to decide where to have their next evangelistic campaign. So,

> when they had gone through Phrygia and the region of Galatia, they were forbidden by the Holy Spirit to preach the word in Asia. After they had come to Mysia, they tried to go into Bithynia, but the Spirit did not permit them.
>
> Acts 16:6-7

We don't learn how "they were forbidden by the Holy Spirit" or how "the Spirit did not permit them" to go to those places, but they were directed the same ways we are. And they obeyed. Some revelations come with more intensity, but each is a treasure. Elijah learned that lesson on the mountain when God came several ways, but even the gentle way was to be revered. God led Elijah often—to Ahab, to Cherith, to Zarephath, to Elisha, to the wilderness. The Lord's leading shows exactly where we are, or are not to put our foot.

Holy Spirit's leading is as concrete now as when Jesus led these men to the mountain. What we discover as we follow His direction is purpose and fulfillment. This mountain isn't identified, but tradition says it's Mt. Tabor.[3] Tabor was instrumental in Deborah's battle plan (see Judg. 4:6), which Gideon also mentioned (see Judg. 8:18). Jeremiah prophesied the coming of the king of Babylon and swore on two geographical areas: "'Surely as Tabor is among the mountains And as Carmel by the sea, so he shall come'" (Jer. 46:18). This quote mentions two locations significant in Elijah's ministry. God showed up on *Tabor* at the Transfiguration when glory fell thick and on Mt. Carmel when He defeated Baal's prophets, fire fell on the sacrifice, and then rain came. Though "so he shall come" refers here to the Babylonian king, the use of these two locations indicates God's glory will show up for us as surely as He did for Elijah in those places.

Tabor was in the Valley of Jezreel, where much of Ahab and Jezebel's judgment was spoken. Its meaning, "choice; purity; bruising"[4] would be appropriate for a mountaintop experience before Jesus's sacrifice a few months later. He chose to die, He was pure, and He was bruised but not broken. Carmel's meaning of "circumcised lamb; harvest"[5] also describes Jesus, the Lamb of God, Whose death and resurrection brought forth a harvest of souls. Both the Tabor and Carmel experiences occurred when God's judgment and mercy were shown to those who followed Baal and by His Son's death and resurrection. Then, Holy Spirit's rain fell.

As Jesus led them to the mountain, Luke adds a detail that they went there so they could pray (see Luke 9:28). Isn't that Jesus's way, praying constantly? Matthew and Mark called it a high mountain (see Matt. 17:1). Oh, how prayer changes our perspective. Like Elijah in the upper room or on Mt. Carmel, from the high mountain of prayer, we see answers not visible from a valley perspective. Luke adds a detail that Jesus's appearance changed while He prayed (see Luke 9:29). He gave this same detail that while Jesus prayed at His baptism (see Luke 3:21), heaven opened. Prayer is an oft-neglected aspect of Christian life, perfunctorily performed, and employed as an afterthought. Powerful biblical saints prayed often and intensely.

THE TRANSFIGURATION

Like Elijah, Jesus was a man of prayer; and that powerful act changed His very countenance. As He prayed, He was transfigured before them. "Transfigured" is *metamorphoo*, "to transform, change."[6] There, in front of His disciples, Jesus had a metamorphosis from His earthly body into a glorified one— His face changed and robe turned white and glistened (see Luke 9:29). Clothing like mantles symbolizes Holy Spirit's anointing or authority. Transfigured means "To change in outward form or appearance…so as to glorify or exalt."[7] Through prayer, Jesus was changed into His glory appearance to be exalted. Mark added another vivid detail about Jesus's clothes: they "became shining, exceedingly white, like snow, such as no launderer on earth can whiten them" (Mark 9:3). After Jesus arose, an angel at the tomb was described similarly as having a face like lightning and snow-white clothes (see Matt. 28:3). Saul also saw the Lord's brightness during his encounter on the road to Damascus and later described Him as being more brilliant than the sun (see Acts 26:13). His glory is beyond what our minds can conceive. As I read these descriptions, I wonder if that glimmering whiteness of Jesus and the angel could have been gold dust covering their garments and faces as it does many modern-day saints?

A face changing in God's presence is not uncommon in the Bible. As Stephen sat before the council which would ultimately condemn him to death, his face shone like an angel (see Acts

6:15). After his burning bush experience, Moses donned a veil over his glowing face when he spoke to others, but took it off when he talked with God (see Exod. 34:29-35). This glory experience shone on these men's countenance as "the brightness of His glory" (Heb. 1:3) shone on Jesus. Until this time, He had hidden His Glory in the veil of His human body. When His godly nature was revealed, that glory changed Him, so others knew He was more than just a dynamic man. He shone forth as God in a human body.

Paul used *metamorphoo* in two references translated differently. He said, "But we all, with unveiled face, beholding as in a mirror the glory of the Lord, are being *transformed* into the same image from glory to glory, just as by the Spirit of the Lord" (2 Cor. 3:18). Like Moses, we too can see God with our unveiled face as we stand in His glory and become more like Him. We're transformed, *metamorphooed*, with each glory experience. How could we possibly remain the same after we see God's power and ability? How could these disciples on the mountain ever be the same? Paul used that word again when he said, "Do not be conformed to this world, but be transformed by the *renewing* of your mind, that you may prove what is that good and acceptable and perfect will of God" (Rom. 12:2). This glory transformation renews our minds. Jesus's luminosity on that mountain is the same transformation and renewing that occurs and changes us as we're in His presence—our appearance, our minds, our desires. His glory takes us to new levels.

MOSES AND ELIJAH

Along with Jesus, Moses and Elijah appeared on the mountain and talked with Him. Much speculation exists regarding why these two men were chosen. Both were great Old Testament prophets who'd left earth in strange ways: Elijah didn't taste death, and no one saw Moses's death and burial because God had buried him (see Deut. 34:5-6). They both had wilderness experiences and sufferings. Both had worked diligently for God. Both are linked in end-time prophecy and signify the ways people will be taken—the raptured (Elijah) who won't taste death and the dead (Moses) who will rise upon Jesus's return. They each represent certain aspects of God. Because he brought the Ten Commandments from the mountain, Moses represents the law. Elijah is the quintessential example of the prophet's life in Holy Spirit. They both had experienced intimacy with God on Mt. Sinai. Moses was a man "whom the Lord knew face to face" (Deut. 34:10), and Elijah had talked to Him there. This was a grand reunion.

For whatever reason these men were chosen, a purpose existed for them to witness the greatest recorded glory scene ever. Luke included one detail about the interaction among the men that other accounts didn't: the three "spoke of His decease which was about to accomplish at Jerusalem" (Luke 9:31). This detail makes great sense because this mountain event preceded the crucifixion and resurrection, which occurred around six months later. It also has another meaning. "Decease" literally means "exodus."[8] Who better than Moses would understand an exodus, which he'd experienced for forty years as he led His people from Egypt's bondage, suffering, and hatred into the Promised Land? Elijah had gone through a supernatural exodus in his ascension, and Jesus was to experience His exodus from earth. By His death, resurrection, and ascension, He would become the sacrifice to create an exodus greater than from Egypt because He would lead people from the slavery of sin and death and bring them life eternal. As they stood on that mountain, they discussed the event soon to come that would also allow men to go from their own land of servitude into a land of promise of eternal life in Holy Spirit. His wasn't just a death but an exodus to a better land.

On that mountain Moses and Elijah confirmed Jesus was truly the One Whom the law and prophets foretold. Moses brought law, but Jesus brought grace and truth (see John 1:17). Their being on the Mount of Transfiguration with Jesus reaffirmed that

He fulfilled prophecies and the law. The law had been exchanged because where it brought death, the law of the Spirit of life made us no longer slaves to the law of sin and death inherited from Adam (see Rom. 8:2). In other words, Holy Spirit brings a higher law that supersedes the one Adam's sin brought on us.

JOHN THE BAPTIST

Elijah not only had the unique honor of not tasting death but he also was the prophet linked closely to Jesus's forerunner cousin, John the Baptist. John is called the second Elijah. Before John's birth, his dad was told that his son would be called in Elijah's anointing (see Luke 1:17, from Mal. 4:5-6). Though some in Jesus's time believed John the Baptist was actually Elijah, several times when John was asked if he was Elijah or Jesus, he said he was not (see John 1:21). Another time the disciples told Jesus that people thought He was John the Baptist, Elijah, or another prophet (see Mark 8:28). Their names were linked together other times too. When Jesus's fame grew, his name reached Herod. When he asked Who Jesus was, he was told Jesus was John who had been resurrected, Elijah, or a prophet (see Luke 9:7-8).

Their appearances were similar. John wore camel's hair and a leather belt around his waist (see Matt. 3:4), and Elijah probably wore animal skins and a leather belt around his waist (see 2 Kings 1:8). Both prophets spent time alone in the desert (see 1 Kings 17:3; Luke 1:80). Both were politically active and rebuked kings (see 1 Kings 18:17-18; Matt. 14:4) who tried to kill them (see 2 Kings 1:9-16; Matt. 14:10) and queens who hated them (see 1 Kings 19:1-7; Matt. 14:3) because they spoke judgment against their sins (see 1 Kings 21:19; Matt. 14:4). Both suffered discouragement despite extraordinary callings and experiences (see 1 Kings 19:4; Matt. 11:2-3). Both preached righteousness (see 1 Kings 18:21; Matt. 21:32), had great influence over Israel (see 1 Kings 18:24-40; Matt. 3:5), and ministered amazingly (see 1 Kings 17:241; Matt. 3:5-6). Neither is credited as a great writer.

John was the prophet, preparing the way for Jesus. He baptized with water for repentance and introduced Jesus, Who would baptize with Holy Spirit. Jesus mentioned John and Elijah together: "For all the prophets and the law prophesied until John. And if you are willing to receive it, he is Elijah who is to come" (Matt 11:13-14). The prophets and the law prophesied until John, when a new covenant through Holy Spirit was to be released. Jesus had come to fulfill those Old Testament prophecies, and John was the crier to announce His arrival. John, Spirit-filled before his birth, issued the prophetic word announcing Jesus, but not just as the Messiah. He also said Jesus would bring the baptism of Holy Spirit's fire (see Matt. 3:11) to ignite and burn dead religion. Elijah had known about and operated in that fire nearly one thousand years before. As John preached, he announced that power just as Elijah had demonstrated it. Many then, as now, rejected the idea of Holy Spirit's fire.

Another time when Jesus was asked,

> Why do the scribes say that Elijah must come first? Then He answered and told them, "Indeed, Elijah is coming first and restores all things. And how is it written concerning the Son of Man, that He must suffer many things and be treated with contempt? But I say to you that Elijah has also come, and they did to him whatever they wished."
>
> Mark 9:11-13

In this passage, Jesus again refers to Elijah as the quintessential example of Holy Spirit's role. The Spirit Who dwelt in Elijah would come "first and restor[e] all things." These words are repeated in an allusion to Holy Spirit's role when Jesus's ascension would allow Him to come for "the times of restoration of all things" (Acts 3:21). Even then, people recognized Elijah's extreme power because as Jesus died and called to God, some around Him thought He was pleading for Elijah to rescue Him (see Mark 15:35-36). However, they didn't make the connection between the wonders Elijah performed through God's Spirit and the Holy Spirit about Whom John preached. Elijah was elevated by the Jews, but they didn't recognize his anointing operating in another vessel, John. That defines religion today too. The Spirit through Whom Elijah operated is the hope for lives. He's come to restore all things on earth, yet much of the earth, even God's people, has rejected and treated Him contemptuously.

END-TIME PROPHECY

Another aspect of comparison between John, Elijah, and Moses is that much end-time prophecy applies to them. Malachi indicates that John the Baptist is the forerunner and messenger of Messiah to prepare the way (see Mal. 3:1). Jesus alluded to this prophet as He spoke about Elijah in the Gospels (see Matt. 17:11-13). Malachi also describes Elijah's role in Jesus's second coming in the last words written at the Old Testament's end:

> Behold, I will send you Elijah the prophet Before the coming of the great and dreadful day of the LORD. And he will turn The hearts of the fathers to the children, And the hearts of the children to their fathers, Lest I come and strike the earth with a curse.
>
> Mal. 4:5-6

Today, hearts of children and fathers need desperately to turn back to each other because in large part we're a nation of fatherless children. This is a promise to cling to for change in this generation. Fathers and children could also be symbolic of Holy Spirit's purpose. Jesus validated Elijah's end-time role. Since Elijah often represents Holy Spirit's gifts, could this statement be prophesying about revival bringing restoration and recognition of the Spirit's power in the last days as God raises Elijahs to bring believers along in the gifts? Is this a pronouncement of both natural and spiritual fathers arising?

CONNIE HUNTER-URBAN

Elisha's question at the Jordan, "Where is the Lord God of Elijah?" resounds today. We've become a powerless church, not drawing those looking for what's real. Having just a denomination with rhetoric but not Holy Spirit's power, many churches meet on Sundays for little more than fellowship but not to utilize the power Jesus's death made available to us. Seekers can get the fellowship dynamics anywhere, even in the world. Sons of the prophets' pronouncement at the Jordan—that "the spirit of Elijah rests on Elisha"—is also appropriate and prophetic for these end-times. The spirit of Elijah needs to overpower us today so we boldly speak God's words and do His signs, wonders, and miracles to testify to the lost. We have no biblical evidence Elijah was an earthly father, but he mentored many in Holy Spirit. Today, God hasn't lost His prophetic voice, but He needs vessels through whom those words will come and who will instruct those He has called. Prophets are chosen; but as Elisha shows, a training time must occur for them to step into that role with anointing, authority, and maturity. The influx of people who'll need more mature prophets to teach them how to operate becomes our responsibility.

Zechariah gives end-time prophecy regarding Moses and Elijah. Two olive trees and two lampstands are described as "the two anointed ones, who stand beside the Lord of the whole earth" (Zech. 4:14). Revelation also discusses witnesses in Jerusalem, which ties to Zechariah's passage by this statement: "These are the two olive trees and the two lampstands standing before the God of the earth" (Rev. 11:4). Much disagreement exists about the witnesses's identities, olive trees, and lampstands, but the rest of this passage clarifies.

> These two olive trees and the two lampstands...have power to shut heaven, so that no rain falls in the days of their prophecy; and they have power over waters to turn them to blood, and to strike the earth with all plagues, as often as they desire.
>
> Rev. 11:4, 6

These events describe two men—Elijah and Moses. Of all biblical prophets, Elijah's role in end-time prophecy is crucial. That, in itself, says we should study his ministry. By the way, I love the addition of the words "as often as they desire." Doesn't that describe Elijah's translation gift?

THE GLORY

When Jesus, Moses, and Elijah spoke on the mountain, they said He would "accomplish [the exodus] at Jerusalem" (Luke 9:31). The word for *accomplish* is the Greek *pleroo*, meaning "fulfill, (be, make) full, perfect, supply."[9] The word translated here as "accomplish" is used as "filled" when Paul says "be filled with the Spirit" (Eph. 5:18). This is no coincidence that Jesus's decease was to be an accomplishment of salvation and release of Holy Spirit. Jesus's leaving ushered us into Holy Spirit's Promised Land. This tense "be filled" implies this infilling is perpetual and "does not stop with a single experience, but is maintained by continually being filled."[10] Can we get that? Jesus came so we wouldn't taste death and would have a never-ending Holy Spirit walk.

Luke added another significant phrase to this scene: "Moses and Elijah, who appeared in glory" (Luke 9:30-31). This phrase "in glory" makes me wonder. It's been described as "of a glorious appearance...like that which the saints have in Heaven."[11] So, these two men appeared as they would in Heaven. The New Testament word for glory is *doxa*, "splendor, radiance, and majesty centered on Jesus."[12] In the Old Testament, the word is *kabod*, "weightiness, that which is substantial or heavy."[13] It's the weightiness which filled Solomon's temple (see 1 Kings 8:11) and which appeared in the cloud as Aaron spoke to people in the wilderness (see Exod. 16:10). That weightiness was God's blanket on that mountain too and may explain the unbelievable statement that Peter and the others were sleepy (see Luke 9:32). How could they think of sleeping during such an amazing event? Several explanations are possible. This was probably nighttime since we're told later in the passage that they didn't go down from the mountain until the next day. No one knows what physical demands this journey with Jesus put on their bodies, so this may have been a time of extreme fatigue? Luke clarified that they were awake to see the glory with Elijah and Moses. Who can sleep with such an intense light?

Unlike later in the Garden when Jesus scolded Peter for sleeping, He didn't say anything this time. As I considered this passage, Peter, James, and John were involved in one of the most intense glory occurrences ever on earth, and they may have been experiencing one of those glory manifestations—such a heavy peace people struggle to stay awake. Often, that peace has entered our presence with extreme weightiness, and we felt like we'd fall asleep too. That's probably what happened to these men. When the glory comes, manifestations occur. This extreme peace was probably one of those manifestations.

When the men were awake and saw what was happening, Peter suggested building three tabernacles, one for each man. Several reasons may have prompted him to say this. This event was occurring during the Feast of the Tabernacles, which included dwelling in tents to commemorate the wilderness journey. Peter probably wanted to include them and prolong the celebration. He suggested this as Elijah and Moses were leaving (see Luke 9:33), so perhaps he wanted to extend that time with them. Luke says Peter said this, "not knowing what he said" (Luke 9:33). People interpret this different ways. Maybe he was still sleepy and spoke without thinking. Perhaps he said this without considering that Elijah and Moses couldn't dwell in earthly habitats. Perhaps he didn't know what he said because God, not him, was speaking through his mouth.

Mark phrases his words differently: "because he did not know what to say" (Mark 9:6). I like that detail. Peter tended to "not know what to say" often and stuck his foot in his mouth. Boy, I can relate! Peter talked when he didn't know what to say like we often do. That goes for our prophetic words too. Sometimes, when we give words of knowledge or wisdom and people are confused or don't see the meaning immediately, we attempt to help Holy Spirit and put our own spin on it. We can learn from Peter.

One day, while driving to a local flea market, I thought about a vendor there. Wade and I had prayed for his wife for quite a while to be healed from a debilitating illness, and she'd improved tremendously by the Master's touch. She and her husband had been thrilled as God worked His healing power on her. That day, on my way to the sale, the Lord spoke to me that she should, "Expect more." I thought of what that could mean: she wasn't expecting enough from God or she should expect more healings. When I saw her husband, I told him what God had said and what it might mean. Then the next time I saw him, he was excited. Two days after I heard those words, she began to exhibit symptoms again, so they grew afraid. Then they remembered God had said to "Expect more." They held onto those words and the knowledge that God had warned them in advance, and she was fine in just two days. They knew God's word had been telling them to expect more attacks and not the meanings I'd suggested. Holy Spirit is never wrong although Connie often is. If He doesn't reveal the full picture, we shouldn't speculate.

HEAR HIM

As Peter suggested building the tabernacles, a glory cloud overshadowed them. Then God's voice erupted from the cloud saying, "This is My beloved Son. Hear Him" (Luke 9:35) and further acknowledged Jesus. People heard God's voice often in the Bible. From Adam (see Gen. 3:8-10) to Paul (see Acts 9:3-7), God talked audibly to men and directed them. This wasn't the first time God had audibly declared Jesus's majesty. As He was baptized at His ministry's beginning, Holy Spirit descended upon Him as a dove, "And suddenly a voice came from heaven, saying, 'This is My beloved Son, in whom I am well pleased'"

(Matt. 3:17). God spoke nearly the same words when Jesus was filled with Holy Spirit and when He was transfigured. I love the difference though. In the baptism, God said He was pleased. Now, as His Son faced a terrible ordeal in the near future, God said to "hear Him."

"Hear Him." God had reiterated Moses's prophesy about Jesus: "The Lord your God will raise up for you a Prophet like me from your midst, from your brethren. Him you shall hear" (Deut. 18:15). Did a part of this Inner Circle still wonder if Jesus could in fact be the Messiah despite what they'd seen before this day? Was God's voice necessary for them to hear His cryptic words of life? This word for *hear* is *akouo*, and one of its definitions is "understand."[14] Was God telling this Inner Circle that as much as they'd walked with Him, they still didn't comprehend His purpose? Jesus had commented about that several times Himself when they didn't learn lessons He taught. The next months before the crucifixion and resurrection would bring revelations, and they would eventually understand His Person. Do we commit the sin of presumption when we don't "hear Him"?

As the voice ceased, Elijah and Moses were gone. Then, the men's reactions were like ours in a new, holy situation: they fell down in fear (see Matt. 17:6). They were just plain scared. This detail told only in Matthew says much. Falling on one's face shows their awe at being in God's presence. When God comes, we should respond with awe but not fear, although our human side is afraid. Jesus's response to that fear, though, wasn't frustration or anger, but He "touched them and said, 'Arise and do not be afraid'" (Matt. 17:7). *Arise* is the same word the angel spoke to Elijah when he brought the cake and water to prepare him for the trip. Then God told Elijah to "go out" of the cave. When we hunker down instead of arising, we can't see the wonder that's occurring.

Jesus "touched them." Can you imagine the power of that touch of the human hand of God? The Master's touch calms the storm, heals the sick, raises the dead, or calms the fears of cowering disciples. When we're overwhelmed, His touch calms us too. Like when Jacob's hip was touched by Jesus as they wrestled in the dirt (see Gen. 32:25), our walk is never the same after the Master's touch. That touch, *haptomai*, is "to attach oneself to."[15] His touch attaches Him to us no matter what answer we need. Whether His touch is to us or our touch is to His garment (see Luke 8:45), we're inextricably attached. Doesn't that thrill you? Jeremiah discovered that touch's importance when he said, "the LORD put forth His hand and touched my mouth, and the LORD said to me: 'Behold, I have put My words in your mouth'" (Jer. 1:9). The Lord's touch accomplishes anything, even birthing the prophetic. Now, as His human hands on earth, we too can bring about much through Holy Spirit.

THE CHARGE

In Matthew and Mark, when Moses and Elijah had left, Jesus instructed them not to tell anyone about the experience until after His resurrection (see Matt. 17:9). Though that request is similar to those today who don't want to tell the over-the-edge stuff that may make others think they're crazy, Jesus wasn't thinking of people's opinions. He certainly didn't care if anyone thought He was too out there, nor did He think God's ways were weird. He said not to tell anyone because they couldn't understand the implications of His glory and what had happened until after His resurrection. Most of these men wrote about it later. John alluded to the experience when he said, "And the Word became flesh and dwelt among us, and we beheld His glory, the glory as of the only begotten of the Father, full of grace and truth" (John 1:14).). He saw Jesus in His glory a second time during his great Revelation vision. He described Him as having a face that shone like the sun (see Rev. 1:16).

Peter wrote,

> For we did not follow cunningly devised fables when we
> made known to you the power and coming of our Lord
> Jesus Christ, but were eyewitnesses of His majesty. For He
> received from God the Father honor and glory when such
> a voice came to Him from the excellent glory: 'This is My
> beloved Son, in whom I am well pleased.' And we heard this
> voice which came from heaven when we were with Him on
> the holy mountain.
>
> 2 Peter 1:16-18

These men had a life-changing glory experience. Unbelievable events then and today aren't "cunningly devised fables" but true and powerful. Like when Wade and I were forever changed with the wonder of Wade's gold tooth, that day, those men's lives were forever changed too. They'd walked with Jesus all those years, but they'd known Him in His humanity. That day, they discovered Him in His deity. The glory didn't fall upon Him; He *was* the glory. He was God, and they saw Him in His fullness. How could they ever consider anything else but to live and to die for their Friend, Mentor, Teacher, and Lord of Glory? The glory isn't to fear or ridicule but rather to reverence because Holy Spirit ushers in that glory, just like on this mountain with Jesus, Moses, and Elijah.

We would like to stay in those mountaintop glory experiences, but usually, we go back to the valley of ordinary living. After this great experience, the next day, the men left the mountain and were greeted by a large group of people (see Luke 9:37). Jesus went back into His realm of the ordinary and was met by those desperate for His touch. For Jesus and His disciples, life proceeded as usual because He had little time to reflect on what *was* because so much of what *is* needed addressed in the few short weeks He had left on earth. Elijah went from glory experience to glory experience too, and in between he just lived and grew.

CONCLUSION

Jesus's Inner Circle wouldn't agree with scoffers about the glory because they didn't need to think about what *could* happen since they knew what *would* and *did* happen. Although many of the glory manifestations people experience now are mentioned in the Bible and many aren't, not everything Jesus did was recorded in Scripture. In the last verse of his gospel, John says, "there are also many other things that Jesus did, which if they were written one by one, I suppose that even the world itself could not contain the books that would be written" (John 21:25). John saw for himself, and naysayers couldn't change that. When we get self out of the way, we'll see God's glory like on this mountaintop. Amazingly, Holy Spirit wasn't yet given because Jesus wasn't yet glorified (see John 7:39). Imagine the glory experience that can happen today because of Holy Spirit. Whatever the rest of the world thought didn't matter to that Inner Circle or Moses or Elijah or Jesus. And it shouldn't to us. What happened on that mountain was a preview of glory to come.

MY HUSBAND'S THOUGHTS

Epilogue by Wade Urban

This book has generated increased excitement and determination in our spirits. I believe we're in a time which mirrors that of Elijah. Just as the prophet was called to challenge a nation lost in idolatry and moral corruption, so also many reading this now (the remnant) have been called to cry out for righteousness and purity in the church where God's judgment first begins (see 1 Pet. 4:17). This will demonstrate God's love and power to turn the blinded and deceived back to Him. Until the church awakens from its slumber, nations will continue to march on to their destruction. Many are hearing the sound of marching in the tops of the mulberry trees (see 2 Sam. 5:24) and know the time for action has come! What's our mission? How can it be accomplished? I believe Elijah's mandate holds a key to our own assignment in this time. The truths you've gleaned from this book and your increased sensitivity to Holy Spirit will both confirm and lead you into all truth—that's His promise.

THE MANDATE

The role of the prophet is to intercede through Holy Spirit, causing the substantiation, materialization, and manifestation of what already exists as a spiritual reality to be transferred to the earth realm. This is a season for promotion for those Prophets-In-Training (PITs), or Elijah's sons of the prophets, who seek to go beyond hearing revelatory words from Holy Spirit to going deeper into the prophet's gift of intercession to see the reality of His promises birthed in earth. This requires leaving comfort zones and entering a new realm of intimacy, experiencing His presence and power, acting out what you see Him doing, and re-sounding what you hear Him saying as prophetic declarations and decrees. This is the spirit of prophecy (see Rev. 19:10). From this elevated perspective—in the glory zone of His presence—instantaneous answers to prophetic declarations and actions manifest.

Even before Connie began to write this book, Holy Spirit impressed on me that we're at the start of a prophetic mandate which is illustrated when on the mountain God revealed to Elijah his assignment:

> Then the Lord said to him: 'Go, return on your way to the Wilderness of Damascus; and when you arrive, anoint Hazael king over Syria. Also you shall anoint Jehu the son of Nimshi as king over Israel. And Elisha the son of Shaphat of Abel Meholah you shall anoint as prophet in your place.'
>
> 1 Kings 19:15-16

This was one of Elijah's last recorded prophetic assignments. I believe this is significant as a present-day prophetic assignment to prepare the church for Holy Spirit's end-time move. This threefold mandate is essential for building a foundational platform for continuous flow of Holy Spirit's power to be released and increased in intensity. Those with a prophetic calling are being equipped for this time (see Est. 4:14). This prophetic role will not just be prophesying God's revelatory words but also causing those revelations to be birthed in earth. When a prophet receives a *rhema*, the reality of that word has already been created in the

Spirit realm, so the prophet becomes the transfer agent to the natural realm (see 2 Cor. 1:20).

Elijah, the prototypical scriptural example of the prophetic gift, was given the assignment to release an anointing to three people: Hazael, Jehu, and Elisha. Here's our assignment:

1. Hazael means "that sees God." The first assignment (anoint Hazael) is to release a visionary anointing to the church. Proverbs 29:18 states the importance of having a vision. The church has lost its vision for equipping people for ministry (see Eph. 4:12). Equipping is a lost concept today. Most people think ministry is the pastor's job, not theirs. This is the purpose of the church—for all believers to be equipped to do the works of Jesus and greater works (see John 14:12). The apostle, prophet, pastor, evangelist, and teacher are offices of equippers to train people in their callings and purpose. Leaders must receive fresh vision to equip and train an army, not entertain and draw audiences. Paul's prayer in Ephesians 1:17-23 is for the church to receive Holy Spirit revelation to know their calling, covenant promises, and resurrection power of Holy Spirit. Father, we declare that the church will regain vision and purpose with leaders who understand and equip the saints in the power of Holy Spirit. Move on leaders with Your power; and if they resist, remove and replace them with those who have Your heart, Your mission, and Your vision.

2. Jehu means "himself who exists" and was the son of Nimshi, meaning "rescued from danger." The second assignment (*anoint Jehu*) is to release an anointing for power gifts of Holy Spirit for power evangelism and deliverance to the body of Christ. Too many have completely ignored Holy Spirit and His purpose in believers' lives. Holy Spirit's gifts are God's power to know, do, and say (see 1 Cor. 12:4-11) what God desires to release. Without Holy

Spirit being alive and functioning in our churches, we've relegated our lives to the transitional period of the gospels, never entering the New Covenant reality of life in Holy Spirit, the very purpose for which Jesus Christ came to earth. He was the Door, and the Way, Truth, and Life (see John 10:9, 14:6), the only Way—Entrance—to the Father. Jesus is the Doorway into a New Covenant life in Holy Spirit. Without Holy Spirit, God's power tangibly demonstrating His love, our churches become little more than fraternal organizations with an animal head over the front door! Power evangelism with healings, miracles, signs, and wonders provides an awesome platform for the true gospel of God's kingdom to be preached. If you really want to draw crowds, allow Holy Spirit to move in your city's streets then watch the church fill up! Father, release a new boldness to demonstrate Your love through Holy Spirit's gifts and power. Put sensitivity and awareness in lives for the divine intersections You set up daily to demonstrate Your ability to transform life's messes into miracles. Empower through Your transfer agents to bring heaven's reality to earth.

3. Elisha, "salvation of God," was the son of Shaphat meaning "judge" of Abel Meholah meaning "mourning of sickness." The third assignment (anoint Elisha) is that of anointing the next generation of ministers (protégés). The modern church hasn't been successful at passing on a true move of God to the succeeding generation. It seems each generation must reinvent the wheel and relearn kingdom principles and the deep truths of God's Word. Many churches flourished in the healing and miracle revivals of the 1940s and '50s, but many children of those moves didn't continue to expand it. They sat in a defensive position and, today, seem to be some of the sickest people in town! It appears satan sets up his operations center in

the very place he was kicked out of years before, much like he's mocking the memory of Holy Spirit's healing move. Each succeeding generation must continue to expand spiritual ground previously secured by past generations. This is true spiritual inheritance! We must pull back the curtain and allow our children to experience what's already theirs in Holy Spirit—spiritual endowments waiting to be revealed! If we're not reproducing our ministry through our children, we're being deceived by the evil one. This assignment for protégés releases a "double anointing" in their lives to demonstrate the "salvation of God" (Elisha) as God "judges" sin (Shaphat) and people are delivered from "mourning of sickness" (Abel Meholah). Father, move on our hearts to raise up the next generation to flow in Your love and demonstrate Your life and power as a lifestyle.

This prophetic assignment will be accompanied by three distinct anointings:

1. Holy Ghost Arsonist (1 Kings 18:20-40)—Elijah's confrontation with Baal's prophets resulted in God's fire consuming his sacrifice. Holy Spirit fire will accompany those who pursue this mandate. We see the reality of this anointing regularly. Most times when hands are laid on people, they testify of a sensation like an electric current flowing through their bodies. At times, the current becomes so intense, it feels like fire. Healings and miracles often result from this heavenly transfer of power to the present need. This anointing provides a tremendous platform for truth to be proclaimed!

2. Rainmaker (1 Kings 18:41-46)—After having shut up the heavens by his word, Elijah prayed for rain. The rainmaker anointing will release all heaven's resources to meet every ministry need. This is an intercessor's anointing to transfer

kingdom reality from the spiritual realm to the natural. It's one thing to stand under the glory cloud of God's presence and feel the blessings of His *kabod* and see and experience glory manifestations of His presence; but it's altogether something different to intercede from His Mercy Seat and see His answers rain on earth. This is our calling and destiny in Christ!

3. Wind-walker (2 Kings 2:1-11)—Elijah was taken to heaven in a chariot of fire by a whirlwind. The wind-walker anointing is fearless empowerment to release the whirlwind of God's power to destroy, tear down, uproot, and change the spiritual landscape as directed by Holy Spirit. Angelic protection and power will accompany this anointing. Many times satanic barriers must be displaced and destroyed before God's plan can be initiated. You have been assigned an area of operation in the Spirit for which you have responsibility and authority to displace the enemy and build kingdom reality. As you seek His face, you'll discover this assignment which will grow as you demonstrate your willingness and obedience to His word.

This mandate is a release to action for those reading this, specifically whose spirits are jumping with confirmation that they've been called for this time. Study Scripture diligently for confirmation; seek Holy Spirit for direction, timing, and His open doors (see Isa. 22:22). Don't push them open yourself; He'll open them as you step forward in faith. We stand in a *kairos* time for God's will to manifest and for reformation of His church to begin.

AFTERWORD

I've spent more than a year studying and writing about this man Elijah. I've cried often as Holy Spirit tugged at my heart to see something more in a scripture. I've excitedly shared revelations with Wade and others as God dropped them into my spirit. But no matter how enthusiastic I was, this study's relevance comes back to the question I posed in my "Introduction"—why Elijah, why now? As operators in the gifts, we know those wondrous tools have been given to us for an overcoming lifestyle, but not for us alone. A whole nation depends upon us to hear from God and to bring His will into being. A whole nation can be saved by our intercession. A whole nation can find its way back to God by our obedience to step up. A whole nation can experience revival as we bring the fire of God to burn up dead religion. Elijah's nation did.

Though a common man, Elijah showed wonders, from drought, to resurrection, to transfiguration, to escaping death, to participating in a glory scene. This prophet lived an amazing Spirit-filled life, performed signs and wonders, didn't taste death, participated in the resurrection, and will have an end-time role. All of us can learn from Elijah as a prophet who knew how to tap into heaven's resources and experienced miracles most of us have never fathomed. He didn't question when God sent him on suicide journeys or heavenly flights because he understood his

Source. Much of Elijah's Holy Spirit ministry is told through alluding to occurrences, so who knows what else Elijah did? His walk culminated in the Transfiguration, the most powerful glory scene ever, and who knows what else we'll see in these end-times.

Today's events show the world is rapidly deteriorating into turmoil: news of impending national economic disaster, news of wars and rumors of wars, news of shortages of food and starvation even in a wealthy nation. Elijah faced the same challenges as we, but did with confidence. He didn't let those reports be his reality as he ate his meat and bread at Cherith, nor as he feasted on years of cakes baked by supernatural oil and meal. His story tells us that nothing is impossible with God, and no matter what we see coming down our own roads, He's in control. We can learn a lot from Elijah.

APPENDIX[1]

Elijah's and Elisha's Travels

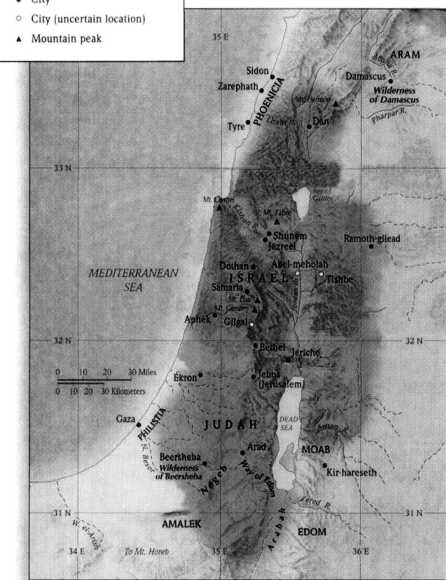

ARAM

Sidon
Zarephath
Damascus
Wilderness of Damascus
PHOENICIA
Mt. Hermon ▲
Tyre
Dan

33 N

Mt. Carmel ▲
Mt. Tabor ▲
Sea of Galilee
Shunem
Jezreel
Ramoth-gilead

MEDITERRANEAN SEA
Dothan
Abel-meholah
I S R A E L
Tishbe
Samaria
Mt. Ebal ▲
Mt. Gerizim ▲
Aphek
Gilgal

32 N   32 N

Bethel
Jericho

0   10   20   30 Miles
0 10 20 30 Kilometers

Ekron
Jebus (Jerusalem)

Gaza
PHILISTIA
DEAD SEA
J U D A H
Arad
MOAB
Kir-hareseth
Beersheba
Wilderness of Beersheba
Negeb

31 N   31 N

AMALEK
EDOM

34 E   To Mt. Horeb   35 E   36 E

NOTES

INTRODUCTION

1. Hayford, Jack W., et al. "Word Wealth." In *New Spirit Filled Bible*. Nashville: Thomas Nelson, Inc., 2002. 366.
2. Ibid.
3. Hayford, "Word Wealth," 1291.
4. "Understanding the Anointing." Kenneth Copeland Ministries. http://www.kcm.org/real-help/article/understanding-anointing (accessed September 2, 2013).
5. Strong, James. *New Strong's Exhaustive Concordance*. Nashville, Tenn.: Thomas Nelson Publishers, 2001. H4886.
6. Ibid. G5548.
7. Ibid. G5530.
8. Theprophetsoil.com. "The Prophets Oil." 2013. http://www.theprophetsoil.com/prophetblog/categories/listings/what-is-anointing-oil (accessed September 2, 2013).
9. Pfeiffer, Charles F., Howard F. Voss, and John Rea. "Plants: Myrrh." In *The Wycliffe Bible Encyclopedia*. Reprint. Chicago: Moody Press, 1975.
10. Ibid. "Plants: Cinnamon." 1357.
11. Ibid. "Plants: Calamus." 1355-56.
12. Ibid. "Plants: Cassia." 1356.
13. Ibid. "Plants: Olive." 1366-67.
14. Strong's G5547.

WHO IS HOLY SPIRIT?

1. Hayford, "Introduction to Ezekiel," 1051.
2. Ibid., "The Kings and Prophets of Israel and Judah Chart," 444.
3. Ibid., "Word Wealth," 923.
4. Strong's G4151.
5. Ibid. H7307.
6. Hayford, "Word Wealth," 431.

ELIJAH AND THE DROUGHT

1. "An Interpreting Dictionary of Scripture Proper Names." In *The Holy Bible: Original King James Version*. Gordonsville, TN: Dugan Publishers, Inc. 1984:10.
2. Ibid. 4.
3. Strong's H8664.
4. Harper (Historian), Douglas. "Recourse." Dictionary.com. http://dictionary.reference.com/browse/recourse (accessed September 20, 2013).
5. Strong's H8453.
6. Ibid. H2919, from H2926.
7. Ibid. H4306, from H4305.
8. Ibid. H1653, from H1652.
9. Ibid. H3068.
10. Ibid. H430.
11. A Division of The American-Israeli Cooperative Enterprise. "The Jezreel Valley." Jewish Virtual Library. http://www.jewishvirtuallibrary.org/jsource/Society_&_Culture/geo/Jezreel.html (accessed September 10, 2013).
12. Ryken, Leland, James C. Wilhoit, Tremper Longman III. "Water." In *Dictionary of Biblical Imagery*. Downers Grove, IL: Intervarsity Press. 1998:931.
13. Strong's H2416 and H4325.
14. Ibid. G2198 and G5204.

15. Ibid. H5641.

16. "Interpreting" 3.

17. U.S. Department of the Interior U.S. Geological Survey. "Migration of Birds: Flight Speed and Rate of Migration." Northern Prairie Wildlife Research Center. http://www. npwrc.usgs.gov/resource/birds/migratio/speed.htm (accessed September 20, 2013).

18. Smith, Dr. William. "Raven - Meaning of 'Raven' in Smith's Bible Dictionary (Bible History Online). http://www.bible-history.com/smiths/R/Raven/ (accessed September 20, 2013).

19. Avian Web LLC (Wikipedia). "Common Raven." Avian Web.com. http://www.avianweb.com/commonravens.html (accessed September 20, 2013).

20. Dickert, Lori Thomas. "Dog Saliva Has Healing Properties." All Pet News. http://www.allpetnews.com/dog-saliva-has-healing-properties (accessed September 20, 2013).

ELIJAH AND THE WIDOW OF ZAREPHATH

1. Strong's H3427.

2. Ibid. H490.

3. Ibid. H6886, from H6884.

4. "Interpreting" 10.

5. Strong's H7197.

6. Hayford, "Word Wealth," 78.

7. Cook, F.C., Ed. "I Kings 17, Bottom Note." In *The Bible Commentary of the Old Testament: I Samuel-Esther*. Reprint, Grand Rapids: Baker Book House, 1974:202.

ELIJAH AND THE PROPHETS OF BAAL

1. "Interpreting" 7.

2. Strong's H5234.

3. Ibid. H5375.

4. Ibid. G726.
5. Ibid. H5916.
6. Dictionary.com. Unabridged. Random House, Inc. "Roil." Dictionary.com. http://dictionary.reference.com/browse/roil (accessed September 21, 2013).
7. "Interpreting" 3.
8. Cook 205.
9. Ibid. 206.
10. Strong's H4196, from H2076.
11. Cook 206.
12. Strong's H8585.
13. Cook 206.
14. "Interpreting" 6.

ELIJAH AND THE DROUGHT'S END

1. Strong's H6635, from H6633.
2. Ibid. H6963.
3. Ibid.
4. Cook 207.
5. Strong's H5927.
6. Hayford, "Word Wealth," 101.
7. "Interpreting" 6.
8. Cook 207.
9. Israel-a-history-of.com. "The Walls of Jericho." http://www.israel-a-history-of.com/walls-of-jericho.html (accessed March 8, 2013).
10. "How long would it take to walk the perimeter of 1 acre?" Answer Party. http://answerparty.com/question/answer/how-long-would-it-take-to-walk-the-perimeter-of-1-acre (accessed March 8, 2013).
11. Strong's H8615.
12. Wood, Bryant. "The Walls of Jericho: Archaeology Confirms: They Really Did Come A-tumbling' Down." Answers in

Genesis. http://www.answersingenesis.org/articles/cm/v21/ n2/the-walls-of-jericho (accessed August 8, 2013).

13. Hayford, "Bottom Note," 470.

14. Strong's H2296.

Elijah and Depression

1. "Interpreting" 4.

2. Ellis, Edward S., and Charles F. Horne. "Ethbaal of Phoenicia." http://www.publicbookshelf.com/public_html/ The_Story_of_the_Greatest_Nations_and_the_Worlds_ Famous_Events_Vol_1/ethbaalp_cd.html (accessed July 9, 2013).

3. "Interpreting" 2.

4. Cook 208.

5. Dictionary.com. "Theophany." Dictionary.com. http://dictionary.reference.com/browse/Theophany (accessed August 23, 2013).

6. Strong's H2722, from H2717.

7. Hayford, "Bottom Note," 471.

8. Strong's H5401.

Elijah and Naboth's Vineyard

1. "Interpreting" 10.

2. Strong's H5022.

3. Hayford, "Middle Note," 475.

Elijah and the Other Prophets

1. U. S. Bureau of Labor Statistics. "Occupational Employment and Wages, May 2012: 21-2011 Clergy." United States Department of Labor. http://www.bls.gov/oes/current/ oes212011.htm (accessed August 24, 2013).

2. Cook 213.

3. Dake, Finis Jennings. "1 Samuel Notes: Man of God." In *Dake's Annotated Reference Bible.* Dake's Publishing, Inc. Lawrenceville, Georgia:555.
4. Ibid. 708.
5. "Interpreting" 7.
6. Ryken, "Threshing, Threshing Floor," 867.
7. Strong's H2199.

ELIJAH AND AHAZIAH

1. "Interpreting" 2.
2. Ibid. 3.
3. Strong's H784.
4. Ibid. H226.
5. Ibid. G4592.
6. Ibid. H4159.
7. Ibid. G5059.
8. Hayford, "Word Wealth," 1519.

ELIJAH AND ELISHA'S JOURNEY

1. Pink, A. W. *The Life of Elijah by A. W. Pink.* "Chapter 28: Elijah's Recovery." http://www.pbministries.org/books/pink/Life_of_Elijah/elijah_28.htm (accessed August 25, 2013).
2. Strong's H155, from H117.
3. Hayford, "Bottom Note," 471.
4. Strong's H5288.
5. Ibid. H8334.
6. Hayford, "Word Wealth," 537.
7. Ibid. G2323.
8. Godfire.Net. "Elijah x 2 = Elisha." Re-think No. 60. http://www.godfire.net/rayknight/60_Elijahx2.pdf (accessed September 19, 2013) .

9. Halley, Henry H. "2 Kings, Chapter 2:Elijah's Translation." In *Halley's Bible Handbook*. Reprint, Grand Rapids, Michigan: Zondervan Publishing House, 1965:201.
10. Strong's H1537, from H1534.
11. "Interpreting" 2.
12. Cook 228.
13. Strong's H3405, from H7306.
14. Ibid. H3383, from H3381.
15. Ibid. H5591, from H5590.
16. Ryken, "Whirlwind," 943.
17. Shirley, Delron. "June 2010 Meditation: Father's in a Fatherless World." Teach All Nations Mission to the World. http://teachallnationsmission.com/medjune2010.html (accessed August 26, 2013).
18. Knight, Ray.

ELIJAH AND THE TRANSFIGURATION

1. Hayford, "Introductory Notes," 1346.
2. Frew, Robert, Ed. "Matthew-Mark, Bottom Note." In *The Bible Commentary: Matthew-Mark*. Reprint, Grand Rapids: Baker Book House, 1981:177.
3. Ibid., 176.
4. "Interpreting" 9.
5. Ibid. 3.
6. Strong's G3339.
7. Dictionary.com. "Transfigured." Dictionary.com. http://dictionary.reference.com/browse/transfigured (accessed August 27, 2013).
8. Hayford, "Bottom Note," 1404.
9. Strong's G4137, from G4134.
10. Hayford, "Bottom Note," 1652.
11. Frew, Robert, Ed. "Luke-John, Bottom Note." In *The Bible Commentary: Luke-John*. Reprint, Grand Rapids: Baker Book House, 1980:60.

12. Hayford, "Word Wealth," 1446.

13. Ibid., "Word Wealth," 944.

14. Strong's G191.

15. Strong's G680.

APPENDIX

1. "Elijah and Elisha." *Bible Land Maps.* Searching the Scriptures. Maps Courtesy of Access Foundation. Set 9:062. June 2012. Date Accessed Oct. 14, 2013. http://www.searchingthescriptures.net/main_pages/free_bible_land_maps.htm

CPSIA information can be obtained at www.ICGtesting.com
Printed in the USA
LVOW12s0412060715

445077LV00018B/253/P